MORMONISM AND AMERICAN POLITICS

RELIGION, CULTURE, AND PUBLIC LIFE

Religion, Culture, and Public Life
Series Editor: Karen Barkey

The resurgence of religion calls for careful analysis and constructive criticism of new forms of intolerance, as well as new approaches to tolerance, respect, mutual understanding, and accommodation. In order to promote serious scholarship and informed debate, the Institute for Religion, Culture, and Public Life and Columbia University Press are sponsoring a book series devoted to the investigation of the role of religion in society and culture today. This series includes works by scholars in religious studies, political science, history, cultural anthropology, economics, social psychology, and other allied fields whose work sustains multidisciplinary and comparative as well as transnational analyses of historical and contemporary issues. The series focuses on issues related to questions of difference, identity, and practice within local, national, and international contexts. Special attention is paid to the ways in which religious traditions encourage conflict, violence, and intolerance and also support human rights, ecumenical values, and mutual understanding. By mediating alternative methodologies and different religious, social, and cultural traditions, books published in this series will open channels of communication that facilitate critical analysis.

After Pluralism: Reimagining Religious Engagement, edited by Courtney Bender and Pamela E. Klassen
Religion and International Relations Theory, edited by Jack Snyder
Religion in America: A Political History, Denis Lacorne
Democracy, Islam, and Secularism in Turkey, edited by Ahmet T. Kuru and Alfred Stepan
Refiguring the Spiritual: Beuys, Barney, Turrell, Goldsworthy, Mark C. Taylor
Tolerance, Democracy, and Sufis in Senegal, edited by Mamadou Diouf
Rewiring the Real: In Conversation with William Gaddis, Richard Powers, Mark Danielewski, and Don DeLillo, Mark C. Taylor
Democracy and Islam in Indonesia, edited by Mirjam Künkler and Alfred Stepan
Religion, the Secular, and the Politics of Sexual Difference, edited by Linell E. Cady and Tracy Fessenden
Boundaries of Toleration, edited by Alfred Stepan and Charles Taylor
Recovering Place: Reflections on Stone Hill, Mark C. Taylor
Blood: A Critique of Christianity, Gil Anidjar
Choreographies of Shared Sacred Sites: Religion, Politics, and Conflict Resolution, edited by Elazar Barkan and Karen Barkey
Beyond Individualism: The Challenge of Inclusive Communities, George Rupp
Love and Forgiveness for a More Just World, edited by Hent de Vries and Nils F. Schott
Relativism and Religion: Why Democratic Societies Do Not Need Moral Absolutes, Carlo Invernizzi Accetti
The Making of Salafism: Islamic Reform in the Twentieth Century, Henri Lauzière

MORMONISM AND AMERICAN POLITICS

Edited by Randall Balmer
and Jana Riess

Columbia University Press   New York

Columbia University Press
Publishers Since 1893
New York   Chichester, West Sussex
cup.columbia.edu

Copyright © 2016 Columbia University Press
All rights reserved

Library of Congress Cataloging-in-Publication Data
Mormonism and American politics / edited by Randall Balmer and Jana Riess.
    pages cm
  Includes bibliographical references and index.
  ISBN 978-0-231-16598-3 (cloth)—ISBN 978-0-231-16599-0 (pbk.)—
ISBN 978-0-231-54089-6 (ebook)
  1. Church of Jesus Christ of Latter-day Saints—Political activity. 2. Mormon Church—Political activity. 3. Religion and politics—United States. I. Balmer, Randall Herbert, editor. II. Riess, Jana, editor.
BX8643.P6M67 2015
322'.108828973—dc23

2015018974

COVER DESIGN: Chang Jae Lee
COVER IMAGES: Mitt Romney © AP Photo/Rogelio V. Solis & Harry Reid © AP Photo/Carolyn Kaster

Contents

List of Illustrations   vii
Introduction   ix
Randall Balmer and Jana Riess

Part I: Origins and Tensions

1. Joseph Smith's Presidential Ambitions   3
   Richard Lyman Bushman

2. Unpopular Sovereignty: Brigham Young and the U.S. Government, 1847–1877   14
   John G. Turner

3. Polygamy in the Nation's Capitol: Protestant Women and the 1899 Campaign Against B. H. Roberts   32
   Jana Riess

4. Eternal Progression: Mormonism and American Progressivism   53
   Matthew Bowman

Part II: Shifting Alliances

5. Ezra Taft Benson and the Conservative Turn of "Those Amazing Mormons"   73
   Jan Shipps

6. Testimony and Theology: The Mormon Struggle with America's Civil Religion   85
   Russell Arben Fox

7. Chosen Land, Chosen People: Religious and American Exceptionalism Among the Mormons   102
   Philip L. Barlow

8. Like Father, Unlike Son: The Governors Romney, the Kennedy Paradigm, and the Mormon Question   115
   Randall Balmer

Part III: Into the Twenty-first Century

9. A Politically Peculiar People: How Mormons Moved into and Then out of the Political Mainstream   133
   David E. Campbell, Christopher F. Karpowitz, and J. Quin Monson

10. "Twice-told Tale": Telling Two Histories of Mormon-Black Relations During the 2012 Presidential Election   155
    Max Perry Mueller

11. Mormon Women Talk Politics   175
    Claudia L. Bushman

12. On the "Underground": What the Mormon "Yes on 8" Campaign Reveals About the Future of Mormons in American Political Life   192
    Joanna Brooks

13. Mitt, Mormonism, and the Media: An Unfamiliar Faith Takes the Stage in the 2012 U.S. Presidential Election   210
    Peggy Fletcher Stack

List of Contributors   227
Index   231

List of Illustrations

2.1 Brigham Young, ca. 1850   16
2.2 The Lion House and the Beehive House, ca. 1855   17
3.1 The Mormon Octopus (ca. 190?)   35
3.2 B. H. Roberts on a train to Washington, D.C. (political cartoon)   39
5.1 Utah presidential and gubernatorial election results, 1896 to 2012   75
5.2 Utah presidential election results, 1896 to 2012   75
9.1 Utah moves into, then out of, the political mainstream   136
9.2 Mormons and the GOP   142
9.3 Mormon views on abortion   144
9.4 Mormon views on same-sex marriage   145
9.5 Mormon views on immigration   147
12.1 The Mormon hierarchy (1904)   206
12.2 8: The Mormon Proposition (2010)   207

Introduction

Randall Balmer and Jana Riess

The story of Mormonism in America is inextricably tied to politics. Joseph Smith's youthful run-ins with the law over divination and treasure-hunting had political overtones, as did the accusations of his inappropriate behavior toward young women. Persecution fueled the Mormons' peregrinations from Fayette, New York, to Kirtland, Ohio, to Far West, Missouri, where they ran into a buzz saw of political opposition, culminating in Governor Lilburn Boggs's infamous "Extermination Order" of 1838 that chased the Mormons back across the Mississippi to Nauvoo, Illinois. Although Smith had negotiated favorable political terms for his Nauvoo settlement with Illinois authorities, his own political machinations hastened his demise. His run for the presidency in 1844, cut short by his murder at the hands of an angry mob on June 27, may have represented an attempt, however quixotic, by the perennial outsider to become the ultimate insider.

Politics, both internal and external, continued to buffet the Mormons. Brigham Young's emergence as leader of the majority of Latter-day Saints during the succession crisis following Smith's death showcased his political skills, and his genius as a leader was never more in evidence than in the great trek to the Salt Lake Basin to create the political entity that Young called Deseret. Politics followed the Mormons there as well, especially when Deseret came under the jurisdiction of the United States at the conclusion of the Mexican War in 1848. The ensuing decades were replete with political tugs-of-war between the federal government and the Church of Jesus Christ of Latter-day Saints over territory, jurisdiction, and especially polygamy.

The Mormon prophet Wilford Woodruff's Manifesto of 1890, which officially abandoned plural marriage, paved the way for Utah's statehood six years later. The new state, populated then (as now) by a majority of Mormons, was entitled to send representatives to Washington. Although elected to Congress in 1898, B. H. Roberts was denied his seat in the House of Representatives because he was a polygamist. Reed Smoot, though not a polygamist himself, had to fight for his seat in the Senate from 1904 to 1907 as Congress conducted what amounted to a proxy war over the persistence of plural marriage. Despite the 1890 Manifesto, some Mormons had continued to practice polygamy through the turn of the twentieth century, but in 1904 Woodruff issued a second manifesto that made plural marriage an excommunicable offense. Smoot finally took office in 1907 and served until 1933.

By the middle decades of the twentieth century, Mormons were no longer outsiders in the political process. Ezra Taft Benson, who would later become president of the Church of Jesus Christ of Latter-day Saints, served the entirety of Dwight Eisenhower's two presidencies as secretary of agriculture and exercised a significant role in strengthening the Mormon people's political affiliation with the Republican Party. Throughout most of the twentieth century, Utah and many of the adjacent states in the so-called Mormon Corridor were represented by Mormons in Congress and in various state legislatures.

Still, the ultimate political office, the presidency of the United States, eluded Mormons, though not for lack of trying. Mormon aspirants to the presidency have ranged from the serious to the symbolic and have included Jon Huntsman, former Republican governor of Utah; Morris Udall, Democratic member of Congress from Arizona; Orrin Hatch, Republican senator from Utah; and Sonia Johnson, excommunicated Mormon feminist who ran a third-party campaign for the presidency in 1984. Two Mormons who mounted the most serious quests for a major-party nomination were George and Mitt Romney, father and son, both of them Republicans and both of them governors, who pursued their bids for the presidency forty years apart, in 1968 and 2008. Mitt Romney also ran a second time in 2012, clinching the Republican nomination after a bitter primary fight.

The papers in this volume, with the exception of three essays (John G. Turner on Brigham Young and "unpopular sovereignty," Jana Riess on the removal of Congressman B. H. Roberts, and Randall Balmer on the contrast between George and Mitt Romney on the "Mormon question"), were first presented at a conference on Mormonism and Politics, held at Columbia University, February 3–4, 2012. Pundits for months had been proclaiming the "Mormon Moment." Just a few blocks to the south of the conference, *The Book of Mormon* musical was taking Broadway by storm. Jon Huntsman, the former governor of Utah and former ambassador to China, had ended his quest for the Republican presidential nomination just a couple of weeks earlier, throwing his support to Mitt Romney, who would soon emerge as the presumptive Republican nominee.

In organizing the conference, we sought, first of all, to provide historical context for understanding the relationship between Mormonism and politics. We wanted a mix of Mormon and non-Mormon scholars, and we also wanted an interdisciplinary approach to the topic. We are confident that we were able to assemble the "A-list" of scholars on the topic. (If memory serves, only one person we asked to participate turned us down.)

On behalf of both the participants and the attendees, we should like to thank Emily Brennan, Chelsea Eben, and Joseph Blankholm of the Institute for Religion, Culture, and Public Life for their superb work in organizing the conference. We are grateful to Mark C. Taylor, chair of the religion department at Columbia and head of the Institute, for suggesting the idea. Finally, we wish to thank Wendy Lochner, Christine Dunbar, Roy Thomas, and the other professionals at Columbia University Press for shepherding this volume to publication.

Mormonism and American Politics is organized chronologically, beginning with Richard Lyman Bushman's analysis of Joseph Smith's emphasis on freedom and equality during his abortive presidential campaign of 1844. John G. Turner places Brigham Young in the context of nineteenth-century debates about popular sovereignty, and Jana Riess explores the antipolygamy rhetoric that bedeviled Mormons generally and effectively terminated the political career of B. H. Roberts. Matthew Bowman charts some of the progressive impulses within Mormonism in the early twentieth century.

Following the Woodruff Manifesto of 1890 and Utah's admission to statehood six years later, Mormons sought to integrate themselves more fully into American culture and politics during the first half of the twentieth century. Jan Shipps underscores the importance of Ezra Taft Benson in pushing Mormons away from the New Deal and toward the political right. Russell Arben Fox demonstrates that, along with many other Americans, Mormons were enamored of American civil religion, and Philip Barlow's essay explores Mormonism's relationship to the discourses of American and religious exceptionalism. Randall Balmer contrasts the handling of the "Mormon question" on the part of father and son, George and Mitt Romney. George Romney willingly talked about his faith, whereas Mitt Romney, in a very different historical context, studiously avoided the topic.

In the final section, David Campbell, Christopher Karpowitz, and Quin Monson employ social-scientific methods to analyze Mormons' political attitudes and behavior. One might expect that a people who endured persecution themselves would assume a more forceful role in advocating for the rights of other minorities, but that has not always been the case. Max Mueller examines the vexing issue of race throughout the history of the Latter-day Saints, and Claudia Bushman shows that although Mormon women do not speak with one voice, many yearn for equality, fuller recognition, and leadership possibilities within the Church of Jesus Christ of Latter-day Saints. Joanna Brooks uses the notion of "undergrounding" to understand Mormon efforts to pass Proposition 8 in California and thereby overturn same-sex marriage. Finally, Peggy Fletcher Stack analyzes media coverage of Mitt Romney's campaigns for the presidency in 2008 and 2012.

Collectively, these essays raise important questions: What is the status of the outsider in American political culture? What drives outsiders to seek a place at the table, and how does cultural acceptance affect their sense of identity? After overwhelming support for Franklin Roosevelt's New Deal, for example, Mormonism's surprising turn toward political conservatism in the mid-twentieth century might be seen against the background of Mormons' political, economic, and cultural coming-of-age. That is, apart from the idiosyncrasies of personalities and politics, as Mormons became more assimilated into American life, they became increasingly conservative. They came to believe that they had interests to protect, including the protection of the traditional nuclear family and an investment in the American enterprise that lured them toward the right of the political spectrum in the expectation (misguided or not) that more conservative policies might protect those interests. Mormons' political views have changed with their shifting cultural locations, from the literal borderlands of the United States to the centers of power, thereby becoming insiders, invested in the political process and deeply committed to patriotism.

That turn toward the right was not always comfortable. George Romney would be considered a liberal by today's political standards, and his son Mitt Romney's governorship in Massachusetts was liberal in many ways, though he later actively disowned his accomplishments in his quest for the Republican presidential nomination. Mormon politicians, like all good politicians, know how to read the political winds and trim their sails accordingly.

For all of their political success, however, Mormons still fell short of capturing the ultimate political prize, the presidency of the United States, an office replete with both power and symbolism. Ever since the victory of John F. Kennedy, a Roman Catholic, in the 1960 presidential election, various groups have viewed the presidency as the ultimate validation of their transition from outsider to insider status. For those inclined to see the glass as half full, the grand narrative of American culture, including American political culture, has become increasingly inclusive, and nothing illustrates that better than the election of an African American as president in 2008 and 2012. But as one group wins cultural acceptance, there's always another waiting in the wings—women, Jews, gays, Hispanics, Asians, Mormons, and, perhaps in a more distant future, Muslims or secularists. All seek the legitimation of political success, which often pits one group against another. Barack Obama's reelection in 2012 came at the expense of Mitt Romney, the first Mormon to win the presidential nomination of a major political party.

Despite Mormons' success at local and state levels, no Mormon has yet captured the presidency. Joseph Smith's unlikely campaign was more than a century premature, but the fact that Mitt Romney was a plausible candidate provides an index for how far Mormons have progressed from outsiders to insiders. The "Mormon Moment" of 2012 may not have culminated with the White House, but the opportunity to win the presidency, and thereby attain the ultimate prize and validation in American politics, will almost certainly present itself again.

MORMONISM AND AMERICAN POLITICS

PART I

Origins and Tensions

1 Joseph Smith's Presidential Ambitions

Richard Lyman Bushman

On May 17, 1844, the Democratic Party met in Baltimore to select James K. Polk as their presidential candidate. It featured the usual hullabaloo of nineteenth-century party politics. The same day in Nauvoo, Illinois, another convention met in the office of Joseph Smith to nominate the Mormon prophet for the presidency as an independent candidate. The formalities were followed by a scaled-down version of the Baltimore festivities. That night Smith's friends lit a barrel of tar in front of his house and twice carried him around the fire while a band filled the air with music.

The miniature convention and tar-burning ceremony publicized a campaign that had been moving forward for four months. The Twelve Apostles, the church's highest governing body after Smith and his two counselors, had first nominated him on January 29 after a frustrating autumn when the five prospective candidates of both parties had refused to promise the Mormons protection from their enemies. In November of 1843, Smith had posed the question to each of them: "*What will be your rule of action, relative to us as a people?*" None of them had answered satisfactorily. Henry Clay said he could not bind himself to any constituency in advance of the election. John C. Calhoun said typically "the case does not come within the Jurisdiction of the Federal Government," igniting an explosion of vexation from Smith: "The States rights doctrines are what feeds mobs. . . . They are a dead carcass, a stink."

The Mormon newspaper, the *Times and Seasons*, accounted for Smith's candidacy by explaining that "under existing circumstances we have no other alternative, and if we can accomplish our object well, if not we shall have the satisfaction of knowing that we have acted conscientiously." Smith himself said he would never have allowed his friends to nominate him if the Saints "could have had the privilege of enjoying our religious & civel [sic] rights." He presented himself as a protest candidate.[1]

The sequence of events in 1843 and 1844 can be seen as an encapsulated version of the overall trajectory of Smith's political career. Reluctance followed by involvement was the pattern he followed throughout his life. He did not want to get mixed up in politics in 1830, the year the church was organized, any more than he did in 1844, but was drawn in by the needs of the church. He had begun his religious career as a millenarian with no interest in America as a nation. When the Church of Christ was organized in 1830, the expectation of an immediate return of Christ made man-made governments irrelevant. All of them would be erased when the Savior installed the millennial order. "Ye will have no laws but my laws when I come," one revelation informed the Saints.[2]

Change came because of the Saints' need for government protection. In 1831 they had laid the foundation for a new Zion in Jackson County, Missouri, on the edge of American settlement. Two years later they were expelled and forced to move north where they began again in Caldwell and Daviess Counties. In 1838 they were dislodged once more. The Missouri governor, Lilburn Boggs, led to believe the Mormons had attacked the state militia, issued his infamous "Extermination Order," forcing the Mormons to move once more, this time to Illinois where they began again in Nauvoo.

This recurring hostility convinced Smith that he could not build his Zion without state protection. His tiny band of Saints could not stand alone against attacks from the communities where they lived. Without the intervention of the state militia or federal troops, Mormons would be at the mercy of their persecutors. Almost immediately after news of the 1833 expulsion, Smith had appealed to the Governor of Missouri, and when no aid was forthcoming, he petitioned President Andrew Jackson. With locals as his enemies, the higher levels of government were his only hope. Again in 1839 he appealed to President Martin Van Buren for succor, and in 1844, as pressures built up in Illinois, his first instinct was to call upon Washington.

Smith's revelations sustained his growing conviction that the only hope for peace lay with the federal government. One said that the principles of the Constitution in protecting people in their rights came from heaven: "That law of the land which is constitutional, supporting that principle of freedom in maintaining rights and privileges, belongs to all mankind, and is justifiable before me."[3] From an irrelevance at the beginning of Smith's prophetic career, government became a necessity after 1833. He saw in the constitutional guarantee of freedom of worship the ideological grounds for demanding federal protection. He valued the founding document almost entirely for its role in protecting personal rights such as freedom of worship. He threw himself into the presidential race determined to protect all abused minorities, such as slaves and prisoners, but with the needs of his own people foremost in his mind.

Indifference followed by involvement, then, appears to have been the trajectory of Joseph Smith's overall political career. His interest appears to have been spurred almost entirely by his need to protect the church. He was a political innocent with little interest in politics until the attacks on his people required government help. That conclusion seems to follow from his history between 1830 and 1844, but it is not the whole story. When we bring the Book of Mormon into the picture, a book published in 1830 at the beginning of his political career, Smith's later interest in national affairs appears in a new light.

Smith claimed the Book of Mormon was a translation of an ancient record that had come into his hands by divine means. It was not a modern history but one written by ancient prophets much like the Bible. It began hundreds of years before Christ and ended in 421 CE. It had no bearing on nineteenth-century American politics, but in its own terms it was a highly political book. Its prophets were deeply involved with the government, and its concerns were national more than individual. If the Book of Mormon represents Smith's thought in 1830, he had politics and good government on his mind from the beginning.

From the opening pages, authority, rule, and power are at the forefront of Book of Mormon history. Nephi, the first prophet-recorder who left Jerusalem around 600 BCE and with his father's family headed for a new promised land, presents himself as the mistreated younger son who suffered at the hands of his older brothers Laman and Lemuel. Their quarrels and eventual separation established a framework for the entire book. For a thousand years, the descendants of the brothers did battle with one another until in the end the Lamanites eradicated the Nephites. On one level these brotherly battles were familial; they warred as rival siblings and their descendants as antagonistic cousins. But the issue, as Laman and Lemuel saw it, was authority. Who had the right to govern the band of migrants? Nephi had taken charge when, by custom and right, Laman should have succeeded to his father's headship. Nephi wrote his account of the family's history to show that he was the legitimate leader despite his status as a younger brother. The older two, his account argued, had forfeited their rights of leadership by consistently resisting their father, their inspired younger brother, and God. Nephi was the obedient son blessed with visions and backed by divine power. Laman and Lemuel had opposed God's purposes at every turn. That division set up the framework for the entire book: the wars between Nephites and Lamanites always turned on the question of Nephi's usurpation of authority. The overarching plot of the Book of Mormon grew out of Nephi's claim to rule.

From Nephi on, the narrative dwelt almost continuously on the interplay of prophecy and politics. Government was never very far from the action. Kings, chief judges, generals, successions of power, changes in the form of government, dissenting factions, political assassinations, civil-military relationships, and the descent into anarchy when government broke down all figure in the book. For one span, the record-keepers omitted politics from their account to concentrate on the spiritual, but the separation did not work. Without politics, the history foundered. The recorders seemed to feel superfluous and wrote less and less. The Nephite record revived only when the record-keepers began to talk again of the nation's political life and turned the record over to a king.[4] From then on, the record came back to life. For much of the time, kings and chief judges were the prophets and kept the record. When they left the judgment seat to preach, they were always in touch with the rulers and generals. Events at the center of power were never far out of the picture. The book was written from within the beltway.

Even when not in office, the prophets concerned themselves with the well-being of the nation. They were not like revivalist preachers who wanted to make a few converts and start a church. Individual conversions in the Book of Mormon usually involved kings and chief judges. More often than not, the prophets spoke to the whole nation rather than to individuals. The prophets were not always rulers themselves, but they always considered themselves the monitors of the nation's goodness. Like the prophets in the Hebrew Bible, they thought corporately and focused on the righteousness of rulers and the people as a whole. Religion and the state were not separated; religion thoroughly infused thinking about the state. The great issue was the religious condition of the people and their rulers; if righteous, the nation flourished; when wicked, it declined. The prophets' threats and promises dealt with the fate of the nation—its prosperity and its decline and fall. That is the way the Hebrew Bible thought, and the same outlook pervades the Book of Mormon. The word "nation" appears 744 times in the Book of Mormon; the word "people" 3,997 times. The book has a national consciousness.

With the Book of Mormon in his background, it would not be the least unnatural for Joseph Smith to think nationally and to be concerned with the righteousness of the nation and its rulers. That is the factor we must introduce into the picture as we trace Joseph Smith's political outlook. The Book of Mormon precedent made attention to politics a natural part of his prophetic identity. In the Book of Mormon, prophets slipped in and out of political leadership as kings, chief judges, or generals; why not a modern prophet?

We get an idea of how the Book of Mormon may have shaped Smith's political thought by examining his 1844 political platform, *General Smith's Views of the Powers and Policy of the Government of the United States* (Nauvoo: John Taylor, 1844). W. W. Phelps authored the document, but Phelps probably thought as much like Joseph Smith as any of his followers. When the Prophet showed the platform to guests, he expressed pride in the document as if it were his own. The Nauvoo Press printed 1,500 copies which were mailed to President John Tyler, the Supreme Court Justices, all the members of Congress, and newspapers all over the country. The 300 missionaries who were sent out to promote Smith's candidacy saw to printings in Pittsburgh, Philadelphia, New York, and Pontiac, Michigan. *Views* was the face of Smith's campaign.[5]

The platform has been ransacked by modern Mormons for hints about Joseph Smith's opinions on twenty-first-century political issues.[6] Modern Mormons rejoice in his vigorous opposition to slavery and his ingenious plan to buy out slaveholders with revenues from the sale of public lands. Latter-day Saint Democrats take comfort in his phrase the "fostering care of government" applied to the encouragement of industry through tariffs and the establishment of a national bank.[7] But efforts to identify Joseph Smith's political position on contemporary issues are no more conclusive than the claims of both Democrats and Republicans to the mantle of Thomas Jefferson. Conditions in the country have altered too radically to translate political views of the 1840s to the 2010s.

It is more suitable to ask if traces of Book of Mormon prophetic politics turn up in Smith's political platform. One possible carryover is the apparent link to the alteration in government in the middle of the book, about 92 BCE. At that point, government went from a monarchy to a government by judges chosen by "the voice of the people." That alteration on first glance appears to constitute an obvious endorsement of American democracy, a kind of American Revolution in ancient garb with the end of monarchy and the beginning of democracy.

The parallel, however, is not as close as it first appears. While popular election of judges certainly has a democratic tone, the results were not recognizably American. To begin with, monarchy in the Book of Mormon was not overthrown by popular demand or by revolution. The sitting king relinquished the throne against the wishes of the people. They wanted a king, and he had to persuade them that rule by judges was a more secure form of government. He installed a chief judge with layers of lesser judges below him who were selected by the voice of the people and then served as checks on one another. Once chosen, however, the voice of the people figured only irregularly. The chief judge served for life, and when he died, the office passed to his son in kingly fashion. Moreover, the chief judge made laws without recourse to a legislature. Representation did not figure at all in Nephite government; there was no congress.

The transition from monarchy to judgeships was less a reenactment of the American Revolution than a reversal of ancient Israel's passage from government by judges to rule by a king. Israel's prophets had resisted the popular desire for a king and only reluctantly agreed to the anointing of Saul. The Book of Mormon corrected that error. It abolished kingship and reinstated judges. Its inspiration seems to have been the Hebrew Bible rather than the Declaration of Independence and the Constitution.[8]

Views, by contrast, went far beyond any Book of Mormon text to endorse democracy. Book of Mormon prophets nowhere declared anything like *Views*'s enthusiastic declaration that "in the United States, the people are the government; and their united voice is the only sovereign that should rule; the only power that should be obeyed."[9] In the Book of Mormon, ultimate obedience would be granted only to God and His law. The book's prophets never implied that the nation's officers "are nothing more or less the servants of the people."¹⁰ The nation's officers in the Book of Mormon were nothing more or less than the servants of God. *Views* says that "the aspirations and expectations of a virtuous people . . . ought to be treated by those to whom the administration of the laws are intrusted with as much sanctity, as the prayers of the saints are treated in heaven."¹¹ That kind of exaltation of popular sovereignty is not heard in the Book of Mormon where the reason for giving the people a voice is much more sober. Mosiah advocated election of judges to make the people morally responsible for the good of the nation, rather than putting the whole burden on kings.¹² Neither the saintliness of the people nor their God-given rights underlay the "voice of the people."

In *Views* the people are given more power but, in a sense, less responsibility. The Book of Mormon is filled with warnings straight out of Jeremiah about a covenanted people displeasing God and suffering for it. The prophets bend their efforts to call the people to repentance to prevent the decline and fall of the nation. The people are the ones responsible for the ultimate demise of Nephite civilization: The nation was to fall because its people first fell into wickedness.

Views's only venture in this direction was to quote the scripture: "Righteousness exalteth a nation, but sin is the reproach to any people."¹³ Otherwise, responsibility for the failings of the nation was laid at the feet of the rulers. Good leaders rather than good people were the best hope for bringing the nation back from ruin. The problem with the United States was that the nation lacked those leaders. Instead "wicked and designing, men have unrobed the government of its glory, and the people, if not in dust and ashes, or in sack cloth, have to lament in poverty, her departed greatness: while demagogues build fires in the north and south, east and west, to keep up their spirits till it is better times."¹⁴ The people as a whole were not responsible for decline; the powerful were the ones to bring the nation down. *Views* feared that "the nobility of the nations," the "great men," would corrupt the country. "They will dally with all rights in order to smuggle a fortune at 'one fell swoop,' mortgage Texas, possess Oregon, and claim all the unsettled regions of the world for hunting and trapping: and should a humble honest man, red, black, or white, exhibit a better title, these gentry have only to cloth [*sic*] the judge with richer ermine, and spangle the lawyer's fingers with finer rings, to have the judgment of his peers, and the honor of his lords."¹⁵ *Views*'s call for reform was less directed at popular morality than at the designs of the powerful. At most, the platform called on the nation to "turn unto the Lord and live; and reform this nation. Frustrate the designs of wicked men."[16] Almost nothing was said of popular repentance.

With these fairly sharp contrasts between the two, did the Book of Mormon and *Views* converge anywhere? Primarily they agreed on the value of harmony in politics. On his visit to the Nephites, Jesus had said that doctrinal contention was of the devil and the principle held true for politics as well. When wickedness infected Nephite society, factions arose and contention followed. Mormon measured the well-being and righteousness of society by the absence of dissent. The Book of Mormon values a politics of harmony. More often than not, defeated dissenters fled the country and established themselves as robber bands in the mountains. Alternately, they sought to overthrow the government to achieve their ends. They resorted to assassination or alliances with the Lamanites. There seemed to be no concept of a loyal opposition as an ongoing and possibly healthy element in government. Dissent led to breakdown; peace and harmony was the only stable state.

In that same spirit, *Views* states on the first page:

> Unity is Power; and when I reflect on the importance of it to the stability of all governments, I am astounded at the silly moves of persons and parties, to foment discord in order to ride into power on the current of popular excitement.[17]

Joseph believed, unrealistically we would say, that government could be based on trust and friendship. The South, he believed, would end slavery voluntarily and happily if compensated for their slaves' value. His plan was to recompense southern slaveholders out of funds collected from sale of public lands. That would end the problem, he was sure: "The southern people are hospitable and noble: they will help to rid so free a country of every vestige of slavery, when ever they are assured of an equivalent for their property."[18] Although opposed to slavery, Joseph disliked abolitionists because they stirred up controversy and protest. Joseph wanted peaceful resolution of the problem where all would join in willingly.

The same held true for the disputes with neighbors that riled the political waters in 1844. There was controversy over the boundary with Canada and a ferocious debate about acquiring Texas from Mexico. The solution of *Views* was to welcome them both into the United States:

My voice would be, come: yea come Texas: come Mexico; come Canada; and come all the world—let us be brethren: let us be one great family; and let there be universal peace.[19]

Smith had the same hope for all foreign relations. *Views* borrowed from James Madison to say:

To cherish peace and friendly intercourse with all nations, having correspondent dispositions; to maintain sincere neutrality towards belligerent nations; to prefer in all cases amicable discussion and reasonable accommodation to intrigues and foreign partialities so degrading to all countries, and so baneful to free ones.[20]

He believed even prisoners (probably thinking imprisonment for debt) could be treated kindly.

Petition your state legislatures to pardon every convict in their several penitentiaries: blessing them as they go, and saying to them in the name of the Lord, go thy way and sin no more. . . . Rigor and seclusion will never do as much to reform the propensities of man, as reason and friendship. . . . Let the penitentiaries be turned into seminaries of learning, where intelligence, like the angels of heaven, would banish such fragments of barbarism.[21]

On the whole, Smith wanted to do away with political parties which he, like so many other Americans, saw as the source of needless contention: "We have had democratic presidents; whig presidents; and a pseudo democratic whig president; and now it is time to have a president of the United States."[22] Smith and Phelps may have gone further with his pleas for peace and harmony than Book of Mormon prophets, but the same desire for dissent-free politics underlay both *Views* and the book.

Joseph Smith did not derive his politics entirely from the Book of Mormon by any means. He adapted his political platform to the world he lived in—a nation that prided itself on its republican form of government. *Views* is far more democratic than the Book of Mormon. The people were a backdrop in the Book of Mormon, politically visible only in the rare instances when there was a dispute over the chief judge. They were not represented in a legislature or said to possess the right to govern. The Book of Mormon does not advocate government by the people.

The closer affinity between *Views* and the Book of Mormon lies in a shared distaste for dissent and contention. In *Views* Smith hopes that brotherhood and friendship will prevail. "Let us be brethren: let us be one great family; and let there be universal peace."[23] *Views* does offer a series of policies to alleviate the miseries of slaves and prisoners and to increase the prosperity of the nation, but Smith's contribution was more a prophetic vision than a blueprint for change. His theology is noted for its high anthropology. He thought humans bore the seeds of godhood within them, and in time could enjoy the fullness of godly power. We can see that exalted optimism at work in *Views*. The discouraging realities of American politics did not weaken his hopes for a union of hearts and minds ruled by benevolence and virtue. He conceived his role not as a policy expert to create a blueprint or a politician to win an election, but as a prophet, like his predecessors in the Book of Mormon, to tell a society of its own possibilities. So he could exclaim at the end: "The very name of 'American' is fraught with friendship! Oh! Then, create confidence! Restore freedom!—break down slavery! Banish imprisonment for debt, and be in love, fellowship and peace with all the world."[24]

Joseph Smith, as his brief history shows, only reluctantly involved himself in national politics. Government came into his field of vision only after 1833 when he needed protection from the church's persecutors. His political interests seemed restricted to his people's right to practice their religion unhindered. But the Book of Mormon opened another dimension of his thought. It measured political success by righteousness, peace, and unity. Smith's *Views* drew upon that aspiration and installed it in his platform for American government. Smith wanted to calm and pacify American politics, to drain it of its vitriol and partisan contention. His great wish was to show the nation how to live together in peace and friendship. The appeal of these ideas in the election of 1844 was never tested. Four months before the election, while his corps of missionaries was promoting his candidacy across the land, Smith was shot by a mob, a victim of the hatred that he had yearned to dispel.

Notes

1. For quotations and supporting citations, see Richard Lyman Bushman, *Joseph Smith: Rough Stone Rolling* (New York: Knopf, 2005), 514–15.

2. *The Doctrine and Covenants* (Salt Lake City: The Church of Jesus Christ of Latter-day Saints, 1981), 38:22. The Saints' Zion was to be formed at the very edge of American settlements, not near the population centers, as if national geography

was irrelevant. The designation of the site for the New Jerusalem spoke of "the place which is now called Independence," as if the political name for the city was a temporary expedient that was not to last. *Doctrine and Covenants*, 57:3.

3. *Doctrine and Covenants*, 98:5.
4. *The Book of Mormon*, trans. Joseph Smith (Salt Lake City: The Church of Jesus Christ of Latter-day Saints, 1981), Omni 12.
5. Richard D. Poll, "Joseph Smith and the Presidency," *Dialogue: A Journal of Mormon Thought* 3 (Autumn 1968): 17–21.
6. For a balanced evaluation, see Martin B. Hickman, "The Political Legacy of Joseph Smith," *Dialogue* 3 (Autumn 1968): 22–27.
7. *Views*, 4.
8. Richard L. Bushman, "The Book of Mormon and the American Revolution," *BYU Studies* 17 (Autumn 1976): 3–20.
9. *Views*, 8.
10. *Views*, 8.
11. *Views*, 1.
12. Book of Mormon, Mosiah 29.
13. *Views*, 5.
14. *Views*, 4.
15. *Views*, 6.
16. *Views*, 6.
17. *Views*, 1.
18. *Views*, 8.
19. *Views*, 8.
20. *Views*, 4.
21. *Views*, 6–7.
22. *Views*, 8.
23. *Views*, 8.
24. *Views*, 7.

2 Unpopular Sovereignty

Brigham Young and the U.S. Government, 1847–1877

John G. Turner

On June 27, 1854, Brigham Young and John Taylor spoke in the Salt Lake Tabernacle on the tenth anniversary of Joseph Smith's martyrdom.[1] It was a sweltering day, so hot that Young ordered thirty barrels of water brought to the tabernacle to provide for the congregation. During Young's morning address, he repeatedly affirmed his abiding love for and fealty toward his beloved prophet. "I am the apostle of Joseph Smith Jr. that brought forth life and salvation to the world," Young stated. Just like the disciples of Jesus saw him in the flesh and then examined his wounds, so Young had known Joseph. "I was not in jail to be sure when he was shot...," he explained, "[but] I saw his body since his death and saw where the bullets pierced him." "I can testify that Joseph is prophet by revelation," he continued, "[and] I can testify he was for I felt him I slept with him I embraced him and kissed him ... I ate with him drank with him walked with him handled him." With firmness and conviction, Young testified to his knowledge that his beloved Joseph was indeed God's prophet. It was a gut-wrenching, heart-churning occasion for the second president of the Church of Jesus Christ of Latter-day Saints, especially as John Taylor talked at length of the events in Carthage jail. "I want those things kept by those who know them," he said the next day, "I do not want to hear them until the time comes." Joseph's murder had left an open wound within Brigham Young's psyche. He preferred not to think about it.[2]

The subject of Joseph's death stirred up both sadness and bitterness, bitterness at the governments of Missouri, Illinois, and the United States. "The government of God and the government of the children of men in their wickedness," Young explained, "is so diametrically opposed to each other [that they] never can become friends and see eye to eye." The United States, he continued, was established "by the hand of [the] Almighty," but the nation no longer honored its revolutionary principles. The United States and other governments of the world feared "the whole proposition of holy priesthood because it would take away the foundations of their government." That priesthood, Young concluded, "is a fair system of government that governs all God's angels and heavenly beings." A portion of that government had come down to earth "for men to govern his earth by that he may be prepared to enter in."[3]

Ten days later, Young delivered another long discourse, this time on the commemoration of American independence from Great Britain. He continued on the theme of the nation's political apostasy from its founding principles. The United States might have developed a true republican and democratic government, one "perfect in its laws and ordinances, having for its object the perfection of mankind in righteousness." Jacksonian democracy, however, was anything but true democracy. Instead, political parties and mobs "tear down and destroy Catholic churches, drive citizens from the ballot box, disallowing them the right of franchise, and persecute, plunder, drive from their possessions, and kill a great people." Whiggery and Democracy both presided over outrages antithetical to democracy and republicanism. Young speculated how his people should proceed were they an independent nation. They should "govern themselves by a Republican system of government" and select "a man from their midst to preside over them." Without any restrictions on length of service, he should be their "President, dictator, lawgiver, controller, and guide in a national capacity." Under this government, there would be unity instead of division. It would protect the rights of all people instead of sanctioning mob rule. Young had not entirely given up on the nation. It might yet return to its founding principles and select enlightened rulers who would guard the rights of all Americans. More likely, however, was a continued descent into corruption and despotism until the Latter-day Saints stepped forward and saved the nation from utter destruction.[4]

FIGURE 2.1
Brigham Young, ca. 1850. (Courtesy of the Church History Library, Church of Jesus Christ of Latter-day Saints)

Brigham Young was no political philosopher. "Brother Phelps calls this kingdom a theodemocracy," he observed in a June 1861 discourse, "call it what you please."[5] What mattered, he said, was that people "be of one heart and mind, and not give our strength and substance, and treasure to the wicked world." Young's political principles were simple, straightforward, and largely unconcealed. Embittered by the murder of Joseph Smith and the repeated expulsions of the Saints from their homes in Missouri and Illinois, he deeply distrusted any non-Mormon political authorities and accordingly sought to preserve the Saints' political autonomy. The Mormons, he insisted, possessed the republican right to self-rule. A republican people, Young said on another occasion, possess the right "to choose their own rulers."[6]

Theodemocracy, however, also meant priesthood rule in opposition to how most other Americans understood republicanism. Thus, during the early years of the Utah Territory, Young and other high-ranking church leaders selected candidates for office that duly received the near-unanimous approval of voters. When Young built his Lion House and Beehive House mansions on the southeastern corner of what became known as

Temple Square, the "Church President's Office" and the "Governor's Office" both stood between them. Young, of course, occupied both offices, a visible symbol of the intermixture of church and state in early Utah. In Young's mind, this was entirely consistent with American republicanism. The people had submitted to the authority of the priesthood through their baptism, through their sacred covenants, and through their decision to follow their leaders to the West. "Our system should be Theodemocracy," apostle George A. Smith explained in 1865, "the voice of the people consenting to the voice of God."[7] Theodemocracy, the "democracy of heaven," brought about unity, whereas the "democracy of earth" generated only division. Furthermore, Young insisted on his own political authority as the church's president. When he reorganized the church's First Presidency in 1847, he told the hesitant apostles of his need to be "perfectly untrammeled."[8]

Utah and Washington were at odds for over half a century, from the earliest days of Brigham Young's governorship in 1851 until the 1907 resolution of the controversy over Reed Smoot's seat in the U.S. Senate. The reasons for the long conflict are rather simple. The Latter-day Saints claimed the republican right to govern themselves under the spiritual and

FIGURE 2.2 Lion House and Beehive House, ca. 1855. In the center of the photograph are the "Church President's Office" and the "Governor's Office." (Courtesy of the Church History Library, Church of Jesus Christ of Latter-day Saints)

temporal authority of the priesthood. Washington, by contrast, claimed the right to influence Utah affairs through political appointments, congressional oversight of territorial laws, and congressional statutes. Similar dynamics rankled other American westerners who lived under the territorial system, and the doctrine of popular sovereignty encouraged westerners to aspire to a greater degree of self-government. Utah, however, was a special case. The past persecution of the Latter-day Saints, coupled with steadily rising American outrage over Mormon polygamy and theocracy, made the conflicts in Utah more intense and dangerous. With each conflict, Mormon theodemocracy became increasingly unpopular and untenable within a nation gradually exercising its claimed sovereignty over the American West.

In July 1847, Brigham Young arrived in the Salt Lake Valley determined to assert his people's right to self-determination. Undoubtedly, Young took pleasure in the pioneer camp's safe passage from the Missouri River to the church's Rocky Mountain refuge from its Eastern persecutors. Yet when Young contemplated the way that Gentiles (i.e., non-Mormons) had treated his people, his blood still boiled. He spoke of the need for the "Kingdom of God" to "rise independent of the Gentile nations," an independence that hinged on economic self-sufficiency. "I am determined to cut every thread of this Kind," recorded Norton Jacobs, "and live free and independent, untrammeled by any of their detestable customs and practices. You don't know how I detest and despise them." According to Wilford Woodruff, Young recounted the persecutions of the Saints in the East, including the murder of his beloved Joseph Smith. Young insisted that Smith would still be alive "if the Twelve had been in Nauvoo" when he crossed the river from Montrose and allowed himself to be arrested. Young maintained he would never have permitted Smith's self-sacrifice. He spoke of his people's repeated expulsions from their homes. Their persecutors, "in the day of the Lord Jesus," could only have saved themselves if they had "come forward voluntarily and let their heads be cut off and let their blood run upon the ground and gone up as a smoking incense before the heavens as an atonement." Young was not prepared to forgive the murderers of Joseph and Hyrum Smith or those church members who had encouraged or allowed the prophet to submit to arrest.

The Saints had left the United States behind when they made their involuntary exodus from Nauvoo, but the nation of their birth had refused to leave them alone. At Young's behest, five hundred Mormon men had offered their services to the U.S. Army in the ongoing war against Mexico, but that decision was pragmatic, not patriotic. One year later, Young was not in a reconciliatory mood. He blamed President James Polk for weakening the Saints through the creation of the Mormon Battalion, and he alleged that the U.S. government had asked Missouri governor John C. Edwards to annihilate the Latter-day Saints should they have refused the enlistment request.

In light of this history, Young threatened dire consequences should the United States ever send "men to interfere with us here." "They shall have their throats cut and sent to hell," he warned. Young suspected that "many of the government men had a hand in the death of Joseph and Hyrum, and he "with uplifted hands to heaven swore by the Gods of Eternity that he would never cease his exhortation while he lived to make every preparation and avenge the blood of the Prophets and saints." He expected the Saints to exercise political autonomy. "No officer of the United States should ever dictate to him in this valley," he vowed, "or he would hang them on a gibbet as a warning to others." Having suffered under the rule of others, they would govern themselves.[9]

With rather less hyperbole, Young made similar comments on other occasions during these years. In August of 1846, he sent Polk an extended letter. At the time, he noted that reports of Polk's favorable disposition toward the Mormons had "kindled up a spark in our hearts which has been well nigh extinguished" by a history of neglect and persecution. Young also apprised the president of the Saints' plans to settle in the Great Basin and their desire for a territorial government. That patriotic spark, however, was still fragile. Young cautioned that "while we appreciate the constitution of the U[nited] States, as the most precious among the nations, we feel that we had rather retreat to the deserts, Islands or mountain caves than consent to be ruled by governors and judges whose hands are drenched in the blood of Innocence and virtue, who delight in iniquities and oppressions." (Young was alarmed at a rumor that former Missouri governor Lilburn Boggs was seeking the governorship of California.) The Saints could live under the political umbrella of the United States, but they feared hostile outside officials and judges.[10]

In late 1848, the church's Council of Fifty, which functioned as a secretive provisional legislature at this time, decided to petition Congress to create a territory named "Deseret," named after a Book of Mormon word connoting industriousness and cooperation. Mormon leaders asked Washington to allocate much of the American West to Deseret, including most of present-day Arizona, Nevada, and Utah as well as portions of Oregon, California, Wyoming, Colorado, and New Mexico. Soon, however, church leaders became alarmed by the specter of non-Mormon office-seekers coming to Deseret with only their own financial interests in mind. Thus, the Council of Fifty changed course, holding elections for the "State of Deseret" in March. The Saints unanimously affirmed a slate of candidates headed by Young, their choice for governor. Deseret quickly developed the trappings of an independent nation, with its own currency, flag, and army. Mormon leaders quickly wrote a state constitution, fabricated the results of a constitutional convention, and drafted a new memorial to Congress, requesting admission into the Union as a state, hoping as was California to bypass territorial status.

The church's petitions reached a Congress at loggerheads over the issue of slavery, particularly as it pertained to the incorporation of territory wrested from Mexico in the recent war. Beginning in 1846, some antislavery Democrats in the North endorsed what became known as the Wilmot Proviso, which would have prohibited slavery in any territory acquired from Mexico. At the same time, South Carolina senator (and former vice president) John C. Calhoun insisted that no territory possessed the constitutional power to restrict slavery. In 1849, Young expressed himself in favor of "free soil," but he simultaneously stated that "we do not wish a prohibitory clause to attach itself to our Territory." The Wilmot Proviso clashed with the church's desire for territorial autonomy.[11] Young keenly appreciated the emerging doctrine of popular sovereignty, a maddeningly vague concept designed to bridge differences between moderates in both the North and the South. Popular sovereignty, as outlined by proponents such as Lewis Cass and eventually Stephen Douglas, insisted that the people of a territory possessed the right to decide whether to legalize or prohibit slavery.

It quickly became apparent that Deseret's bid for statehood had no support in Congress. Getting wind that territorial status was more likely, Young angrily dictated a letter to John Bernhisel, one of his representatives in Washington. He complained that it would be a novelty "to see the people and authorities quietly yielding up the Government into the hands of those it was the pleasure of their oppressors to appoint." Young wished to remind Washington that "all Republican Governments emenats [emanates] from the people and that it is they who have the right to dictate that they are the Parents and not the child."[12]

Despite Young's protestations and Bernhisel's efforts, the Compromise of 1850 created the Territory of Utah instead of admitting the State of Deseret. Congress allowed that "when admitted as a State, the said Territory, or any portion of the same, shall be received into the Union, with or without slavery, as their constitution may prescribe at the time of their admission."[13] The bill was silent about Utah's right to either codify or prohibit slavery prior to statehood. With relatively little fanfare, the measure overturned the thirty-year-old Missouri Compromise line, as Utah lay north of the of the 36° 30´ parallel.

Young and other church leaders understood the utility of popular sovereignty for Mormon Utah. In their minds, the federal government had no right to interfere in Utah's domestic institutions. Young suggested in a September 1852 letter that "as for Congress they might as well abolish slavery in the South as plurality in Utah."[14] If popular sovereignty made black slavery a territorial matter, surely plural marriage also fell outside federal control. What Young probably did not fully understand was the tenuous standing of popular sovereignty throughout the 1850s. Southern and northern Democrats understood the doctrine differently, with those differences primarily hinging on when the people or legislatures of territories could choose to codify or prohibit slavery.[15] At best, the doctrine as advanced by Stephen Douglas in the early 1850s rested upon an extremely fragile consensus. Any protection it offered to Utah would collapse with that consensus. As it turned out, conflict between Utah and Washington would play a role in hastening its collapse.

In the meantime, Utah's white residents received the prerogative of deciding the matter of slavery for themselves. In a move that gained surprisingly little attention in a capital city increasingly preoccupied with the issue, Utah's territorial legislature in early 1852 created a legal framework for black and Indian slavery. As citizens of a territory, however, they did not receive the right to select all of their own leaders. President Millard Fillmore's appointment of Brigham Young as the territory's first governor created some ephemeral authority, but once Washington asserted its parental rights of appointment and legislation, conflict was inevitable.

Beginning in 1851, Washington appointed a mixture of Latter-day Saints and non-Mormons to Utah territorial offices and judgeships. The first batch of appointees arrived in the summer of 1851; the non-Mormon appointees remained in Utah for only two months before fleeing the territory.[16]

Shortly after their arrival, Young dressed down his own Washington representative, Almon W. Babbitt, in the presence of territorial secretary Broughton Harris. "Politicians are a stink in my nose," Young declared. Utah's governor apparently intimidated the young secretary. Clerk Thomas Bullock recorded that it was a "new scene for Mr. Harris to behold the Power of the Priesthood."[17] The next day, the church held its annual July 24 celebration, with Harris and Chief Justice Lemuel Brandebury in attendance. Responding to reports that late President Zachary Taylor had opposed even territorial government for the Mormons, Young observed that "as incidental providence would have it, he is in hell and we are here."[18] The appointees did not appreciate Young's humor. For their part, the appointees almost certainly arrived with deep suspicions about Mormonism, suspicions obviously confirmed when they observed both plural marriage and theocracy at close hand.

After weeks of steadily rising rancor, conflict between church leaders and the appointees became public at a Sunday church meeting. Associate Justice Perry E. Brocchus delivered an address in which he questioned the patriotism of Mormon leaders and—quite unwisely—the virtue of Mormon women. According to reports of the meeting, church members were nearly ready to attack Brocchus, who had arrived in Utah hoping to return to Washington as the territory's congressional delegate. Young expressed sympathy with the crowd's angry response to Brocchus's speech, but he stated that he would not encourage anything that might lead to the "pulling of hair or cutting of throats."[19] Several weeks later, the non-Mormon appointees all fled the territory, convinced that more than their political careers were in danger. "Mormonism was a little to[o] warm for their relish," Young wrote apostle Amasa Lyman. "I felt like kicking the poor curses['] arse out of the territory," Young recounted the next summer.[20] He attributed the Saints' harsh reaction to their fear of persecution. "Many in their imagination," he explained two years later, "saw us all hung, shot, drown, murdered massacred in evry imaginable shape that you could think off."[21] For the Latter-day Saints, persecution at the hands of non-Mormon politicians was not a distant memory but a live future possibility.

The "runaway judges," as church leaders cleverly named the group, returned to the East. A war of words ensued, as the appointees denounced the theocratic elements of "theodemocracy" and Mormon leaders denounced their character and manners. In all likelihood, the appointees and their successors exhibited levels of political opportunism and morality similar to their counterparts in other territories. Moreover, the personalities and details in both this and similar subsequent episodes distract from the fundamental divide between Washington politicians and church leaders. Both sides regarded the other as wielding illegitimate political authority.

Over the next several years, popular sovereignty remained the regnant but fragile solution to intersectional disputes over slavery in western territories. The doctrine never fully satisfied antislavery northerners, nor did it satisfy firebrands who insisted that territories could not restrict the property rights of southerners. It did, however, defer decisions and allow southerners and northerners to hope that future territorial decisions would accord with their wishes.

Utahans closely followed eastern news, whenever riders or mail brought newspapers and rumors. In April 1854, Brigham Young's Sunday prayer circle spent an evening engaged in "conversation on the new nebraska bill."[22] The next month, Congress passed the Kansas-Nebraska Act, which more explicitly overturned the Missouri Compromise and opened the territories of Nebraska and Kansas to slavery should their residents so choose. Church leaders hoped the legislation's doctrine of popular sovereignty would shield Utah from federal interference in its domestic institutions.[23]

Meanwhile, non-Mormon army officers and politicians passed through Utah and usually passed out again with negative comments about the church and its leaders. By 1855, Young's four-year term as territorial governor had expired. President Franklin Pierce offered Lieutenant Colonel Edward Steptoe the governorship. Steptoe, along with 325 soldiers, had stopped in Salt Lake City during the winter of 1854–55. Initially on good terms with Young, he changed his mind by the time he departed. The lieutenant colonel declined the gubernatorial appointment, but he wrote President Pierce a scathing indictment of what he termed "fanaticism in the mass of the people, and a religious oligarchy, or rather Monocrasy."[24] Young, meanwhile, openly declared his belief in the sovereignty of the priesthood. "If I continue to be Governor," he insisted, "I will make my Governorship submit to the priesthood."[25] Utah's Chief Justice, the non-Mormon John F. Kinney, considered Young's rhetoric treasonous. "The avowed doctrine of the 'great Apostle,'" he wrote U.S. Attorney General Caleb Cushing two weeks after Young's sermon, "is that the authority of the Priesthood is and shall be the law of the land."[26] Kinney left the territory in 1856, though he eventually resumed relations with the church hierarchy on warmer terms.

When the Steptoe Expedition left the territory in the spring of 1855, a sizeable number of Mormon women left in the company of U.S. officers. Over the winter, moreover, there had been a number of clashes between soldiers and church members. In a fiery discourse, Young expressed regret that the soldiers had escaped punishment for their immorality. "We ought to have slain them in the middle of the day," he asserted, "and hung up their bodies or thrown them to the wolves." Young equated the soldiers' actions to those of the anti-Mormon mobs that had victimized the Saints in Missouri, and he threatened that the Saints possessed every right to "get redress by the same laws of mobocracy." If any "more mobs come [to Utah]," he warned, the Saints would be justified in "cut[ting] their damned throats." Given the likelihood of future army expeditions and forts, Young's words portended conflict. Indeed, Young's rhetoric resembles that of southern "fire-eaters" who threatened secession and violence in the face of perceived northern slights.[27]

Church leaders ardently expressed their belief in popular sovereignty as the 1850s progressed. A March 1855 *Deseret News* editorial, written while Lieutenant Colonel Steptoe debated Pierce's proffered governorship, suggested that in a republican government, "a person might reasonably expect to see the principle of 'popular sovereignty' . . . carried out to the fullest extent, and not only each state but also each territory be left to operate untrammeled so long as they kept within the bounds of the Constitution." The paper alleged that the territorial system was rank despotism, akin to the way that Great Britain had treated its colonies. "All the territories of our boasted Republic," it argued, "although contributing their full quota to swell the public revenue, are entirely at the mercy of men for whom they are denied the right of casting one vote for or against."[28] Utah contended that popular sovereignty should allow it to cast off the quasi-colonial shackles of territorial government.

The passage of the Kansas-Nebraska Act, however, accelerated the demise of popular sovereignty. An assortment of former Whigs, Free Soilers, radical antislavery Democrats, and nativists coalesced into a new Republican Party. Dedicated to "free soil, free labor, free men," the Republican Party platform in 1856 called on "Congress to prohibit in the Territories those twin relics of barbarism—Polygamy and Slavery."[29] In 1857, Vermont Representative Justin Morrill called on Congress to pass legislation that would extirpate a "Mohammadan barbarism revolting to the civilized world."[30] The *Deseret News* responded that regardless of whether Morrill's proposed legislation passed, the people of Utah remained "decidedly more in favor of 'popular sovereignty' than of 'popular institutions,' [and] they will pursue the even tenor of their ways as heretofore."[31]

Much as many Republicans despised it, polygamy was a sidebar to the ongoing violence between proslavery and antislavery settlers in Kansas. Nevertheless, Democrats correctly understood the Republican position on polygamy as a backdoor attempt to justify the regulation of territorial slavery. Thus, Illinois's Stephen Douglas as well as many southern Democrats opposed early efforts to pass antipolygamy legislation. If Congress could declare territorial polygamy a crime, why could it not prohibit slavery's further expansion? According to Utah congressional delegate John Bernhisel, Douglas expressed his opposition "to any interference with any local or domestic institution, for the reason that if the principle were once recognized it would apply everywhere, to all religious sects, slavery, etc." Douglas's position gave Mormon leaders hope that popular sovereignty would shield Utah from federal interference, and antipolygamy legislation did not pass until secession left the Republican Party with a solid majority in Congress.[32]

In early 1857, church leaders made a tactless attempt to resolve their longstanding feud with Washington over political appointments. In January, with Governor Young's approval, the territory's legislative assembly composed a memorial for incoming president James Buchanan. The memorialists warned that if Washington continued to appoint "office seekers and corrupt demagogues," Utah's citizens would "send them away." At the time, Mormon leaders were at odds with Utah's three federal justices (two of whom had left the territory) and an assortment of federal Indian agents and surveyors. A draft of the memorial had been even more incendiary, threatening federal appointees engaged in "swindling operations" with "summary punishment." The draft had also rejected the right of the national government to "distress" Utah by "locating in our midst an ungovernable and reckless soldiery." Still, even with some especially inflammatory portions excised, Utah's legislators—and Young—had issued an undiplomatic challenge to Washington.[33]

In mid-March, Utah delegate John Bernhisel delivered the memorial to newly inaugurated president James Buchanan, who instructed him to pass the document along to Secretary of the Interior Jacob Thompson. The next day, Thompson informed Bernhisel that he regarded the memorial as a "declaration of war."[34] "It is impossible for us to enforce the laws in this Territory," asserted justice W. W. Drummond in a letter published in the *New York Herald* several days after Bernhisel met with Thompson. "Every man here holds his life at the will of Brigham Young." Drummond suggested that non-Mormons were exposed to murder, robbery, castration, and imprisonment for questioning the church's authority.[35] Taking note both of Drummond's letter and the church's request for an all-Mormon slate of appointees, the *Washington Star* suggested that the "Mormons are practically in a state of rebellion."[36] The city's abolitionist *National Era* called the Latter-day Saints the "freaks of popular sovereignty."[37] Chief Justice Kinney and Utah's Surveyor General David Burr also submitted complaints to Washington about this time, both recommending that a military force accompany a new, non-Mormon governor to the territory.

Buchanan did just that, dispatching the U.S. Army to escort newly appointed governor Alfred Cumming safely to Salt Lake City. At first, Stephen Douglas hesitated to denounce the Mormons, suggesting that "Mormonism in Utah is not so bad as represented." He added that the "idea of Gov. Young taking an airing in a carriage with his twenty-six wives, with their three children each, seems to me to be beyond the bounds of credibility." However, Douglas concluded that "the popular sovereignty doctrine is not intended for Utah." Former Illinois representative Abraham Lincoln, whom Douglas would best in an 1858 bid for a Senate seat, noted that Douglas's rejection of popular sovereignty for Utah proved that his "doctrine was a mere deceitful pretense for the benefit of slavery." When he revised his remarks for publication, Douglas fully abandoned his former Mormon allies and declared it "the duty of Congress to apply the knife and cut out this loathsome, disgusting ulcer." Mormon Utah had become too unpopular for Stephen Douglas to defend.[38]

Brigham Young responded by mobilizing Utah's militia, the Nauvoo Legion, to defend the territory from the approaching U.S. Army. The traumas experienced by the Latter-day Saints in Missouri and Nauvoo continued to shape Young's leadership. Young worried about a reprisal of past horrors. "The mail not coming in regularly is ominous," Young had said during an interruption in service two years earlier, "they always stopd the mails in Kirtland, Missouri, & Nauvoo when there was a fuss on hand."[39] In his mind, if the Saints allowed the army to march into the territory they would be inviting their own destruction, and he considered his own life very much at risk. As he prepared Utah's defenses, Young called on Mormon men to "lift the sword and slay" the U.S. soldiers should they enter the valley.[40] It may well be that throughout the 1850s Young and his followers misread, exaggerated, or otherwise distorted the danger that U.S.

officials and soldiers posed to the Mormon people. Still, the past reality of persecution and martyrdom shaped their perception of events. As historian William Freehling once observed of the sectional crisis that led to the U.S. Civil War, the "ensuing fury, by producing confusion and paranoia, may explode in wild and violent political decisions. The fury, however, must be followed back to the reality that caused it as well as ahead to the delusions about it."[41] For Young and many Latter-day Saints, the decisive reality was the history of what had happened to them in Missouri and Illinois.

After several months of maneuvering and skirmishes in northern Utah and after a bloody massacre in southern Utah, Young reluctantly backed down. The Utah War, for all practical purposes, foreshadowed the eventual resolution of the conflict over political sovereignty between the church and Washington. During the early 1860s, church leaders persuaded President Abraham Lincoln to remove an unpopular governor and several other appointees, and Young vehemently complained about the U.S. Army's decision to station Col. Patrick E. Connor's regiment of California volunteers in Salt Lake City. Through the early 1870s, there were constant threats and rumors of war, but the outcome of the Utah War had revealed the hollowness of Young's rhetoric. The Saints claimed the republican right to choose their own rulers, but they had established that they would not fight for that right.

In 1862, Washington opened another chapter in the conflict over Utah's political sovereignty with the passage of the Morrill Anti-Bigamy Act, which threatened polygamists with fines and imprisonment, annulled the implicit legal sanction of polygamy, and, in a blatant attempt to strip the church of its economic power, ruled that no territorial religious corporation could possess more than $50,000 in property. The law remained a dead letter until the mid-1870s, when Congress passed additional legislation that ensured that non-Mormon judges could impanel juries willing to convict Mormon polygamists.

Church presidents from Brigham Young to Joseph F. Smith were faced with a choice between defending the practice of plural marriage on the one hand and greater political assimilation into the United States on the other. U.S. officials made it clear to Young, John Taylor, and Wilford Woodruff that the abandonment of polygamy was the price for Utah's statehood. Young and Taylor were unwilling to pay that price and fiercely defended the principle of plural marriage, but in 1890 Woodruff publicly surrendered the practice of polygamy when government pressure had grown to the point that it imperiled the church's future. Utah gained its statehood, though some high-ranking church leaders quietly continued to contract and sanction plural marriages. Publicity over those marriages created difficulties for the church, but Joseph F. Smith, the Mormon prophet whose tenure began in 1901, eventually took firm action to prevent additional plural marriages. Smith also dropped from the Quorum of the Twelve Apostles two members whose post-1890 plural marriages had embarrassed the church. As Kathleen Flake has argued, through those actions Smith subordinated his church's authority to that of the state.[42]

Joseph F. Smith's life, even more directly than Brigham Young's, was shaped by the June 1844 murders of his father and uncle. Like Young, Joseph F. Smith (the son of Hyrum Smith) preferred not to think about the violence in Nauvoo. As Flake observes, the murders "so traumatized the five-and-a-half-year-old Smith that he did not visit the site of his father's death until 1906, notwithstanding his having been in the vicinity several times." Nevertheless, Smith could eventually move beyond those traumas to a much greater extent than could Brigham Young.

Brigham Young, by contrast, lived in fear of assassination until the end of his life. In the fall of 1871, Young fled to southern Utah because he feared for his life should he be arrested on a murder charge. Utah's attorney general might "spring a trap upon me," he wrote back to Salt Lake City, "get me to camp and let men come in there who would assassinate me."[43] Only months before Young's own August 1877 death, the church president still feared arrest in connection with the 1857 Mountain Meadows Massacre, in which Mormon militiamen in southern Utah had butchered around 120 non-Mormon travelers. For Young, the scars of Nauvoo remained too fresh. It would take more time and a recognition on the part of Young's successors that accommodation with the United States promised more benefits than an ongoing and ultimately futile quest for political autonomy.

The Mormon bid for political sovereignty was both unsuccessful and intensely unpopular outside of the Great Basin. Indeed, opposition to Mormon polygamy and theocracy was one of the very few issues that spurred southern Democrats in the years following the Civil War to abandon their opposition to an interventionist national government.[44] Retrospectively, Brigham Young's provocative confrontations with representatives of the U.S. government and military seem reckless and misguided. Young was playing a losing hand, as became increasingly obvious. The Republican Party's ascendancy, coupled with its interest in asserting greater control of the American West, eliminated any possibility of achieving greater territorial autonomy. Brigham Young was an advocate for states' rights without a state, an unpopular sovereign in a country that cast aside the pre–Civil War doctrine of popular sovereignty.

NOTES

1. Some material is adapted from John G. Turner, *Brigham Young: Pioneer Prophet* (Cambridge: Harvard University Press, 2012). I am grateful to Edward Blum for reading a draft of this essay.

2. Brigham Young discourse of June 27, 1854, transcript of George D. Watt's shorthand notes by LaJean Carruth, Papers of George D. Watt, Church History Library (hereafter, CHL), Church of Jesus Christ of Latter-day Saints, Salt Lake City, Utah; minutes of June 28, 1854 (box 2, folder 55, General Church Minutes [GCM], CR 100 318, CHL). See LaJean P. Carruth and Mark L. Staker, eds., "John Taylor's June 27, 1854 Account of the Martyrdom," *BYU Studies* 50.3 (2011): 25–62.

3. Brigham Young discourse of June 27, 1854.

4. Brigham Young discourse of July 4, 1854, revised and published in *Journal of Discourses by Brigham Young, His Two Counsellors, the Twelve Apostles and others . . .* 26 vols. (Liverpool and London: various publishers, 1854–1886), 7: 9–11.

5. Brigham Young discourse of June 9, 1861 (box 4, folder 12, CR 100 317, CHL).

6. Discourse of July 5, 1852 (box 1, folder 27, CR 100 317, CHL).

7. "Conclusion of President Young's Trip to Sanpete," *Deseret News*, July 26, 1865, 2. See Patrick Q. Mason, "God and the People: Theodemocracy in Nineteenth-century Utah," *Journal of Church and State* 53 (Summer 2011): 349–75.

8. "perfectly untrammeled" in minutes of November 16, 1847, excerpted in Gary J. Bergera, *Conflict in the Quorum: Orson Pratt, Brigham Young, Joseph Smith* (Salt Lake City: Signature Books, 2002), 60.

9. I have relied on several reports of this speech, including those by Thomas Bullock, Wilford Woodruff, and Norton Jacob. See Will Bagley, ed., *The Pioneer Camp of the Saints: The 1846 and 1847 Mormon Trail Journals of Thomas Bullock* (Spokane, WA: Arthur H. Clark, 1997), 243–44; Scott G. Kenney, ed., *Wilford Woodruff's Journal, 1833–1898: Typescript*, 9 vols. (Midvale, UT: Signature Books, 1983–84), 3:240–42; Ronald O. Barney, ed., *The Mormon Vanguard Brigade of 1847: Norton Jacob's Record* (Logan: Utah State University Press, 2005), 226–29.

10. Young to Polk, August 8, 1846 (copy in box 16, folder 8, Brigham Young Papers [hereafter, BYP], CR 1234 1, CHL). See Ronald W. Walker, "The Affair of the 'Runaways': Utah's First Encounter with the Federal Officers," *Journal of Mormon History* 39 (Winter 2013): 2.

11. Young to Bernhisel, July 19, 1849 (box 16, folder 17, BYP).

12. Young to Bernhisel, July 29, 1850 (1844–1853 Letterpress Copybook, box 1, BYP).

13. *Statutes at Large and Treaties of the United States of America* [31st Congress, 1st sess.] (Boston: Little and Brown, 1851), 9:453.

14. Young to Bernhisel, September 14, 1852 (1851–1862 Letterpress Copybook, box 14, page 94, BYP).

15. See the discussion in Christopher Childers, "Interpreting Popular Sovereignty: A Historiographical Essay," *Civil War History* 57 (March 2011): 48–70.

16. For the most extensive narrative history of this episode, see Walker, "The Affair of the 'Runaways.'"

17. Minutes of July 23, 1851 (box 2, folder 31, GCM, typescript by LaJean Carruth and John Turner); "Power of the Priesthood" in July 23, 1851, Journal of the Church Historian's Office (CR 100 1, CHL).

18. Minutes of July 24, 1851 (box 2, folder 31, GCM).

19. Minutes of September 8, 1851 (box 2, folder 32, GCM, typescript by LaJean Carruth and John Turner).

20. Young to Amasa Lyman, March 31, 1852 (box 17, folder 1, BYP).

21. Wilford Woodruff Journal, February 20, 1853, in Kenney, ed., *Woodruff's Journal* 4:206.

22. April 16, 1854, Journal of the Church Historian's Office.

23. On the passage of the Kansas-Nebraska Act, see Nicole Etcheson, *Bleeding Kansas: Contested Liberty in the Civil War Era* (Lawrence: University of Kansas Press, 2004), ch. 1.

24. Steptoe to Pierce ("My dear General"), April 25, 1855 (MS2/0278, Idaho State Historical Society Public Archives and Research Library).

25. Minutes of February 18, 1855 (box 3, folder 1, GCM).

26. John F. Kinney to Caleb Cushing, March 1, 1855, in Records Relating to the Appointment of Federal Judges, Attorneys, and Marshals for the Territory and State of Utah, National Archives, microfilm copy at Harold B. Lee Library, Brigham Young University.

27. Young, discourse of July 8, 1855 (box 3, folder 7, GCM). On the Steptoe Expedition, see William P. MacKinnon, "Sex, Subalterns, and Steptoe: Army Behavior, Mormon Rage, and Utah War Anxieties," *Utah Historical Quarterly* 76 (Summer 2008): 227–46.

28. *Deseret News*, March 8, 1855.

29. Kirk H. Porter and Donald Bruce Johnson, eds., *National Party Platforms*, vol. 1: *1840–1956* (Urbana: University of Illinois Press, 1956), 27.

30. Remarks of February 24, 1857, in *Appendix to the Congressional Globe*, 34th Congress, 3rd sess. (Washington, D.C.: John C. Rives, 1857), 286.

31. *Deseret News*, May 13, 1857.

32. JMB to BY, January 13, 1854 (box 60, folder 15, BYP). See the discussion in Sarah Barringer Gordon, *The Mormon Question: Polygamy and Constitutional Conflict in Nineteenth-Century America* (Chapel Hill: University of North Carolina Press, 2002), 54–65.

33. January 6, 1857 memorial and draft (box 54, folder 7, BYP).

34. Bernhisel to BY, April 2, 1857 (box 61, folder 1, BYP). See William P. MacKinnon, *At Sword's Point, Part I: A Documentary History of the Utah War to 1858* (Norman, OK: Arthur H. Clark, 2008), 106–107.

35. "Utah and Its Troubles," *New York Herald*, March 20, 1857. See MacKinnon, *At Sword's Point*, 102–103.

36. *Washington Star*, March 21, 1857.

37. *National Era* (Washington), April 2, 1857, 54. See MacKinnon, *At Sword's Point*, 103.

38. Douglas, speech of June 12, 1857, *Illinois State Journal*, June 13, 1857; Lincoln, speech of June 26, 1857, *Illinois State Journal*, June 29, 1857; *Remarks of the Hon. Stephen A. Douglas on Kansas, Utah and the Dred Scott Decision* . . . (Chicago: Daily Times Book and Job Office, 1857), 13.

39. Minutes of November 25, 1855 (box 3, folder 8, GCM).

40. BYP; discourse of August 16, 1857 (box 3, folder 24, CR 100 317, CHL). See MacKinnon, *At Sword's Point*, 239–43.

41. William W. Freehling, "Paranoia and American History," *New York Review of Books*, September 23, 1971, 37–38.

42. Kathleen Flake, *The Politics of American Religious Identity: The Seating of Senator Reed Smoot, Mormon Apostle* (Chapel Hill: University of North Carolina Press, 2004).

43. Brigham Young cipher telegram to Wells, December 14, 1871 (box 73, folder 34, BYP).

44. See Patrick Q. Mason, *The Mormon Menace: Violence and Anti-Mormonism in the Postbellum South* (New York: Oxford University Press, 2011), ch. 5.

3 Polygamy in the Nation's Capitol

Protestant Women and the 1899 Campaign Against B. H. Roberts

Jana Riess

In December of 1898, Mrs. M. C. Reynolds, the secretary of the Woman's American Baptist Home Mission Society, sent a memorable package to the editor of *The Kinsman*, an anti-Mormon newspaper that had started the previous year in Salt Lake City.[1] It was a Bible, "wrapped in the protecting folds of an American flag." The Baptist women who sent it used those symbols to indicate that patriotism and Protestant Christianity were the keys to unraveling Utah's persistent depravity. "If the Rocky Mountain states are to be saved to righteousness and America," wrote Mrs. Reynolds, "it will be because its people are taught to love and honor them both."[2] An event had recently occurred that threatened the values of patriotism, Protestantism, and domesticity these women held so dear: Brigham H. Roberts, a polygamous man from Utah, had been elected to Congress the month before.

Eight years after a Manifesto prohibited Mormons from undertaking new plural marriages, congressman-elect Roberts was candid about having three wives, pointing out that he had married all three women before the 1890 declaration. In his mind, he had broken no law; and technically, such a position was tenable according to the agreement the Mormons had reached with the federal government. Prior polygamists were "grandfathered" in after 1890, and could continue to support their extant plural families, though they were forbidden from entering into new plural marriages. Public sentiment was a very different story, however, as Roberts was soon to discover.

This chapter traces the roots of the B. H. Roberts controversy by exploring Mormonism's uncertain situation in 1890s America. How would the renegade religion get along in the Union after Utah achieved statehood in 1896? The election of B. H. Roberts struck a nerve during this liminal time, with many Americans expressing anxiety about a future in which Mormons might hold federal office. As we shall see, the anti-Roberts campaign drew upon the foundation that Protestant women had established during their victorious antipolygamy and missionary activities in the 1880s. One key difference, however, was that men also joined in the fray against Roberts, alarmed at the prospect of the allegedly tyrannical system of Mormonism mixing with their democratic government. Although the campaign to unseat Roberts was successful, it was a pyrrhic victory, the last such triumph for activists who failed in subsequent attempts to pass a national antipolygamy amendment and unseat a Mormon U.S. senator.

Mormonism on the Rise: Statehood and Missionary Advances, 1890–1898

In the years before Roberts's election, Mormons began to enjoy an unprecedented role on the national stage. In 1896, Utah was admitted to the Union as the nation's forty-fifth state. This action followed nearly half a century of Mormon petitions, pleas, and finally the major concession of LDS president Wilford Woodruff's agreement to end the practice of polygamy. For Utah's Mormons, statehood was a prize long sought and finally attained through compromise and sheer perseverance.

Many Protestants, however, viewed Mormon statehood as a severe blow to Christian nationhood. Some had opposed Utah statehood for as long as the Mormons had desired it; in 1887, for example, Presbyterian minister Robert McNiece had referred to it as a political "disaster" which should be averted at all costs.[3] In this same letter Reverend McNiece sneered that the Mormons had "rented an elegant house in Washington," which they would use to entertain members of Congress and arrange to "smuggle a Mormon state into the Union." In Salt Lake City, missionary teacher Mina Morford returned to the field in 1896 after a year's absence. She felt a renewed opposition to herself and her mission, and sensed a new potency among Mormon residents, who were now "asserting their power in the legislature."[4]

Anti-Mormon activists had warned that statehood would provide the Mormon majority in Utah with two senators and several congressional representatives. Some Protestants believed that the Mormons had merely made a show of compromise on plural marriage to gain political power on a national scale. Statehood, they felt, allowed the Mormons to relax their façade of conciliation and resume an aggressive posture toward the American nation. Utah's statehood symbolized the Mormons' successful forays into the corridors of national power, where, it was feared, they would sneak their doctrines into national legislation.

But it was not only Utah's political aspirations that concerned American Protestants; the Mormons' entry into large-scale missionary work essentially meant that positions had been reversed. By the mid-1890s, Protestants noted with discomfort that instead of consenting to be the objects of missionary work and charity, Mormons had the nerve to send their own missionaries abroad. "The Book of Mormon is not only printed in English," complained the Utah Methodist Episcopal Conference in 1891, "but in Welsh, Polynesian, Italian, Danish, French, [and] German."[5] Protestant churchwomen expressed grave concern about the spread of Mormonism in foreign lands, and especially the success LDS missionaries were enjoying in Scandinavia.

Even more dangerous than Mormon conversions in Europe was the threat of Mormonism closer to home, as Mormon elders set out in pairs to proselytize their American homeland. Eastern Protestants were enraged by the hubris of this upstart heresy; not content to be evangelized, Mormons dared to convert others.[6] After recounting some of Mormonism's oft-rehearsed evils on the floor of Congress, one Indiana representative exclaimed, "And these are the people who are sending out missionaries all over our land to convert us to their religion!"[7] Protestants scrambled to fight Mormons on their own Eastern turf, dispatching tracts and pamphlets that could be distributed "among all the families who are likely to be influenced by the work of the Mormon 'missionaries,'" said one Presbyterian teacher in 1900.[8]

Mormons also improved their public relations back home, becoming savvy about marketing Salt Lake City as a tourist attraction in the early twentieth century. Full-time guides were assigned to Temple Square to answer visitors' questions and take them through the Tabernacle and the

FIGURE 3.1 The Mormon Octopus. Protestant tracts claimed that Mormon missionaries had to be challenged on non-Mormon turf or their influence would spread like a disease. (Home Mission Echoes, 190?, Interdenominational Council of Women for Christian and Patriotic Service, New York City)

gardens. Tourists were welcomed and offered a very positive view of the Latter-day Saints—a view that did not include, as Protestants noted with some scorn, the truth about the persistence of underground polygamy, or Mormonism's unorthodox beliefs about godhood and prophecy. To counter this carefully scripted presentation, Salt Lake Protestants founded their own tourist information center, the "Gentile" Bureau of Information. Its founders, members of the Salt Lake Ministerial Association, aimed to expose Mormon theology and to undermine the Mormons' "domination" of Utah's economy and politics.[9]

Mormons had a harder time gaining respectability away from home, however. Historian Spencer Fluhman has noted how Mormonism was systematically excluded from the World Parliament of Religions in 1893. The LDS Church, led by an apostle named B. H. Roberts—the same man who would five years later be elected to Congress from Utah—attempted, in vain, to procure an invitation to the parliament. All such requests for Mormonism to be represented as a religion were denied. However, the larger Columbian Exposition was a secular success for the fledgling state of Utah. "Where the Mormon religion had failed," Fluhman writes, "Mormon arts and agriculture met with huge success.... Utah's agricultural displays were widely heralded, and the Mormons' choir finished second in the choral competition to considerable acclaim."[10]

Internally as well, the 1890s were a decade of tremendous change within Mormonism. With the jettisoning of polygamy came something of an identity crisis; historian Jan Shipps has noted that with the disappearance of this defining feature of the faith, other elements of the Mormon religion rose in prominence, such as tithing and keeping the Word of Wisdom (the Mormon dietary code).[11] Other changes, like LDS president Woodruff's creation of the Genealogical Society of Utah and growing emphasis on Mormons doing proxy temple work for their deceased ancestors, unfolded through the 1890s, as Mormons sought to understand how to be a "peculiar people" without polygamy.[12] A de-emphasis on Utah as a central gathering place for the Latter-day Saints coincided with a demographic move outward that would gain momentum in the twentieth century, cementing Protestants' fears about Mormon infiltration throughout the country. As their physical "center place" of Zion morphed into more of a spiritual sense of being a Zion people no matter where they were living, Mormons sought to reinvent themselves as the consummate Americans.

The Antipolygamy Movement Confronts B. H. Roberts

While in many ways the 1890 Manifesto breathed new life into Mormonism as the LDS Church realigned its temporal and spiritual priorities without plural marriage, the declaration dealt a heavy blow to the antipolygamy movement that had thrived among Protestant women in the 1870s and 1880s. Historian Peggy Pascoe has shown that Protestant women established missions to Utah during those years as part of a quest for female moral authority in the West.[13] Bolstered by their own expanding influence and missionary status, they sought to bestow some of their newly found freedoms on Mormon women, who appeared to suffer the worst kind of oppression.

The women's missionary efforts had been funded for the better part of two decades by the urgency behind embellished tales of white slavery, marauding Danites, and maidens sullied by polygamy. The 1890 Manifesto left them without a *raison d'être*, at least in the eyes of their financial backers. In the 1890s, try as they might, Protestant activists could not convince their donors back East that polygamy was still a grave problem.

The numbers told the story. A month after the Manifesto, a New West missionary teacher wrote of "speaking every day for a week in mid-October to raise funds."[14] Despite such plucky efforts, by 1891, the New West Education Commission was a month behind in paying its teachers, and the payroll account was $3,000 overdrawn.[15] Other denominations suffered a similar tightening of the purse strings. When a financial panic in 1893 closed thousands of businesses, Protestant churches reined in their expenditures for missions, refocusing their energies on those missions that seemed to be producing the most results. That did not include Utah.

But the antipolygamy movement was not dead yet, experiencing a swift revival in 1899 after the election of B. H. Roberts to Congress. Although Protestant women had done little to protest the Democratic candidate's election campaign throughout the autumn of 1898, the year 1899 dawned with a renewed commitment on their part to eradicate polygamy once and for all, starting with this arrogant-sounding politician.

According to the letter of the law, nothing Roberts had done was illegal, but the spirit of the law was another matter. He was still living in polygamy, a fact that his female critics tried to convey delicately by mentioning that his third wife had recently borne twins. In an anti-Roberts circular distributed to churchwomen, the Presbyterian Woman's Board of Home Missions opined that giving Roberts a voice in national legislation would be outrageous, since he had flaunted the law so flagrantly himself. How, they asked, could a lawbreaker function effectively as a lawmaker?[16]

Some Protestant critics tried to paint Roberts as an unrepentant felon by accusing him of entering his third marriage after the Manifesto. This charge was not factually true, but was reprinted so many times that in the public mind it may as well have been.[17] The allegation that Roberts had married his third wife, Dr. Margaret Curtis Shipp, after the Manifesto first appeared in an 1898 issue of the *Salt Lake Herald*,[18] and thereafter recurred in numerous periodicals and flyers as truth. In fact, Roberts had beaten the Manifesto by a matter of months; he and Shipp were wed in April of 1890, the same year that the September "revelation" called a halt to new plural marriages.[19]

Roberts was a devout Mormon. Born in England, he traveled to America as a boy and accompanied his convert family in the great Mormon migration west.[20] He had spent years as a missionary in England and belonged to the Quorum of the Seventy, the LDS governing body for missionary work. He had served a prison sentence during the darkest days of antipolygamy in 1889, having surrendered himself to the authorities for incarceration. He refused to take an oath that he would end his polygamous relationships. His financial situation at that time was so dire that he had to serve an extra month in prison because he could not pay the fine. After his release, he began writing for Mormon periodicals to support his growing plural families, publishing Mormon apologetics in several LDS periodicals in the 1880s and 1890s, and became a noted expert on the Book of Mormon.[21] He also became interested in politics, an arena where he rapidly rose to prominence.[22] Roberts made a name for himself during the state constitutional conventions of 1894, when he stridently opposed both the reinstitution of woman suffrage in Utah and the addition of an enforced temperance clause into the new state's constitution. From these actions, Roberts made enemies among the temperance-loving, suffrage-seeking Protestant churchwomen of the East.[23]

After his 1898 election, Roberts's prolific yield of Mormon scriptural and theological writings came back to haunt him as Protestant women combed through his prodigious treatises on various subjects for signs that he still endorsed polygamy and opposed the policies of the United States government.[24] They found the evidence they were looking for, even when it was indirect. Baptist missionary Rose Webster, for example, noted that since in LDS theology godhood was only possible for polygamous Mormon males, Roberts's statement that "men have got to learn to become gods" meant that he was surreptitiously encouraging men to take new plural wives and increase their celestial status.[25] Another anti-Roberts activist, Helen Gould, scrutinized newspaper accounts and read through several works of Mormon doctrine in her search for Roberts's most incriminating statements. She found much to distress her. Roberts, she claimed, believed not only in having many wives but in worshiping many gods. He was a polytheist, teaching that Christ and God were separate individuals. Worse yet, he believed that each deity had a physical body "of flesh and bone."[26]

In the campaign against Roberts, Protestant denominations fell back upon the deep infrastructure of women's missionary societies that had been solidified the decade before. The *Home Mission Monthly* explained this as a pragmatic decision, in that no other organization of women or men had the capacity to mobilize such a large number of citizens at the grassroots level. This strategy did not disappoint; the women's missionary societies delivered an astounding seven million petition signatures to Congress in 1899, protesting Roberts's election.[27] The decision to utilize the home missions infrastructure was also an ideological declaration, since activists felt "this subject is vital to the sanctity of home and womanhood."[28]

FIGURE 3.2   Political cartoonists had the proverbial field day in 1899, depicting Roberts on a train headed for the U.S. Capitol with several boxcars of wives and children in an entourage behind him. Popular songs ridiculed the situation, with refrains such as: "We're coming, Uncle Samuel / This B. H. Roberts crew / To show the Washingtonians / Three Wives and babies too." "On to Washington," *The Kinsman* (February 1899), 112.

Such fervor ran high in 1899. The *Home Mission Monthly* queried whether "every society ... [was] at work" in the campaign, calling on mission-minded American women to respond immediately with petitions, funding, and prayer. Protestant women became conjoined in "an intense, patriotic purpose ... from ocean to ocean," a unity forged in a common enemy: Roberts and the LDS Church.[29] Denominations thrust aside internecine squabbles and competition for converts, choosing instead to coordinate their efforts. A Presbyterian resolution titled "Ten Reasons Why Christians Can Not Fellowship the Mormon Church," passed by the Presbytery of Utah in 1897, was circulated among other denominations during the anti-Roberts campaign and endorsed by both the Congregational and Baptist Associations.[30]

Various denominational missions organizations handled the campaign differently. Churches throughout America encouraged the faithful to sign petitions opposing Roberts; eventually, they sent these to Washington rolled up in American flags.[31] The Methodist Episcopal Church printed a petition on a page of its regular magazine, so that local subscribers could cut it out and circulate it among concerned women.[32] Similarly, the March 1899 issue of *Tidings*, a Baptist women's missionary periodical, included petition forms for local churchwomen to sign and send to Washington. By the fall of 1899, petition forms were also printed with the *Home Mission Monthly*.[33] The national *Christian Endeavor* magazine featured advertisements for anti-Roberts pamphlets and petitions, so clergy could order the materials in bulk.[34] The magazine requested that clergy preach sermons on the subject, and alert congregants to the grave danger Roberts posed to American values.

As the 1899 public outcry gathered momentum, it became clear that the Roberts controversy hinged upon nothing less than the question of Mormonism's future role in national life. Protestant reformers felt that to allow Roberts to take his seat in Congress would permit the Mormons, a formerly oppressed people, the social and political triumph of seeing one of their own serve in the nation's top legislative body. It was too bitter a pill. Seating Roberts in Congress would give Utah the satisfaction of turning the tables on the federal government; concessions made to achieve statehood would no longer be necessary. Anti-Mormons believed that once in office, Roberts would systematically set about restoring polygamy as a national right, elevating the LDS Church to political power.[35]

Roberts, for his part, remained comfortably sure that the public outcry would diminish and he would have no trouble taking his seat. "There is nothing permanent about this sudden storm of religious fanaticism which is attacking me," he told the *San Francisco Examiner* in January 1899. "It will soon be over. Why, I don't take my seat until next fall. There is a long summer between now and then."[36]

Of those two predictions—that the controversy would soon be over and that Roberts would emerge victorious—only the first proved true. In January 1900, the House of Representatives denied entrance to B. H. Roberts, the first time in American history that an elected congressional representative was refused a seat. The congressional vote tallied in at 268 to 50 against Roberts, with thirty-six representatives abstaining.[37] The process of his ousting took only six weeks.[38] Roberts returned to Utah in disgrace while another Mormon Democrat, who was not a polygamist, was chosen in a special election in early 1900.[39] His political hopes destroyed, Roberts set about rather reluctantly to augment his meager church stipend by writing a comprehensive history of Mormonism. His six-volume history became the standard, definitive church-produced work on the subject—and Roberts got to tell his version of his own defeat at the hands of "the sectarian 'Christian' ministry."[40]

Gender and Power in the B. H. Roberts Controversy

The means of the 1899 antipolygamy crusade had remained the same as always—petitions, lectures, tracts, missionary societies—and at least one part of the old message was intact: the battle for Christian womanhood. For example, "Baptist mothers, with a care for girls" were encouraged to rise up in the name of Christian womanhood to defeat Roberts and also challenge Mormon missionary elders in Appalachia, where the Saints were allegedly inducing "young and ignorant girls" to abandon their families for Mormonism and Utah.[41]

Although idealized womanhood remained a powerful factor in the new antipolygamy crusade, it was not the only slogan that helped to mobilize Protestants against Roberts in 1899. A newer addition to the mix of anti-Mormon rhetoric was the theme of emerging American nationhood—which Mormonism, with its allegedly undemocratic priesthood, threatened to dismantle. The late 1890s marked a shift as Protestants moved from challenging Mormonism on the grounds of Victorian womanhood to contesting its political status and priesthood power. One Baptist missionary queried her readers:

> Will this Nation recognize that Congressman-elect Roberts, the polygamist, and thus drive thousands in Utah and the Great West into a slavery to priesthood rule and degradation, stop the wheels of progress, liberty, and enlightenment in the state, and cause the iron heel of blasphemous assumption to crush the hearts and souls of thousands of its blinded victims, and enable it to extend its deadly power all over the country?[42]

In a nation rallied to jingoistic heights by the farce of the 1898 Spanish-American War, anti-Mormon arguments on patriotic grounds gained even greater cultural currency than the previously foundational rhetoric of sacred womanhood. Some writers even connected Roberts's congressional election with the recent assassination of President McKinley; the menace of a polygamist in Congress provided just one more example of the erosion of American patriotism.[43] To allow a Mormon in Congress would eradicate all of the enlightened "progress" the new nation had made, since Mormonism was a tyrannical system to its core. Mormons, of course, were quick to counter that they were the most patriotic of Americans. They noted repeatedly the distinctive Mormon belief that the U.S. Constitution was a divinely inspired document, framed by God, and also reminded their critics that one of their Articles of Faith called them to be subject to rulers and the laws of the land.[44]

The increasing importance of political power in turn-of-the-century anti-Mormonism affected the gender breakdown of the campaign against B. H. Roberts. Joan Smyth Iversen has postulated that the 1899 campaign against Roberts, in contrast to the antipolygamy crusades of the 1880s, was male-led. Indeed, it is true that men were prominent writers and speakers in the campaign to unseat Roberts. Yet Iversen goes too far in claiming that women were merely marionettes, heeding male control, and she misses an underlying reason for increased male involvement.[45] Women still set a significant portion of the agenda for the 1899 crusade, forming a national organization to further their antipolygamy interests, putting polygamy back in the headlines, and mobilizing local missions organizations across the country to fill out petitions and contact their congressional representatives. In 1899, for example, women encouraged "the inducing of all men who come under our influence to write to their Congressmen-elect, and so overwhelm them with letters that they will feel that there is no chance for their re-election unless they do what their constituents wish."[46] As in the 1880s, women urged their husbands, brothers, fathers, and sons to participate in the crusade against polygamy.

However, the composition of the movement had changed. What differed between the 1880s campaign and this one? Why did men become more prominently involved than ever before in defeating polygamy in such a public way?

The difference was that polygamy had become inextricably linked to a "male" prerogative: politics. Men's and women's interests in toppling polygamy had always followed divergent trajectories. Women became the primary movers in the 1880s when plural marriage had cast its shadow over motherhood, female piety, and women's roles. Those concerns were still very prevalent in 1899—witness the anti-Roberts factions calling for noble womanhood to reassert itself—but a fresh emphasis on the dangers of Mormonism's political power arose to stand alongside it. Protestant men, who had long been more concerned with Mormonism's alleged antidemocratic tyranny than polygamy's treatment of women, became coleaders with women in a more politicized anti-Mormon crusade. Antipolygamy was now one aspect of a more complex movement. Mormonism had always threatened Protestant domination, but until it insinuated itself into the Capitol, women had felt its threat more keenly, more immediately, than men. Roberts's election sent a clear message that not only women should be afraid.

Whereas women's pens had written urgently about the Mormon priesthood's absolute power in controlling female lives, men's writings emphasized the priesthood's dictatorial political style, alleging that Mormons were told how to vote.[47] The priesthood's tyranny extended so far that one tract even claimed that Roberts would seek revenge not only upon those congressional representatives who voted against him, but upon every citizen who dared to sign a petition.[48] Roberts would learn their names and turn upon them with the mighty wrath of the Mormon priesthood.

Men's anti-Mormon writings wrestled conspicuously with issues of democracy and patriotism. William Campbell began his tract on "The Political Aspects of Mormonism" with a succinct characterization of the "polygamous hierarchy" as "not only anti-Democratic and anti-Republican, but anti-American."[49] Campbell and others taught that Mormonism mocked the two-party system; although individual Mormons belonged to both political parties, they would always vote for the LDS Church's interests. Democratic governments would eventually give way to the growing Mormon cancer, according to the male anti-Roberts campaigners. In a meeting of Utah's Presbyterian ministers in 1898, just three months before the congressional elections, the pastors publicly denounced Mormonism in no uncertain terms, issuing a list of its dangers. First upon that list was the LDS Church's alleged entry into politics and its dictatorial priesthood, which chose appropriate political candidates and indicated how church members should vote. A distant third on the list was Mormonism's "peculiar institution," polygamy, which the ministers asserted was still alive and well in Utah. But instead of decrying plural marriage as an insult to womanhood, they asserted that Mormon polygamy had spawned more than a thousand children since statehood was granted in 1896 — in direct violation of Utah's concessions for statehood. These children only added to the menacing Mormon "kingdom," which eventually threatened to dominate American political life.[50]

Roberts was livid at the national outcry against him, pointing out that few had raised so much as an eyebrow during his candidacy and election. Why all the fuss after the fact? He singled out the protest of the "so-called Christian sects" as especially damaging. "Special conferences and conventions of the churches and Sunday Schools adopted resolutions," Roberts later recalled, "and finally by the time Congress was ready to convene, petitions signed by upwards of seven million names were pasted together and rolled up like [a wheel of] cheese and wheeled into the House of Representatives, protesting my being allowed to take my seat."[51]

Roberts saw that his detractors were not only Protestant, but largely female. The fact that Roberts later acknowledged that he had been defeated by "short-haired women and long-haired men" demonstrates that he was himself aware of the gendered character of the outcry against him.[52] One group of women stayed above the fray. Caught in the crossfire, Mormon women remained oddly silent about Roberts. On the one hand, he was one of their own, a Utah resident who shared their faith and history, and he was going to Congress. On the other hand, Roberts was a virulent antifeminist who had already crossed purposes with the pro-suffrage "leading sisters" of Mormondom.[53] Roberts strongly opposed woman suffrage when the Utah constitution was being drafted and ratified, declaring it would cause women to become like men and ruin the family. (As historian Anne Firor Scott has noted, Roberts seemed to miss the fact that women had already voted in Utah from 1870 to 1887 without these desperate consequences.)[54]

Failed Efforts, Changing Times: The Antipolygamy Amendment and the Smoot Hearings

Protestants rejoiced at the exclusion of B. H. Roberts from Congress. Women activists were careful, however, not to rest on their laurels, trying instead to galvanize the anti-Roberts sentiment into a more permanent form of change. Utah missionary Emma Parsons wrote in 1900 that women "must gird ourselves for another conflict and not rest until the states have ratified the proposed constitutional amendment making polygamy a crime punishable with a severe penalty."[55] The Interdenominational Council of Women for Christian and Patriotic Service (ICWPS), of a similar mind, determined to "strike at the root of the matter and make polygamy forever impossible." Its members drafted a proposed constitutional amendment that would make polygamy a federal offense, and set out on an ambitious program to have the amendment ratified.

The amendment proposed to criminalize polygamy in any U.S. state or territory (which then included the Philippines). Polygamists would not be permitted to hold civil or military office, or to vote in state or national elections. Advocates touted disfranchisement as the only measure that could effectively curb polygamists' political power, which they considered mighty indeed.[56] They defined "polygamy" as both unlawful plural marriage and polygamous cohabitation, to avoid any circumvention of the law by informal polygamous relationships.[57]

Protestant missionaries in Utah were among the most influential voices in creating the proposed amendment. The ICWPS acknowledged that it had heeded the voices of missionary teachers in Mormon country, who had written that nothing less than a constitutional amendment would effect lasting change.[58] Antipolygamy activism was again picking up steam, as other prominent women's organizations threw their support behind the proposed amendment. In 1904, the Woman's Christian Temperance Union declared that its primary objective would be to make polygamy a crime.[59]

The amendment drifted in and out of the public consciousness for the next decade. By 1912, it was still a tertiary item on women's reform agendas; rallies were sometimes well-attended, and pro-amendment measures continued to be drafted in American women's groups.[60] In 1903, however, another major crisis arose for America's antipolygamists. LDS Apostle Reed Smoot had been elected as a senator from Utah.

Smoot differed from Roberts in that he was not a polygamist. He had married his sweetheart Alpha Eldredge in 1884, and they had six children; from all appearances, Smoot was the quintessential Victorian monogamist. "I am not and never have been a polygamist," Smoot declared to the Senate in 1907. "I deem it proper to further state that I have never taught polygamy."[61] However, the public perception of Mormons still equated Mormonism to some degree with polygamy, and Smoot was guilty by association because he not only belonged to this wayward religious group, but was one of its twelve Apostles. Smoot had served as an Apostle since 1900 (and would continue to do so until his death in 1941), and was thoroughly dedicated to the LDS Church. He was new to politics, having had successful business interests in textiles, lumber, manufacturing, banking, and the railroad.

While the Senate debated Smoot's case, Protestant women once again mobilized themselves as a lobbying anti-Mormon force. Corinne Allen, an anti-Roberts activist who was married to one of Roberts's political opponents, was the first to carry anti-Smoot measures into national women's groups. In 1904, she consolidated major women's groups, including the WCTU, into the National League of Women's Organizations, a confederation boasting more than a million women, and then organized those women into submitting petitions against Smoot. Chapters in forty-five states did so.[62]

For a time, signs looked favorable for Smoot's hearing to be a repeat performance of Roberts's ousting. The Smoot controversy breathed temporary life into the on-again, off-again campaign for a constitutional amendment to ban polygamy. One activist wrote that while the majority of American families were still safe from "the hideous, slimy monster, polygamy," the eradication of plural marriage was the business of every true American.[63] Unlike the quick routing of Roberts, the ugly fight over Smoot's seating took three years, during which major LDS Church officials were called upon to defend not just Smoot but their entire religion on the national stage. As historian Kathleen Flake put it,

> The Smoot hearing would range far beyond the senator's qualifications for office. Smoot did all he could, even compromising his defense, to stave off the moment to subpoena the church hierarchy. . . . Smoot's sacrifice was to no avail. On the eve of the hearing, Chairman Burrows "very frankly" told Smoot that "he was not on trial, but that they were going to investigate the Mormon Church."[64]

Crucially, the president of the LDS Church had to publicly declare in the proceedings that Mormonism was "solely an ecclesiastical organization" that was "separate and distinct from the state."[65] Smoot's loyalties—and, by extension, all Mormons' loyalties—were in question: would Mormons be loyal first to the prophet or to the nation? Whom would they obey?

Although polygamy remained an issue in the Smoot hearings, the real question was one of Mormon fealty to the United States. Smoot's critics maintained that he would always place his first allegiance with the church, and not the nation. The controversy illustrates that early-twentieth-century anti-Mormon discourse continued to claim that Mormonism was inherently un-American because it ostensibly silenced dissenting voices and expected members to vote along with the dictates of the church. Whereas once Mormonism had outraged the public because it made a mockery of tender wives and mothers, now it was accused of political tyranny. If anything, this accusation was even more prominent during Smoot's hearing than the national debate about Roberts, because the specter of polygamy was largely irrelevant to Smoot's personal life. Issues of tyranny and theocracy displaced polygamy as the most dangerous-seeming elements of Mormonism. The 1906 General Assembly of the Presbyterian Church condemned "the Mormon hierarchy" in a resolution to unseat Senator Smoot. Smoot, the Presbyterians claimed, was "living in harmony" with the church's teaching that the government of the United States would someday be supplanted by "the government of the Mormon priesthood," and as such, was guilty of treason.[66] That priesthood, one petition alleged, "is vested with Supreme Authority in All Things," and constituted a national menace.[67]

In the end, Smoot survived the crucible of his hearing and went on to serve in the Senate for almost thirty years.[68] The ramifications of Smoot's success, and the antipolygamy amendment's contemporaneous failure, rippled throughout the women's antipolygamy movement. Women activists who had once enjoyed a national spotlight found themselves no longer able to mobilize public support for their cause. Ann Eliza Webb Young, the ex-wife of Brigham Young who had once published a scathing bestseller about her experiences in polygamy, tried to use the Smoot controversy as a springboard back into national celebrity. Her efforts to resurrect her once-flourishing career failed miserably. Her revised book did not even sell a thousand copies, and her lectures attracted little public attention.[69]

One of the major reasons for the Senate hearings' failure, and for women activists' inability to resurrect polygamy as a national issue, was that gender itself was being refashioned in early-twentieth-century America. Historian Gail Bederman has postulated that in this era, middle-class white men espoused a "primitive" version of masculinity that included "a primal virility"—a virility that was at least partly measured by sexual conquest.[70] Smoot found an advocate, for example, in President Teddy Roosevelt, whose famous game-bagging African safari excursions stood for a "new manhood." Roosevelt wrote that the Mormons embodied this manhood as much as any religious men could. In 1906, Roosevelt castigated women's efforts to oust Smoot as "hysterical sensationalism," removing all hope that he would stand behind the antipolygamists' cause.[71] He supported Smoot through the entire case, stating that the senator-elect's domestic life was "exemplary in every way."[72]

It was difficult for antipolygamists to fathom the seismic shift of the nation's mood. Women whose activism had been forged in the domestically minded women's movement of the late nineteenth century were displaced by those espousing a "more diverse, individualistic, heterogeneous [women's] movement with a modern agenda" and an emerging, distinct sexual morality.[73] This is not to say that the Victorian discourse of Mormonism as an insult to womanhood entirely disappeared. It found many vocal Progressive Era advocates, such as Mrs. Frances J. Diefenderfer, the president of the National Order of Antipolygamy Crusaders. Her 1915 condemnation of polygamy as an "institution of barbarism and open offense against womanhood" echoed churchwomen's arguments from three decades before.[74] But Diefenderfer's Order of Crusaders never gained the widespread popular support her antipolygamy foremothers had enjoyed, both because polygamy was widely regarded as a "dead" issue and because the concept of womanhood itself had been transformed.

Conclusion

At the turn of the twentieth century, congressman-elect B. H. Roberts symbolized many things that were anathema to turn-of-the-century Protestants. By persisting in his polygamous relationships, he represented Protestants' failure to overcome polygamy once and for all, despite draconian legislation. He stood as an obstacle to women's rights; mainstream Protestant women saw his three marriages and his opposition to legalized temperance as evidence of despotism and depravity.

In his cavalier approach to polygamy, refusal to sanction women's suffrage, and unswerving dedication to the LDS Church, Roberts provided an all-encompassing scapegoat for Protestant women activists. And by his election to Congress, he posed enough of a political threat to galvanize men into protest. However, the activists' stunning success in defeating Roberts was not to be repeated; as the twentieth century wore on, the tenor of the times shifted, and new complexities eroded the single-minded purpose that Protestant activists had once enjoyed. The antipolygamy movement never recovered from its early-twentieth-century failures to pass a national amendment and prevent Reed Smoot's seating in the Senate.

NOTES

1. Utah Presbyterians inaugurated *The Kinsman* in 1897 to call attention to underground polygamous marriages in Utah. Douglas Brackenridge, *Westminster College of Salt Lake City: From Presbyterian Mission School to Independent College* (Logan: Utah State University Press, 1998), 99.

2. "That Flag and Bible," *The Kinsman* (January 1899), 79.

3. Rev. R. G. McNiece to Dr. Agnew, December 22, 1887, 3 (Robert McNiece file, A-1823, Utah State Historical Society, Salt Lake City).

4. Mary G. Burdette, ed., *Twenty-Two Years' Work Among the Mormons* (Chicago: Woman's Baptist Home Mission Society, 1905), 60.

5. "Action of the Utah Methodist Episcopal Church Mission Conference" (Ogden, Utah: July 9, 1891), 1.

6. Mormons were also thought to infiltrate Eastern schools and institutions in a clandestine way. In 1906, one anti-Mormon writer claimed that LDS missionaries were "drawing off the best young blood of the East" to Utah. See Jennie Fowler Willing, *On American Soil: Or, Mormonism the Mohammedanism of the West* (Louisville, KY: Pickett, 1906), 23.

Corinne Marie Allen (1856–1931), the antipolygamy activist who spearheaded the campaign to unseat Brigham H. Roberts, claimed that the Mormon danger was not just limited to Utah. Allen wrote that Mormon students had won places "in all eastern universities, and many co-educational schools to influence girls." Corinne Allen, "The Evils of the Harem Life of Mormon Women, by Mrs. Corinne M. Allen, President, Utah Congress of Mothers," ca. 1910. See Corinne Marie Allen Papers, A-5, 12 (Schlesinger Library, Radcliffe College, Cambridge, Massachusetts).

7. Hon. Landis of Indiana, speech on the floor of the House of Representatives during discussion of the Roberts case, quoted in Edgar E. Folk, *The Mormon Monster: Or, The Story of Mormonism* (Chicago: Fleming H. Revell, n.d.), 107.

8. "How To Meet the Mormon Missionaries: By a Utah Worker" (New York: Literature Department of the Woman's Board of Home Missions of the Presbyterian Church, 1902), 3.

9. "'Gentile' Bureau of Information" (Salt Lake City: Woman's Missionary Union of Salt Lake City and the Utah Ministerial Association, 191?), 2.

10. J. Spencer Fluhman, *"A Peculiar People": Anti-Mormonism and the Making of Religion in Nineteenth-century America* (New York: Oxford University Press, 2012), 130–31.

11. Jan Shipps, *Mormonism: The Story of a New Religious Tradition* (Urbana: University of Illinois Press, 1985), 125, 128.

12. Matthew Bowman, *The Mormon People: The Making of an American Faith* (New York: Random House, 2012), 162–63. Bowman notes, "The bonds that polygamy had created across space would now reach with renewed vigor across time; the old dream of a human race bound together link by link would survive polygamy with renewed strength."

13. Peggy Pascoe, *Relations of Rescue: The Search for Female Moral Authority in the American West, 1874–1939* (New York: Oxford University Press, 1990).

14. Dee Richard Darling, "Cultures in Conflict: Congregationalism, Mormonism, and Schooling in Utah, 1880–1893" (PhD diss., University of Utah, 1991), 213.

15. Darling, "Cultures in Conflict," 214.

16. William R. Campbell, "Reasons Why B. H. Roberts, of Utah, Should Be Expelled from the House of Representatives of the Fifty-Sixth Congress," 1899 (George Martin file, CH-Ma, Westminster College Archives, Salt Lake City). Campbell was chosen by the Interdenominational Council of Women for Christian and Patriotic Service as Field Secretary for Utah.

17. See, for example, *The Kinsman* (December 1899), 62.

18. See the *Salt Lake Herald*, November 6, 1898. This charge was reprinted many times; cf. Campbell, "Reasons Why B. H. Roberts, of Utah, Should Be Expelled," 3.

19. Editor's afterword, Gary James Bergera, ed., *The Autobiography of B. H. Roberts* (Salt Lake City: Signature Books, 1990), 254. This third wife, Dr. Margaret Curtis Shipp, was seven years Roberts's senior. According to historian Jessie Embry, such an age differential would have been unusual in plural marriages, in which husbands continued to select new brides in their late teens even as they

advanced into their mid- to late thirties themselves. See Jessie Embry, "Polygamous and Monogamous Mormon Women: A Comparison," in Patricia Lyn Scott and Linda Thatcher, eds., *Women in Utah History: Paradigm or Paradox?* (Logan: Utah State University Press, 2005), 13.

20. Bowman, *The Mormon People*, 157.

21. For a detailed discussion of B. H. Roberts's role in Book of Mormon apologetics, see Terryl Givens, *By the Hand of Mormon: The American Scripture That Launched a New World Religion* (New York: Oxford University Press, 2002), 106–112.

22. Bergera, ed., *The Autobiography of B. H. Roberts*, 175, 181.

23. Jill Mulvay Derr, Janath Russell Cannon, and Maureen Ursenbach Beecher, *Women of Covenant: The Story of Relief Society* (Salt Lake City: Deseret Book, 1992), 148–49.

24. Roberts's theological works are remarkably convoluted. One female journalist, Annie Laurie, tried to wade through his writing before interviewing him for the *San Francisco Examiner*, but found his work to be "so full of ecclesiastical terms that it is hard for a lay mind to catch the meaning without close study." Annie Laurie, "'Plural Marriage Brings Sorrow and Is Now Dying Out,' Says the Favorite Wife of Congressman-Elect Roberts," *San Francisco Examiner*, January 9, 1899.

25. Rose Glen Webster, "Ye Shall Be As Gods," in Burdette, *Twenty-Two Years' Work*, 83–84.

26. I. D. Marshall, "Miss Helen M. Gould's Fight Against Roberts: She Tells in a Signed Statement Why She Entered the Crusade Against Mormonism," *The (Salt Lake City) Daily Tribune*, December 3, 1899.

27. Thomas G. Alexander, *Mormonism in Transition: A History of the Latter-day Saints, 1890–1930* (Urbana: University of Illinois Press, 1986), 11. Kathleen Flake gives the figure at three million signatures, not seven million. Flake, *The Politics of American Religious Identity: The Seating of Senator Reed Smoot, Mormon Apostle* (Chapel Hill: University of North Carolina Press, 2004), 34.

28. "An Appeal to American Womanhood," *Home Mission Monthly* (August 1899), quoted in *The Kinsman* (August 1899), 294.

29. *Home Mission Monthly* (March 1899), quoted in *The Kinsman* (March 1899), 144.

30. "Ten Reasons Why Christians Can Not Fellowship the Mormon Church" (New York: League for Social Service, 1898).

31. Joan Smyth Iversen, *The Antipolygamy Controversy in U.S. Women's Movements, 1880–1925: A Debate on the American Home* (Hamden, CT: Garland, 1997), 190.

32. *The Kinsman* (September 1899), 340.

33. Iversen, *The Antipolygamy Controversy*, 190.

34. Marshall, "Miss Helen M. Gould's Fight Against Roberts," *The (Salt Lake City) Daily Tribune*, December 3. 1899.

35. Campbell, "Reasons Why B. H. Roberts . . . ," 1.

36. Laurie, "'Plural Marriage Brings Sorrow and Is Now Dying Out,'" *San Francisco Examiner*, January 9, 1899.

37. Bergera, *The Autobiography of B. H. Roberts*, 218.
38. Flake, *The Politics of American Religious Identity*, 26.
39. Alexander, *Mormonism in Transition*, 11.
40. Bergera, *The Autobiography of B. H. Roberts*, 218.
41. Burdette, *Twenty-Two Years' Work*, 72.
42. Burdette, *Twenty-Two Years' Work*, 77–78.
43. Willing, *On American Soil*, 24. Willing denounced polygamy and spoke of the "anarchist who shot President McKinley" in the same breath.
44. See, for example, "'Mormon' Women's Protest: An Appeal for Freedom, Justice, and Equal Rights" (Salt Lake City: Juvenile Instructor's Office, 1886), at www.fairmormon.org/Misc/MormonWomenProtest.pdf. The twelfth Article of Faith states, "We believe in being subject to kings, presidents, rulers, and magistrates, in obeying, honoring, and sustaining the law."
45. See Iversen, *The Antipolygamy Controversy*, 189.
46. "To Overwhelm Congressmen," *The Kinsman* (October 1899), 375.
47. In some respects, this charge was true. When Utah achieved statehood in 1896, the LDS Church was anxious to be perceived as abiding by the two-party system. To this end, some Mormon leaders "routinely visited wards to urge members to vote for one party or the other. Which party often mattered less than the simple act of casting a ballot; anecdotes from the time describe bishops dividing their wards down the middle of the chapel aisle and assigning a party to the congregants on either side." Bowman, *The Mormon People*, 155.
48. William R. Campbell, "The Political Aspects of Mormonism. Mr. Roberts Not a Democrat. . . . " (Salt Lake City, 1899), 1. George Martin file, CH-Ma, Westminster College Archives, Salt Lake City.
49. Campbell, "The Political Aspects of Mormonism," 1.
50. "The Present Situation in Utah," reprinted in "Preachers Resolve: First Presbyterian Ministers See Spooks and Other Things," *Salt Lake Tribune*, August 30, 1898.
51. Bergera, ed., *The Autobiography of B. H. Roberts*, 212.
52. Joan Smyth Iversen, "Antipolygamy Activism in the Nation's Capitol," Mormon History Association panel, May 24, 1998, Washington, D.C.
53. Emmeline Wells, for instance, had never been a Roberts supporter, "but now she had to stand by him because, simply put, the condemnation of Roberts had become a repudiation of the LDS Church." Iversen, *The Antipolygamy Controversy*, 195. See Maureen Ursenbach Beecher, "The 'Leading Sisters': A Female Hierarchy in Nineteenth-century Mormon Society," *Journal of Mormon History* 9 (1982).
54. Anne Firor Scott, "Mormon Women, Other Women: Paradoxes and Challenges," *Journal of Mormon History* 13 (1986), 12.
55. Burdette, *Twenty-Two Years' Work*, 87.
56. See letter of William R. Campbell to members of Congress, November 15, 1899 (George Martin file, CH-Ma, Westminster College Archives, Salt Lake City).
57. "Proposed Antipolygamy Constitutional Amendment," reprinted in *The Kinsman* (December 1899), 63.

58. Memo of the Interdenominational Council of Women for Christian and Patriotic Service, n.p., n.d. (George Martin file, CH-Ma, Westminster College Archives, Salt Lake City).

59. Alexander, *Mormonism in Transition*, 64.

60. Letter of C. E. Mason, President of the Interdenominational Council of Women for Christian and Patriotic Service, to Mrs. Clarence Allen, January 31, 1912 (Schlesinger Library, Radcliffe College, A-5, 12). As late as 1912, Mason reported having 1,200 people attend the Carnegie Hall mass meeting on the amendment, a good turnout considering that the sidewalks were like a sheet of ice, and the Week of Prayer was also under way. Another mass meeting was scheduled to occur in New Jersey, followed by rallies in Maryland and Illinois.

61. "Speech of Hon. Reed Smoot," February 19, 1907, 2.

62. Iversen, "Antipolygamy Activism in the Nation's Capitol," May 24, 1998, Washington, D.C.; and Iversen, *The Antipolygamy Controversy*, 217–18.

63. Willing, *On American Soil*, 13.

64. Flake, *The Politics of American Religious Identity*, 51.

65. Flake, *The Politics of American Religious Identity*, 54.

66. "The Presbyterian Assembly on Mormonism," *The Missionary Review of the World* (November 1906), 364.

67. "In the Matter of Reed Smoot, Senator-Elect from Utah: Protest of Citizens of the State of Utah Against the Admission to the United States Senate of Reed Smoot, Apostle of the Mormon Church" (Salt Lake City, 1903), 2.

68. Gary L. Bunker and Davis Bitton, *The Anti-Mormon Graphic Image, 1834–1914: Cartoons, Characters, and Illustrations* (Salt Lake City: University of Utah Press, 1983), 68.

69. Thomas Edgar Lyon, "Evangelical Protestant Missionary Activities in Mormon-Dominated Areas, 1865–1900" (PhD diss., University of Utah, 1962), 130.

70. Gail Bederman, *Manliness & Civilization: A Cultural History of Gender and Race in the United States, 1880–1917* (Chicago: University of Chicago Press, 1995), 22.

71. See Iversen, *The Antipolygamy Controversy*, 222–27.

72. Arnold K. Garr, "Theodore Roosevelt and the Latter-day Saints," in *Out of Obscurity: The LDS Church in the Twentieth Century* (Salt Lake City: Deseret Book, 2000), 130.

73. Iversen, *The Antipolygamy Controversy*, 247.

74. Mrs. Frances J. Diefenderfer, "National Reform Movement: The Mohammedan Mormon Kingdom: Letter from the President of the National Order of Antipolygamy Crusaders," *Christian Statesman* (February 1915), 83.

4   Eternal Progression

Mormonism and American Progressivism

Matthew Bowman

The chorus to "I Am a Child of God," a popular Mormon children's hymn, originally ran "Lead me, guide me, walk beside me / Help me find the way / Teach me all that I must know, to live with him someday." So the story goes, Spencer W. Kimball, president of the church from 1973 to 1985, asked that the word "know" be changed to "do." As Kimball explained, "To know isn't enough. The devils know and tremble; the devils know everything. We have to do something."[1] The change marks in microcosm the ethos of twentieth-century Mormonism. Its intellectual ideals and organizational culture were characterized by a devotion to effort, an optimistic vision of human potential, and a renewed commitment to bureaucracy and organization as the means by which these visions could be enacted. These ideals reflect a fruitful marriage between nineteenth-century Mormon theology and the progressive movement of the early twentieth century. In that era the phrase "eternal progression" moved to the center of the Mormon lexicon.[2] It encapsulates in two words a theology about humanity's destiny, defined as a process of development and change over time, the slow tempering of the soul toward divinity through the long effort of a lifetime, and perhaps after. These ideas had deep roots in Mormon history, but the encounter with the American progressive movement revitalized them. The early twentieth century was a time of rehabilitation for Mormons, when they worked to reinvent a religion shorn of polygamy and forced into American ways of being, and progressivism gave them the concepts, language, and tools to preserve their distinctiveness within adaptation.

By the late twentieth century the word *progressive* had become a synonym for *liberal*, a word that had in the 1980s and 1990s become a derogatory term in American politics, particularly after Republican presidential candidate George H. W. Bush spoke it with enough scorn to kill in a debate with Democratic nominee Michael Dukakis. Today, those Americans who identify as progressives tend to support the platform of the Democratic Party—but also often want to push the party a bit more to the left. They supported the presidency of Barack Obama but wished Obama had initiated more reforms, pushed Republicans in Congress harder, and generally been less conciliatory.[3] However, slotting the word into the neat polarities of twenty-first-century American politics overlooks the ways that "progressivism" offered a deeply philosophical vision of the possibilities of American life; one as much about the nature of culture, humanity, and civilization as it was about tactical politics. As Theodore Roosevelt, one of their great tribunes, declared, progressives were those who "with fervor and broad sympathy and imagination stand for the forward movement, the men who stand for the uplift and betterment of mankind, and who have faith in the people."[4] This is, of course, pure platitude. But it's deadly earnest, and deadly confident. Progressives, more than anything, were profound optimists.

For instance, listen to Simon Patten in 1907, one of the founders of American sociology, the progenitor of the Wharton School of Business, and a man dedicated to progressivism's particular understanding of human nature, and human potential: "When poverty is gone, the last formidable obstacle to the upward movement of the race will have disappeared . . . it is for us to unite the social activities—whose motive forces are charity, religion, philanthropy, revolt, and unrest—into a philosophy that is social, not sectional, in that it gives to them all a reorganized rational body of evidence upon which to proceed."[5] Patten here expresses a delightful naïveté about the future of American society—those opening four words are memorable—but also a conviction that such grandiose goals could be achieved through rationalized social organization.

Many Americans in the thirty or so years before the First World War shared this rather extraordinary optimism about the capacity of American civilization to improve itself. This, of course, was not new. Americans had been optimistic about their nation from the beginning, particularly evangelical Americans who believed their nation to be God's new Israel. But progressives found their nation's strength in a new place—not necessarily in the favor of God, but in human rationality, education, and science.[6] They believed all these things were well on their way to making the United States the most perfect country in human history. They believed that the social sciences had discerned great truths about human nature and about how human societies functioned, and that therefore it was possible, given the right amount of information, to put together a consumer's league or labor union and tweak society just so: to end poverty or alcoholism or prostitution; to educate, uplift, and civilize everybody. As Albert Shaw, a one-time journalist and professor of politics at Cornell wrote, modern systems of welfare, urban planning, and labor organization meant that "centers of population can be made not only safe and wholesome physically for the masses of people, but also conducive to mental and moral progress."[7]

This sort of confidence in bureaucracy, science, and expertise is one marker of progressivism. The other is confidence in what human potential might achieve given sufficient education and self-discipline. Now, again, this was not entirely new. Many nineteenth-century evangelicals had then and still advocated for a form of Christian perfectionism attained through piety and the Holy Spirit.[8] But again, what is interesting is the extent to which progressives repudiated these metaphysical means while still clinging to the utopian end. Instead, they bound it to the promises of social science, the possibilities of correct education, and, more than anything, to organizations.

We saw this in Simon Patten's exultation about the inevitable upward progress of the race, but it also appears in the thought of Jane Addams, who founded Hull House, a home for immigrant women and children in Chicago that offered job training, food, shelter, and any number of other opportunities designed to uplift the poor. Founded in 1889, Hull House quickly became the centerpiece of American progressivism, and Addams herself a theorist, spokesperson, and leader of the movement, eventually winning the Nobel Peace Prize.[9] Addams declared that the impulse toward progressive political reform was "identical with that necessity, which urges us on toward social and individual salvation." She believed that progressivism taught that "without the advance and improvement of the whole no man can hope for any lasting improvement in his own moral or material individual condition."[10] Like many progressives Addams was not conventionally religious, but her language here indicates the extent to which progressivism fused technocracy, faith in academia and in science and in the intellect, with the messianic. They accomplished these things in a variety of ways: Social scientists organized charity organizations to foster uplift of the poor; pastors organized youth groups and Bible study classes that advocated for the social aid programs called "applied Christianity"; politicians sought ways to better institute educated democracy, like the initiative or referendum. As Robert A. Woods, one of the leaders in the settlement house movement, said, calling for educational reform in the city of Boston: "For poor children whose material welfare and moral salvation very largely turn upon getting started in some skilled trade, our system of education is obviously deficient."[11] Lester Frank Ward, one of the founders of the discipline of sociology, made a similar connection: "Social progress consists in transforming the environment. I will not even restrict it to simple material progress where this is obvious . . . but will predicate it also of all esthetic, moral, and intellectual operations."[12] To be educated was to achieve not merely technical skill but moral discernment: the only thing standing in the way of a righteous American republic was, simply, ignorance. And that might be solved.

The progressives sought not merely to help the poor, but to refine their souls; not simply to educate immigrants, but instill in them American values; not only to feed people, but, in the last analysis, to make them not perhaps Christian, but at least good.

All of this may, I hope, help us answer that knotty old question of why it was that Mormons so readily gave up their Zion in the desert, their marital radicalism, their economic communalism and instead made common cause with that very American society that had just spent a decade punishing them. The Mormons entered the twentieth century with tremendous confidence that the mood of the Progressive Era was eminently suited to the practice of their religion.

Let me be clear what I'm arguing. It's habit for many historians to discuss this period with words like "accommodation" and "adaptation," language which implicitly argues that the Mormons compromised themselves. To some extent, of course, they did.[13] But they also gladly entered into that national project that Addams, Patten, and others had begun. They did so because progressivism spoke to many ideas Mormons already embraced. With other antebellum utopians, Joseph Smith had taught of the limitless possibility of human potential, though unlike many of them he drew the notion from his belief in the ontological continuity between God and humanity. He had created an elaborate priestly hierarchy, binding the promise of salvation to the rituals that his priesthood supervised.[14] And nineteenth-century Mormon thinkers, particularly the brothers Parley and Orson Pratt, had built rudimentary connections between science and scripture.[15] Progressive ideas would have appealed to the Mormons in part because of what they offered—but also, perhaps, because of what they had lost.

Joseph Smith was never a systematic thinker, but in the last years of his life his ideas about religion and the societies which religion might create orbited around the creation of relationships. The heaven he dreamed of was created through the sacralization of human relationships: the sealing of marriages, the linking of ancestors to descendants through proxy ordinance, and, of course, the vaguely dynastic system of polygamous marriages. The leaders of Mormonism which followed Joseph Smith systematized these ideas and taught their flock of a heaven of interlocking kingdoms, each made up of marriages—often polygamous marriages—sealed, their glory measured in numbers. This was presumed to be done in the image of God, the literal father of humankind, who sought to exalt his children as their rise exalted him.[16]

This was all vaguely premodern, and even medieval: a heaven predicated upon ceremony, ritual, and the creation of kinship bonds. And the end of polygamy destroyed it. Nonetheless, Mormons continued to value the ideas central to their religion: the literal nature of humanity's likeness to God and the holiness of the relationships that bound them to him; the promise of humanity's eventual ascendance to divinity; the sacred structures that God's priesthood could create. In the Progressive Era, the leaders of Mormonism, men and women, reformulated, rephrased, and transformed the ways that Mormons understood these ideas. They drew particularly on turn-of-the-century social theorists and philosophers to draw their soteriology away from the static, dynastic polygamous afterlife and toward a language of development, evolution, and the cultivation of character through participation in rationalized institutional structures that replaced the kin-based community of polygamy. First, I will deal with the intellectual work of several Mormon theologians, then, by turning to the women who largely staffed and ran the church's youth and social service auxiliaries, show the ways these ideas were implemented in practice.

The three theologians I will examine most closely were all General Authorities, among the highest leaders of the church in the early twentieth century: John Widtsoe, James Talmage, and B. H. Roberts. The first two served as members of the Quorum of the Twelve Apostles, the second-highest governing body of the church; the last as a president of the Quorum of the Seventy, a rung lower on the ladder than the apostles. They were all European immigrants—Talmage and Roberts from Britain, Widtsoe from Norway—who converted as children with their families. Talmage and Widtsoe were both highly educated, with PhD's in the sciences; Roberts was a brilliant autodidact on top of some college education he had in Utah universities.

Further, these men were taken as authorities both inside and out of their faith. All served among the highest leadership of the church, and their work gained exposure and credibility because of it. Roberts and Widtsoe wrote official manuals of study for the priesthood quorums that incorporated their ideas, and Talmage's writings on Jesus Christ, temples, and other topics were often issued with official approval. They were sent into the public eye as curiosity about Mormonism rose in the aftermath of the 1890 Manifesto and the apostle Reed Smoot's election to the Senate in 1904. All three men regularly booked speaking engagements across the nation and represented their church at various conferences and gatherings. Talmage and Roberts wrote serialized books about Mormonism published in national periodicals.[17]

More important than the topic of their educations were the habits of mind they learned. The educations bequeathed to them a very progressive faith in education and the human sciences. Their optimism was perhaps most readily apparent in their conviction that scientific language could best express the truths of their religion, and that the application of scientific principles would advance the work of redemption. Widtsoe declared that "the only rational philosophy is based on science."[18] Many Protestant progressives dealt with the challenges of scholarship on the Bible, evolution, and the origins of the earth posed to faith through arguing that God's benevolent hand was evident in human progress: in scientific advances that brought medicine, sanitation, and the comforts of technology; in the spread of democratic government, education, and justice; in the spread of charitable organizations, temperance, and piety. To these Protestants, science clarified and enlightened scripture, and revealed truth should be seen through its lens.[19]

These Mormon thinkers would not go that far. They nonetheless believed that the language of progressive social science best expressed what Mormonism taught about the human experience. In so doing, they gave intellectual birth to a revitalized church organization, one targeted at the cultivation of character through education, work, and self-discipline, a church shorn of polygamy and instead based upon Joseph Smith's profound optimism in human potential. With a few alterations, the achievement of Talmage, Widtsoe, and Roberts remains the Mormonism believed by most Latter-day Saints today.

The first task was the reduction of the universe to something understandable and explicable through science. Mormons had a great deal of raw material for the effort in the ideas of Joseph Smith. He repudiated creation *ex nihilo*, the notion that God created the earth out of nothing, depicting God as a great craftsman rather than a creator per se. He insisted that the supernatural and the spiritual was merely matter of another form, and by all of this moved the divine and the human onto the same ontological plane. If God was not wholly other, then logically God's works could be understood through the tools that humans use to understand the world more generally.[20]

To the progressive Mormon theologians all of this meant that God was God because he understood and manipulated science. Therefore, they began to speak about religion in the language of scientific law. Talmage's magnum opus, the 1915 biography *Jesus the Christ*, explained that Christ's suffering and death satisfied apparently universal laws of justice, which bound even God's desire to forgive sin should they not be satisfied.[21] More centrally, Widtsoe's first book was titled, bluntly, *Joseph Smith As Scientist*, and asserted that human existence was governed by what Widtsoe called the "moderate law of evolution." By this Widtsoe meant neither Darwinian brute natural selection, nor blind, aimless change. Rather he understood evolution to be teleological change toward a determined and directed end. Widtsoe found in the moderate law of evolution God's plan for his children: eternal progression, their course through earth life to eventual exaltation. As he asserted, "The Mormon plan of salvation is strictly scientific and rests upon the irrevocable laws of the universe," and that "the truth behind Spencer's law of evolution and the doctrines taught by the Mormon prophet [Joseph Smith] are one and the same."[22]

The "Spencer" referenced here is Herbert Spencer, a British social philosopher whose ideas undergirded much of what progressives believed about the progress of human civilization. Spencer argued that the social application of Darwin's ideas meant that all things were both in ceaseless change, but also were progressing toward increasing complexity.[23] For progressives, this meant that human civilizations, like human beings themselves, were tending toward increased sophistication, refinement, and advancement. This progress derived from a process of growth and change: the struggle with and overcoming of obstacles. For Mormons, his philosophy reconciled their ideas about human progression with the world they lived in better than any other. "Undoubtedly true evolution is true, meaning progress from the lower to the higher, from the simple to the more complex," James Talmage wrote, adopting language of inheritance to describe the goals of Mormonism.[24] The language here closely mirrored Spencer, who argued that the principle of evolution held as true for societies and individuals as it did for species and biology: the natural tendency of living things as for species was toward greater complexity, growth, and progress.[25] In reference to the ways his religion understood the world, John Widtsoe wrote that "the philosophy of Herbert Spencer is considered the only philosophy that harmonizes with the knowledge of today."[26]

The Mormon theologians drew from Spencer's reworking of evolution two key concepts. First, that they might think of their connection with God in terms of evolutionary, ontological inheritance rather than in the dynastic language of polygamy. The traits of divinity they increasingly spoke of as inborn rather than acquired only through covenant relationship. Secondly, they began to think of "eternal progression" as a function of Spencerian evolution—the cultivation of progress through struggle, refining personal character through education, confronting obstacle, and committing to the character-building work of their church. The Mormons stood convinced that godhood was every human's inheritance—provided they would put in the effort.

Joseph Smith had taught that humans were the same type of being God is, but for these Mormons that humans were literally the children of God, an inference that Smith's followers had made, was of prime importance. In 1916, the First Presidency of the Church issued a proclamation called "The Father and the Son: A Doctrinal Exposition." It clarified divine relationships not only within the godhead but among the Father and the Son and humanity. In *Jesus the Christ* James Talmage identified Jehovah or Yahweh, the God of the Hebrew Bible, as the premortal Jesus Christ, acting as the agent of his father.[27] The First Presidency insisted that the distinction was crucial to properly understand humanity's relationship to divinity. As they wrote, "Jesus Christ is not the Father of the spirits who have taken or yet shall take bodies upon this earth, for He is one of them. He is The Son, as they are sons or daughters of Elohim." Talmage noted that understanding these relationships enabled Mormons to properly understand the nature of Christ's mission, lauding "the humble offer of Jesus the Firstborn—to assume mortality and live among men as their Exemplar and Teacher, observing the sanctity of man's agency but teaching them to use aright that divine heritage."[28] As Roberts asserted, the network of these relationships meant that Mormons must "think as Christ did, that it is no robbery to be equal to God," for they could claim the same inheritance as he.[29]

Roberts wove together the ideas of Joseph Smith and those of later Mormons into the radically optimistic understanding of human identity most Mormons accept today. Joseph Smith had never explicitly taught that human beings were the literal children of heavenly parents. His famous King Follet Discourse and Sermon in the Grove emphasized rather that human "intelligence" was co-eternal with divine "intelligence" and of the same type of being. This theology was more clearly enunciated by Joseph Smith's successors, particularly Brigham Young, who taught that human spirits were the products of heavenly procreation.[30] Roberts reconciled these two concepts, teaching that humans were both uncreated, co-eternal beings of the same divine nature as God himself, but also the literal children of God, their identities and intelligence clothed in bodies spiritual and physical through God's creative powers, and destined, ultimately, to achieve the same degree of divinity and glory which their heavenly father enjoyed—though always, as children are always the children of their father, in a position of subordination and respect.

The question became how to cultivate this divine inheritance, and here effort moved to the forefront. Roberts drew on what he called "Spencer's primary doctrine . . . evolution" to elaborate on how this worked. "The principle is an induction from experience," he said, declaring that Spencer's theories demonstrated that growth came only through dealing with challenging trials.[31] Talmage emphasized that in Christ's sufferings in

Gethsemane, "the Savior took upon himself the burden of the sins of mankind," and that the cross "could not exceed the bitter anguish through which he had successfully passed." Douglas Davies has argued that Talmage emphasized Gethsemane to foreground Christ's active choice to suffer, to freely choose trial and overcome it.[32] It was only through suffering that true progress could come. Indeed, a long history of persecution had taught the Mormons to find value and identity in suffering. B. H. Roberts perhaps articulated these ideas most eloquently when he wrote, "I believe it consistent with right reason to say that some of the lowliest walks in life, the paths which lead into the deepest valleys of sorrow and up to the most rugged steeps of adversity, are the ones which, if a man travel in, will best accomplish the object of his existence in this world."[33]

What did these ideas mean in practice? Like many progressives, Mormons came to believe that bureaucratic organization could foster the sort of spiritual progress they hoped for. The institution of the church replaced the old kinship networks of polygamy as the ground on which salvation was worked out, and that salvation increasingly came through the task of self-discipline. In particular, the late nineteenth and early twentieth century found Mormons engaged in a massive project directed at the training of their young people: youth organizations for young men and women, Sunday schools, and a children's organization called Primary. All of these organizations held weekly activities, and offered lessons in Mormon doctrine and scripture study, but also in personal comportment, virtues like honesty, punctuality, and etiquette, and personal grooming. In 1898 the General Superintendency of the Deseret Sunday School Union announced that "The great aim of Sunday School work is to insure right action . . . a desire to obey . . . doctrines and ordinances. In short, to make Latter-day Saints out of them."[34] Just before World War I the LDS Church officially affiliated with the Boy Scouts of America, a progressive organization if there ever was one, and to this day speaks of its benefits in terms of training young men to become leaders in the church. Mormonism had auxiliaries—versions of Sunday school, the Relief Society organization for women, prayer groups and quorum meetings for men—from the middle of the nineteenth century, but under Joseph F. Smith, president of the church from 1901 to 1918, participation in these auxiliaries was standardized and expectations of participation began to rise.[35] By the early twentieth century to be a Mormon meant increasingly meeting a set of standards in personal behavior, achieved primarily through participating in the institution of the church.

The careers of two prominent early-twentieth-century Mormon reformers and politicians demonstrates the persistence of progressive ideology from the abstract world of theology into the public realm.

Nearly all the public work of Mormonism was done largely by women. As with polygamy, Mormon women bore the task of implementing theological transformation, making Mormon life over in the image of its intellectual developments. The career of Amy Brown Lyman in particular demonstrates the gradual shift from the kinship-based Mormonism of the nineteenth century to the rationalized progressive Mormonism of the twentieth. Wife of the apostle Richard R. Lyman, a civil engineer who studied at Cornell University, Lyman accompanied her husband across the country in 1902 on the way to his studies. They stayed the summer in Chicago, where Amy Brown Lyman met Jane Addams. She also discovered sociology, taking a summer course in what was called the "case work" method, which encouraged community activists to involve themselves in the practical needs of a community and devote themselves not to simply dispensing charity, but to encouraging, training, and generally seeking to educate those who suffered from social ills like poverty in methods that might lift them out of their benighted state. Lyman later declared that her studies in Chicago convinced her that "no work could be more important and satisfying than that of helping to raise human life to its highest level."[36]

In 1909, back in Salt Lake City, Lyman joined the General Board of the Relief Society and quickly moved up its ranks, becoming secretary of the organization in 1913 and in 1921 joining the Relief Society general presidency. In 1940 she became president of the Relief Society herself. Additionally, in 1919 Heber J. Grant, who had just become president of the church, placed her in charge of the church's new department of social services, giving her a mandate to organize relief efforts, medical care, and other charitable efforts. Lyman sprang into action. She had already, working through the Relief Society, established milk kitchens for poor children and organized classes for young mothers in Salt Lake City's poorer neighborhoods, and reached out to the Young Women's program as well, hoping to draw the youth of the church into similar campaigns. These would not only serve the poor but would also invest both those served and the Mormon women who served them with charity, moral fiber, and a greater commitment to their faith.

By 1917 Lyman was taking women of the Relief Society out of state for training in sociology, the case work method, and other such progressive innovations. In 1919, she arranged for several dozen Mormons in a few

Salt Lake City congregations to receive training so that a community welfare department could be set up there. It was then that she had a confrontation with Susa Young Gates.

A daughter of Brigham Young, Gates was one of the most prolific and gifted writers in Mormonism at the turn of the century. She edited both the *Young Women's Journal* and the Relief Society journal, the official organs of these auxiliaries, and served on the General Board of the Relief Society and as one of the earliest leaders of the Young Women's association.[37] Gates judged herself a progressive; in part under her guidance the Young Women's association, like the Relief Society in Utah, grew from local, ad hoc, congregational clubs into a church-wide, formally organized institution with an intricate leadership structure and a wide number of tasks and aims. "No one will deny that the women of the church have been magnificently disciplined by their various organizations," crowed Gates. "There is much to encourage the sociologist in the steady improvement and progress of the women of the church."[38]

But though Gates absorbed certainly the ethos and the mood of progressivism, she remained skeptical of its cult of expertise, training, and bureaucracy. Gates was a child of nineteenth-century Mormonism's kinship-based community, and she was consistently suspicious of attempts to modernize, professionalize, or train Mormons to do anything. In January 1920 the two women had a heated confrontation in front of the desk of Heber J. Grant, Lyman defending her attempts to integrate progressive organizational strategies into the Relief Society and Gates attacking them. Grant, generally conflict-adverse, referred the matter back to the Relief Society board.

Why did Gates oppose Lyman's innovations? Both believed that the cultivation of godly character lay near the heart of what it meant to be a Mormon, and both believed that this cultivation came through the rigors of self-discipline, self-abnegation, and the exertion of effort. Their disagreement rather reflects the proper method through which these goals could be attained. Gates, born merely a decade after the Mormons settled the Great Basin, conceived of her church in terms of the communal, familial networks that had been so essential to the success of the pioneers. She feared that Lyman's programs, training, and hunger for expertise and efficiency would lead, inevitably, to the women of the Relief Society being pushed aside, the old sisterhood falling prey to the inexorable march of what she called professional charity. Lyman, for her part, intended no such threat: but she did believe that the church, to meet the demands of a growing population and the ever more urgent need to socialize and train the young, could do no better than to draw upon the best and most advanced knowledge possible. Susa Young Gates resigned from the Relief Society board in 1922, and Amy Brown Lyman remained at the head—both de facto and de jure—of the church's social services efforts.

A similar tension can be seen in the political career of B. H. Roberts, who threw himself into local and national politics in the 1890s, as Utah was pursuing its ultimately successful bid for statehood, achieved in 1896. As mentioned in chapter 3, Roberts twice ran for the House of Representatives as a Democrat, and was elected in 1896, only to be denied his seat because he was a polygamist. Roberts's political platforms were suffused with the language and ideas of his particularly Mormon version of progressivism. For instance, unlike other religious progressives, he opposed Prohibition when it was first proposed, and supported repeal in the last years of his life. While Heber J. Grant, a more conventional political conservative and president of the LDS Church during the Great Depression, opposed repeal, Roberts declared

> There is no identity between the L.D.S. Church's Word of Wisdom and what is known as Prohibition. The former rests upon persuasion, upon teaching, upon education and that without compulsion or constraint. The other, State Prohibition, should be enforced with fines, imprisonment and often it has proven to be at the cost of life in pursuance of such enforcement of law and if the Church undertakes to enforce it by penalties or should turn it over to be enforced by the state through pains and penalties, then the Church would be changing and relegating its discipline to enforcement by the state and thus grossly depart from the high moral and spiritual grounds upon which its supplanted Word of Wisdom has been placed by the Almighty.[39]

Roberts's faith in education and moral self-development shaped his approach to American politics throughout his career. He remained convinced that the church's greatest power—indeed, the greatest power of any institution—lay in its capacity for education, not coercion. Thus he staunchly protested an 1896 statement issued by the First Presidency advising all General Authorities of the Church that they required permission from the "proper authorities" of the church before they engaged in political activity.[40] Roberts declared such policies to be a "violation both of usual political methods and the declared principles of the Church."[41] As he understood it, politics was the delicate and always dangerous art of exerting control, and religion, whose province was the shaping of character, had to tread carefully when it entered that tempting arena. As Roberts put it, he hoped "the church shall make it her sole business to make men, and leave men to make the state."[42]

At the same time, Roberts ascribed profoundly optimistic potential to voluntary organizations. As early as 1914, he endorsed an "empire of humanity"—an international organization devoted to preserving peace, and when Woodrow Wilson proposed the League of Nations, Roberts ascribed millennial possibilities to it. "The next step in the world's progress is to organize a League of Nations," he declared in an address in the Tabernacle in Salt Lake City in 1919. "It has become recognized as a world's need by enlightened minds of all nations." As had Lyman, Roberts urged the church's organizations to mobilize in support of the League of Nations to educate Americans about the possibilities that it offered.[43]

Mormonism still retains this profound devotion to its institution. By the time of the Great Depression, the Mormons had erected the Church Welfare Program, a system of aid to the needy that encouraged recipients to offer labor and cultivate habits of thrift and industry in return for their benefits.[44] But the argument is perhaps most manifest in the church's greatest project of the twentieth century: the systematization, reorganization, and reaggregation that made up the project called Correlation. An attempt to regularize the lines of church authority, bringing all auxiliaries under the supervision of the Quorum of the Twelve, establishing a regular and uniform curriculum used by all members of the church, and overseeing for orthodoxy all church publications. One church leader explained that the process of Correlation was not merely organizational, but rather a necessary tool in "the divine plan of saving souls."[45] The education administered through correlated materials is notoriously simplified, but for a reason: it is targeted less at increasing scriptural or theological knowledge than it is upon encouraging Mormons to become better people. The lesson on the Sabbath day in the current Sunday school manual, for instance, dwells quite briefly upon the scriptural origins of the Sabbath before devoting most of its attention to questions about how faithful Saints can better observe it in their own lives.[46] This is education as moral improvement; it is the language of progressivism at its finest.

The Mormons still retain the unadulterated confidence in organization and education that many Americans left in the trenches of the world wars and the food lines of the Great Depression; they speak with justified pride about their church's welfare program, the capable church bureaucracy that makes Mormonism an identical experience in Provo, Utah, Paraguay, and Poland; their faith's simultaneous dedication to businesslike efficiency and the refinement of souls. They may seem to many Americans technocrats, devoted to a strong and bureaucratic institution—but they are technocrats sure that technocracy can make people better: a peculiar fusion of ideas long since severed on the American political landscape which the Mormons have kept alive.

NOTES

1. "New Verse Is Written for a Popular Song," *Church News*, April 4, 1978, 16. See also Karen Lynn Davidson, Our Latter-day Hymns: The Stories and the Messages (Salt Lake City: Deseret Book, 1998) 303–304.

2. This claim derives from Gordon and Gary Shepherd who track the use of themes, phrases, and concepts in the church's semiannual General Conferences from the mid-nineteenth century through the mid-twentieth in their *A Kingdom Transformed: Themes in the Development of Mormonism* (Salt Lake City: University of Utah, 1984) 237–42.

3. On the process of coding the word "liberal" in late twentieth-century politics, see Thomas Edsall, *Chain Reaction: The Impact of Race, Rights and Taxes on American Politics* (New York: Norton, 1992), 212–15. George Lakoff has traced the rise of the word "progressive" as a replacement for "liberal" in American politics since 2000; see, for instance, *Thinking Points: Communicating American Values and Vision* (New York: Farrar, Straus and Giroux, 2006), 17–19. On progressives in the early twenty-first century, see Gary Dorrien, *The Obama Question: A Progressive Perspective* (Lanham, MD: Rowman and Littlefield, 2012).

4. Ronald J. Pestritto and William J. Atto, eds., *American Progressivism: A Reader* (Lanham, MD: Rowman and Littlefield, 2008), 36. I am guided in my interpretation of progressivism as a largely cultural, visionary, and redemptive movement that nonetheless enthusiastically embraced the social sciences and bureaucracy by a number of authors; most significant are Jackson Lears, *Rebirth of a Nation: The Making of Modern America, 1877–1920* (New York: Harper, 2009); Maureen A. Flanagan, *America Reformed: Progressives and Progressivisms, 1890s–1920s* (New York: Oxford, 2006); Robert Crunden, *Ministers of Reform: The Progressive Achievement in American Civilization, 1889–1920* (New York: Basic, 1982).

5. Simon Patten, *Economics and the New Basis of Civilization* (New York: Macmillan, 1907), 197–98. Patten receives attention in William Leach, *Land of Desire: Power and the Rise of a New American Culture* (New York: Random House, 1994), 238–41.

6. Robert Wiebe, *The Search for Order: 1877–1920* (New York: Hill and Wang, 1967), is the classic defense of this argument.

7. Albert Shaw, "European Town Life," *Chatauquan* 9 (June 1889), 520.

8. See, for instance, Ronald Walters, *American Reformers, 1815–1860* (New York: Hill and Wang, 1997), 28–34.

9. On Addams, her achievements, and her relationship to her faith, see Crunden, *Ministers of Reform*, 16–32, and Addams's own *Twenty Years at Hull House* (New York: Macmillan, 1911).

10. Jane Addams, *Philanthropy and Social Progress: Seven Essays* (New York: Crowell, 1907), 127.

11. Robert A. Woods, *The City Wilderness* (Boston: Houghton Mifflin, 1898), 240.

12. Lester Frank Ward, *Pure Sociology* (New York: Macmillan, 1903), 251.

13. See, for instance, Thomas G. Alexander's essential *Mormonism in Transition: A History of the Latter-day Saints, 1890–1930* (Urbana: University of Illinois Press, 1986), xii; Leonard Arrington, *Great Basin Kingdom: An Economic History of the Latter-day Saints, 1830–1900* (Cambridge: Harvard University Press, 1958), 380–412; Jan Shipps, *Mormonism: The Story of a New Religious Tradition* (Urbana: University of Illinois Press, 1985), 117–18.

14. On Joseph Smith's theology, see Douglas Davies, *Joseph Smith, Jesus, and Satanic Opposition* (Burlington: Ashgate, 2010), particularly 175–95; Richard Lyman Bushman, *Joseph Smith: Rough Stone Rolling* (New York: Knopf, 2005), 436–59.

15. Terryl Givens and Matthew Grow, *Parley P. Pratt: The Apostle Paul of Mormonism* (New York: Oxford, 2011), 334–37; Benjamin Park, "'Reasonings Sufficient': Joseph Smith, Thomas Dick, and the Context(s) of Early Mormonism," *Journal of Mormon History* 38 (Summer 2012): 210–24.

16. On the sacralization of relationships, see Samuel Brown, *In Heaven as it is on Earth: Joseph Smith and the Early Mormon Conquest of Death* (New York: Oxford, 2012), 170–203; I discuss the soteriology of polygamous Mormonism in my "The Crisis of Mormon Christology: History, Progress, and Protestantism," *Fides Et Historia* 40 (Summer/Fall 2008), as does B. Carmon Hardy, *Solemn Covenant: The Mormon Polygamous Passage* (Urbana: University of Illinois Press, 1992), 1–39, and Kathryn Daynes, *More Wives Than One: The Transformation of the Mormon Marriage System* (Urbana: University of Illinois Press, 2001), 17–36.

17. For the careers and activities of these three, see Alexander, *Mormonism in Transition*, 251–58, 273–93.

18. John Widtsoe, *A Rational Theology* (Salt Lake City: General Young Men's Improvement Board, 1915), 103.

19. On liberal Protestantism, see most generally William Hutchison, *The Modernist Impulse in American Protestantism* (Cambridge: Harvard University Press, 1976), and Gary Dorrien, *The Making of American Liberal Theology: Imagining Progressive Religion* (Nashville: Westminster/John Knox, 2001); on liberal Protestantism and the progressive movement more generally, beyond works already cited, see Richard Wightman Fox, "The Culture of Liberal Protestant Progressivism, 1875–1925," *Journal of Interdisciplinary History* 23.3 (Winter 1993): 652.

20. For analyses of these ideas, see Erich Robert Paul, *Science, Religion, and Mormon Cosmology* (Urbana: University of Illinois Press, 1992).

21. James Talmage, *Jesus the Christ* (Salt Lake City: Deseret Book, 1916), 676; see also Talmage's *The Vitality of Mormonism* (Boston: Gorham, 1919), 60. This

remains the way Mormons commonly discuss Jesus's atonement; see for instance the *Gospel Principles* Sunday school manual (Salt Lake City: Intellectual Reserve, 2009), 59–67.

22. Widtsoe, *Joseph Smith As Scientist* (Salt Lake City: Young Men's Mutual Improvement Association, 1908), 112, 115.

23. Spencer's most important works were *Social Statics* (New York: Appleton, 1873), which discusses social evolution from 269–73, and *First Principles* (London: William and Norgate, 1880), which discusses Spencer's principles of evolution and applies them to a wide variety of human endeavors—politics, art, psychology, morality, and justice, among others. Assessments of Spencer include Mark Francis, *Herbert Spencer and the Invention of Modern Life* (Ithaca: Cornell University Press, 2007), and Derek Freeman, "The Evolutionary Theories of Charles Darwin and Herbert Spencer," in John Offer, ed., *Herbert Spencer: Critical Assessments* (London: Routledge, 2000), 5–70.

24. James E. Talmage to F. C. Williamson, April 22, 1933 (James E. Talmage Papers, Church History Library and Archives, Salt Lake City).

25. Robert Perrin, "Hebert Spencer's Four Theories of Social Evolution," *American Journal of Sociology* 81.6 (May 1976): 1339–59; Mark Francis, *Herbert Spencer and the Invention of Modern Life*, 247–61, on Spencer's influence.

26. Widtsoe, *Joseph Smith As Scientist*, 97.

27. Talmage, *Jesus the Christ*, 38–39. This concept had circulated in Mormonism for several decades before the 1915 publication of *Jesus the Christ* but Talmage was its primary popularizer. See Thomas Alexander, "The Reconstruction of Mormon Doctrine," *Sunstone* 22 (July 1999): 15–29; Boyd Kirkland, "Jehovah as the Father: The Development of the Mormon Jehovah Doctrine," *Sunstone* 9 (July/August 1980): 36–44.

28. B. H. Roberts, *The Mormon Doctrine of Deity* (Salt Lake City: Deseret News, 1903), 202; Talmage, *Jesus the Christ*, 8–9.

29. The First Presidency and the Twelve, "The Father and the Son: A Doctrinal Exposition," in James Clark, ed., *Messages of the First Presidency* (Salt Lake City: Bookcraft, 1965–1975), 5:25; Roberts, *Doctrine of Deity*, 75–77, and Roberts, *The Gospel* (Salt Lake City: Deseret News, 1888), 261.

30. Alexander, "The Reconstruction of Mormon Doctrine"; Van Hale, "The Origin of the Human Spirit in Early Mormon Thought," in Gary Bergera, ed., *Line upon Line: Essays in Mormon Doctrine* (Salt Lake: Signature, 1989), 115–21; Blake Ostler, "The Idea of Pre-existence in the Development of Mormon Thought," *Dialogue: A Journal of Mormon Thought* 15.1 (Spring 1982): 59–78; Terryl Givens, *When Souls Had Wings: The Idea of Preexistence in Western Thought* (New York: Oxford University Press, 2009), 212–20.

31. B. H. Roberts, *Seventy's Course in Theology: Doctrine of Deity* (Salt Lake City: Caxton Press, 1910), 153. Roberts cites *First Principles* throughout his works; for instance, in *The Mormon Doctrine of Deity* (Salt Lake City: Deseret News, 1903), 105, to disprove traditional trinitarianism.

32. Talmage, *Jesus the Christ*, 613–14; Douglas Davies, "Gethsemane and Calvary in LDS Soteriology," *Dialogue* 34.3 (2000): 19–30.

33. Roberts, *The Gospel*, 290.

34. B. H. Roberts, *Latter-day Saints Sunday School Treatise* (Salt Lake City: Deseret Sunday School Union, 1898), 13.

35. For this process, see Alexander, *Mormonism in Transition*, 125–57; Matthew Bowman, *The Mormon People: The Making of an American Faith* (New York: Random House, 2012), 144–52. On the Boy Scouts, see, for instance, *Handbook 2: Administering the Church* (Salt Lake City: Church of Jesus Christ of Latter-day Saints, 2010) 8.13.4: "Scouting should help young men put into practice the gospel principles they learn on Sunday."

36. Amy Brown Lyman, *In Retrospect* (Salt Lake City: General Relief Society Board, 1945), 114. Much of Lyman's biography and information about her career is drawn from two sources: David Hall, "Anxiously Engaged: Amy Brown Lyman and Relief Society Charity Work, 1917–1945," *Dialogue* 27.2 (Spring 1985): 73–91, and Hall's "In the Utah Vanguard: Amy Brown Lyman as Progressive Mormon Activist, Welfare State Builder, and Modern Woman in Dual-Career Family" (PhD diss., University of California, Santa Barbara, 2003).

37. The standard biography of Gates is Richard Cracroft, *Susa Young Gates: Her Life and Work* (Salt Lake City: University of Utah Press, 1951). See also Carolyn Person, "Susa Young Gates," in Claudia Bushman, ed., *Mormon Sisters* (Logan: University of Utah Press, 1997), 199–222.

38. Susa Young Gates, *History of the Young Ladies Mutual Improvement Association* (Salt Lake City: Deseret News, 1911), 36.

39. B. H. Roberts, "The Autobiography of B. H. Roberts," 391 (L. Tom Perry Special Collections, Brigham Young University).

40. *Deseret Weekly News*, April 6, 1896, 533.

41. Roberts to J. M. Sjodahl, December 8, 1910 (B. H. Roberts Papers, Church History Library and Archives, Salt Lake City); cited in D. Craig Mikkelsen, "The Politics of B. H. Roberts," *Dialogue* 9.2 (Summer 1974): 42.

42. *Journal History of the Church of Jesus Christ of Latter-day Saints*, November 5, 1910.

43. *Improvement Era* 12.6 (April 1919): 474.

44. On the Welfare Program, see Garth L. Mangum and Bruce D. Blumell, *The Mormons' War on Poverty: A History of LDS Welfare, 1830–1990* (Salt Lake City: University of Utah Press, 1993).

45. Harold B. Lee, quoted in Breck England, "Harold B. Lee: Master Teacher," *Ensign* (January 2002), 17.

46. *Gospel Principles*, 139–45.

PART II

Shifting Alliances

5 Ezra Taft Benson and the Conservative Turn of "Those Amazing Mormons"

Jan Shipps

Whenever election time comes around, the General Authorities of the Church of Jesus Christ of Latter-day Saints remind local leaders across the United States to encourage the members of their wards to take an active part in the political process. Not long ago, in a priesthood meeting in one of the many wards in Provo, Utah, this reminder was delivered by one of the high priests. He said that at a specified time, the Republican men in the ward should gather in a nearby school auditorium; the Democrats should gather in the school's broom closet.[1]

It is possible there may be isolated LDS wards in blue states where there are more Democrats than Republicans, but in virtually every sector of Utah and the other states in the Mormon culture region except the urban areas where non-Mormons live, a staggering disparity now exists between highly conservative Republicans and moderate Democrats. Because this state of affairs has endured without a change in the outcome of presidential elections in Utah since 1968 and in the vote for governor since 1984, and also because a great majority of LDS Church leaders in Utah moved into the Republican Party after the Mormon "People's Party" was forced to give way in order for Utah to become a state in 1896, many modern observers are under the impression that Utah has always been extremely conservative.

Yet the history of Mormonism reveals that throughout the nineteenth century, this movement was not conservative, but virtually revolutionary. Its members experimented with radical social and economic systems, although it was for a time a theocracy—or as it called itself, a theodemocracy—that was both powerfully patriarchal and strictly hierarchical. Moreover, even after the U.S. Congress insisted that in order for Utah Territory to become a state, its citizens must do away with the Mormon People's Party and divide their political allegiances so that the new state would have both strong Democratic and Republican parties, national political ideology was likely less important than the local situation in the mountain west. The lion's share of the Saints in many of the wards (i.e., congregations) preferred to be Democrats. This probably had little to do with whether that party was progressive or conservative; instead it reflected the fact that Joseph Smith, the first Mormon prophet, was a Democrat. In order to balance things out and make statehood possible, many LDS leaders became Republicans, and as the leaders went, so did many of their followers.[2]

Another reason that accounts for the fact that Mormons in Utah were not always conservative is that around the turn of the twentieth century and in the century's early decades, the Republicans were the progressives. But as the two timelines pictured below indicate (figs. 5.1 and 5.2), the predominantly Mormon state did not always vote for Republicans, either for U.S. president or Utah governor.

As is obvious from these two figures that display the vote in Utah for both the governor of the state and the president of the nation, the years from 1932 through 1948 Utah voters were, by far, the most Democratic they ever were. But all through the years of the Eisenhower administration, the state was solidly Republican. Moreover, Mormon Apostle Ezra Taft Benson was Secretary of Agriculture during this period, serving in the highest civil executive office ever held by a Latter-day Saint.[3]

Following President Eisenhower, the state voted for Richard Nixon in 1960[4] and for Lyndon Johnson in 1964. David O. McKay, the president of the Church of Jesus Christ of Latter-day Saints, and his wife became friends with Johnson, visiting the president in Texas and in the White House and welcoming President Johnson and his wife when they paid a return visit to Utah. In fact, McKay had been the first religious leader Johnson asked to the White House after the Kennedy assassination.[5] The state elected Republican governors from 1949 through 1965, but in the following two decades, the nation-state pattern reversed, with the election of

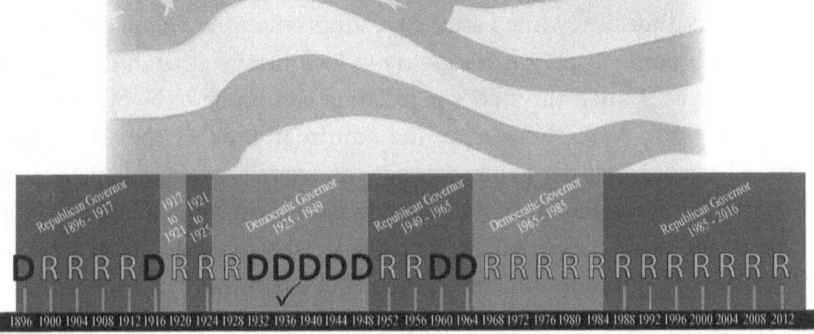

FIGURE 5.1 Utah's voting record in presidential and gubernatorial elections, 1896 to 2012. The checkmark above 1936 indicates that church members were instructed how to vote in this election, the only time LDS leaders have ever given church members direct instructions about how to vote. However, Mormons in Utah voted for FDR instead.

FIGURE 5.2 Utah's voting record in presidential and gubernatorial elections, 1896 to 2012.

Democratic governors and Republican candidates for U.S. president. From 1984 until 2012, however, the state was so solidly Republican and intensely conservative that it seemed unnecessary for national Republican candidates to do much campaigning there.

Before examining this remarkable conservative turn that led to the high priest's jest about the Latter-day Saints who were the Republicans meeting in an auditorium, while Latter-day Saints who were Democrats could meet in a broom closet, it is necessary to look briefly at Utah during the New Deal years when the state's population continued to be overwhelmingly Mormon. As early as 1910, the administration of the Church of Jesus Christ of Latter-day Saints shifted away from its traditional pattern of encouraging all Latter-day Saints, especially new converts, to settle in the Great Basin.[6] As it happened, their advice to "stay in the world, but not of it" was so often honored in the breach that even many historians have failed to take note of the church's decision to cancel "the gathering" that had been so crucially important in the perpetuation of this new American faith. Excepting in a few urban areas outside the mountain west where the church was organized into local stakes, wards, and branches, plus a few areas on the Pacific coast, the Mormon world was still subdivided into Zion and the mission field. The presence of a living prophet, a population of ethnic Mormons, and LDS temples in Salt Lake City, Logan, Manti, and St. George meant that large numbers of the mission-field Mormons wanted to reside in Zion unaware of the reality that the resources of the Mormon culture region could not support all of them.

This was especially true in the state of Utah, Mormonism's center place, where agriculture had been the main source of income throughout the nineteenth century. This situation was much the same in the twentieth century, although the state's economy was increasingly integrated into the national economy through the commercialization of agriculture and manufacturing—most notably the processing of beet sugar and other agricultural products.[7] In addition, a sizeable business sector developed and corporate mining grew as well. The development of railways, aside from the Union Pacific, and the coming of urban utilities, including interurban railways from Salt Lake City to Ogden and to Utah County, allowed the population to take advantage of the new economy by traveling daily to places where jobs in those industries had become available.

As a result, Utah became the most industrialized state in the mountain west. For all that, since so much of the state's manufacturing was tied to agriculture, the agricultural depression that hit the nation in the 1920s was devastating to Utah.[8] As Garth L. Mangum and Bruce D. Blumell note in *The Mormons' War on Poverty*:

> Utah, the center of the Mormon population, was . . . one of the hardest-hit areas of the nation. The regional economy was based on mining, stock raising, farm products, and transportation, industries which had expanded greatly during World War I but which, during the postwar collapse in demand, had slid into a regional depression that lasted throughout the 1920s and then worsened significantly during the 1930s.[9]

In other words, the state was suffering economically long before the advent of the Great Depression, a circumstance that surely added to the vote that defeated Senator Reed Smoot in 1932 and led to the state's choice of a Democratic president. In 1936, Church President Heber J. Grant—once a Democrat, but by this time a strong Republican—placed a letter on the front page of the church's newspaper, the *Deseret News,* on the day before the national election urging all Latter-day Saints to vote against President Franklin Roosevelt, a Democrat.[10] Rather than following his advice, a majority of Mormon voters all across the state voted for FDR.[11] In Utah, 69.34 percent of voters chose to reelect FDR, while only 29.79 percent went for the Republican challenger, Alf Landon. This was nearly a ten-percentage-point jump over the national statistic that had 60.80 percent of voters supporting the Democratic incumbent.[12]

The collapse of the stock market in 1929 and the onset of the Great Depression led to an unemployment rate of 35.8 percent in Utah.[13] Not surprisingly, as New Deal programs were put into place to help the poor and the unemployed, Utah's citizens were quick to take advantage of them. The Utah state government likewise accepted available funds from Washington to establish public welfare and other state programs to assist the unemployed. In 1933, if more than four out of every ten people in Utah were not exactly "on the dole," they were accepting various forms of public help. By late 1932 Utah was receiving, on average, $5.00 of federal assistance per capita in contrast to the U.S. average of $1.87 per person. One Utah family out of four received government help, as opposed to one in seven elsewhere in the country.[14] At the same time, however, LDS leaders encouraged church members to avoid public assistance if at all possible, fearing a culture of dependence.

In these dreadful Depression years, the church moved to establish its well-known Church Welfare Program, designed to help church members who were harmed by the stagnant economy.[15] As soon as it was well under way, LDS leaders encouraged church members to turn to their local wards for assistance, rather than depending on the government. As the First Presidency stated at the program's launch in 1936, its aim was that "the curse of idleness" and "the evils of a dole" would be abolished; the aim of the church, the statement clarified, was "to help them people to help themselves."[16] But the no-strings-attached help the government provided remained the primary source of assistance until the economy rebounded as the nation moved toward World War II. In fact, in the first year of the existence of the church's welfare program, ten times as many Utah citizens relied on public assistance as the number who sought assistance through the new LDS plan.[17] In a discussion about the Depression years in Utah, several Latter-day Saints told this author that one of the incentives for seeking government help was its invisibility. Since the LDS pattern of help asked those who received help to repay the favor by helping others, recipients of church welfare were identified as needing assistance to feed themselves and their families.

Life in Utah was better in the 1940s as the economy recovered and as the Latter-day Saints found themselves at one with the nation in their desire to defeat Japan and the Axis powers. In the immediate postwar years, the church was at pains to regather the Saints who had been scattered during and immediately after the war, organizing or reorganizing the church all throughout the Mormon culture region, as well as along the Pacific coast. Additionally, since many of the church's missions had been halted due to the war, in the late 1940s the church undertook extraordinary mission activities and began to expand, both in numbers and in geographic space organized into stakes, wards, and branches.

The decade of the 1950s was one of astonishing activity in Mormonism's center place. Church growth was occurring outside as well as inside the United States at such an undreamed of rate that the prewar church organization was finding it impossible to keep up with constructing enough buildings and finding enough lay clergy to lead all the new Saints.[18] What to do about the deteriorating urban area around church headquarters was another problem, as was managing all the genealogical material that was being gathered from throughout the world. At the time, the church was still being led by its priesthood organization and its auxiliaries (the Female Relief Society, the Sunday School, the Primary organization, the Young Men's and Young Women's Mutual Improvement Associations), and the heads of departments such as Genealogy, Buildings, Mission programs, and so on. Each auxiliary and department had a few employees, but the church had no real bureaucracy.

What it did have was a first-rate Public Affairs Department which had been in existence for well over a half century. That department caught the excitement of the age and stayed busy issuing press releases disseminating information about the growth of the church, the Mormon Tabernacle Choir (called "America's choir" by President Eisenhower), and its successful members like swimsuit designer Rose Marie Reed, golfer Johnny Miller, and actor Victor Jory. In these and the following exhilarating years, the public perception of the Latter-day Saints grew ever more positive as the *Reader's Digest* and other periodical press outlets published articles about the Saints.[19]

One such article was published as originally written in *Reader's Digest*'s competitor *Coronet* in April 1952. Publication proceeded despite warnings from the Dean of the University of Utah's Graduate School, Sterling McMurrin, to whom *Coronet* sent it for review, that it was filled with falsehoods.[20] Written by Andrew Hamilton, the article was called "Those Amazing Mormons" and it provided a picture of a people with all the Boy and Girl Scout virtues who didn't drink alcohol, didn't smoke, kept a year's larder full of foodstuffs, and, of the greatest importance, "took care of their own."

It was this portrait of an attractive, productive people who had managed to get through the Great Depression without depending on government handouts that was adopted by the LDS Church as it publicized its Church Welfare Program and its food storage policy. Moreover, as lifelong Mormons became models for all the new LDS converts, church members adopted this picture of themselves as well. In an environment filled with concerns about atom bombs and the dangers of communism, the embrace of such a picture called for forgetting the reality of the Great Depression years as well as stories about Mormonism's experimentation with a radical social system that could have changed the nature of the Mormon family and a theodemocracy that would have made the Mormons stand apart from other Americans.

The Mormon who may have celebrated the picture of "Those Amazing Mormons" more than any other was Apostle Ezra Taft Benson. Although his tenure as Agriculture Secretary was difficult and challenging because the nation's farmers wanted more government aid than he was willing to support, his position nevertheless gave him access to the national press where he sometimes referred to the "amazing" farming people in his home state who were not seeking government assistance. His eight-year stay in the nation's capital during the decade of the 1950s also convinced him that communism was the greatest of all dangers to the United States and to the Church of Jesus Christ of Latter-day Saints since World War II.[21]

Although Utah's presidential vote went back to the Democrats when Lyndon Johnson was running for president in 1964, a conservative movement was spreading across Utah at the ground level.[22] The leaders in this radical conservatism were Apostle Benson; his son Reed; Ernest Wilkinson, president of Brigham Young University; and W. Cleon Skousen, a member of the BYU faculty who worked for the FBI and later was the chief of police in Salt Lake City.[23]

Benson had always been conservative, but during his years in Washington as a member of Eisenhower's Cabinet, he became so stridently anticommunist that this view came to dominate his thinking. During his presence in the nation's capital, his fellow members of the Quorum of the Twelve had been so greatly appreciative of his high station in the national government that expressions of pride in the tasks he was accomplishing were the general rule in comments about Benson, even among those Apostles who would oppose his political position in the years after he returned to Salt Lake City.

While not all Latter-day Saints who came from farming backgrounds were deeply conservative, leaning to the right was the tendency of farm folk. This was certainly true of the Benson family. Born in 1899 in Whitney, Idaho, Ezra bore the name of his great-grandfather who had been an Apostle, a member of the Quorum of the Twelve in the days of Brigham Young. The first of eleven children, young Ezra bore heavy family responsibility before the age of ten when his father was called on a mission, leaving his wife and seven children at home.

At fourteen, Ezra entered a church-sponsored high school, graduating at eighteen. Attending both the Utah State Agricultural College (now Utah State University), and Brigham Young University, he earned his bachelor's degree and served a mission in England before he married at age twenty-six. Receiving a research scholarship to attend Iowa State College (now Iowa State University), Benson earned a master's degree in agricultural economics in less than a year.[24] He returned to Idaho to farm after he completed his work in Iowa. His farming experience plus his education made it possible for him to move up the ladder from agricultural economist and marketing specialist for the University of Idaho to executive secretary, first, of the Idaho Cooperative Council and later of the National Council of Farmer Cooperatives.

This responsibility included representing farmers in Congress. He also served on a national agriculture advisory committee to President Franklin Roosevelt in World War II. These posts made Ezra Taft Benson a highly visible representative of U.S. farmers in the nation's capital. His prominence also rested on his outstanding volunteer activity as a national leader of the Boy Scouts of America. It is difficult to tell whether his service as the president of the LDS Washington, D.C., stake or his 1943 appointment to the Quorum of the Twelve of the LDS Church added to his celebrity, but this was probably the least noticeable of all the offices he held.

When President Eisenhower selected Benson to be Secretary of Agriculture in 1952, there was no opposition to his appointment. The fact that it was widely approved pleased LDS Church President David O. McKay and the Apostles. While his actions as Agriculture Secretary were initially endorsed by the nation's farmers, his opposition to increasing the government's financial assistance to farmers that had been initiated during the Great Depression caused him to lose popularity with the very people he was appointed to serve. As time moved forward during his tenure as a member of Eisenhower's cabinet, he became ever more concerned that the United States was threatened by communism, a worry that made him even less willing to support the sort of government assistance that farmers had enjoyed during the New Deal and World War II. If his actions made him far less popular in the farming community, Benson's report of his activities to the Quorum of the Twelve remained upbeat, focusing on his effort to protect the United States from the threat of communism. Through his eight years as Secretary of Agriculture, Benson became ever less acceptable to the farming community, but there was continuing pleasure in Salt Lake City that one of their own held a cabinet post in Washington.

He brought his worry about a communist threat when he returned to Utah in 1961 to fully resume his place in the Quorum of the Twelve. During his first post-cabinet interview with Church President David O. McKay, he was accompanied by his son Reed, who was already active in the John Birch Society. Benson returned to Utah clearly hoping that his church would move directly into the Birch Society's fold. He obviously expected that his advocacy for this extremely anticommunist political organization could convince President McKay to support it. Although McKay never placed the church over which he presided in league with the anticommunist cause, he gave Benson permission to make an anticommunist address to the LDS Annual Conference. Benson had allowed the magazine published by the John Birch Society to use his photograph on the cover and he almost managed to get President McKay to allow his photograph to be used on the cover as well. This was headed off by Apostle Hugh B. Brown, a Democrat.[25] Nevertheless, the radical conservatism of Apostle Benson surely promoted the spread of backing for the cause he supported among Latter-day Saints in local wards and stakes throughout Utah.

In the fall of 1960, I moved with my family to Logan, Utah, returning to school that year and changing my major from music to history. In the course of my studies, I had to take a senior seminar in which students were required to write term papers using primary sources. At least two of the topics selected by the seniors in the class had to do with Utah during the Depression. It was there that I learned that one of Utah's deep dark secrets was the fact that Mormons in Utah had been as likely as any other poor or unemployed citizens of the United States to take advantage of New Deal assistance programs. The other was the existence of polygamy (plural marriage) in Mormon history in the years after church president Wilford Woodruff had issued his 1890 Manifesto indicating that the LDS Church would no longer sanction the marriage of more than one woman to a Mormon man. The picture Mormonism presented to our family when we were visited almost weekly by ward missionaries was the picture of "Those Amazing Mormons."

This effort to forget the past was very much a part of the move toward political conservatism that we saw around us. Consequently, I was not surprised when I was told by the director of the LDS Church Historical Department that when Deseret Books published *Building the City of God: Community and Cooperation Among the Mormons*, by Leonard Arrington, Feramorz Fox, and Dean May, a member of the Quorum of the Twelve was so distressed he asked that it be shredded.[26] So much for remembering and celebrating Mormon history's story of the extraordinary effort the Saints made to live as had the early Christians. To Elder Benson, who had requested the shredding, Christian communitarianism was simply too much like the communism that threatened the world in the twentieth century.

When Ezra Taft Benson became president of the LDS Church in 1985, liberal Mormons were relieved that instead of taking the church further into political conservatism, he turned his attention to important developments in modern Mormonism: reanimating the Book of Mormon as a spiritual text by asking every church member to make reading the Mormon scripture a devotional duty; and building LDS temples and encouraging the Saints to celebrate sacred ordinances therein.[27]

That shift away from politics did not mean that he no longer cared about them. No doubt he died as uncertain about whether it was possible to be a good Democrat and a good Mormon as he had been for nearly a half century. However, his work in the area of politics was done. Utah and the remainder of the Mormon culture region had become as conservative as any other part of the nation, if not more so.

Notes

1. This incident was related to the author by the eminent Mormon folklorist, William A. Wilson.

2. Thomas G. Alexander, *Mormonism in Transition: A History of the Latter-day Saints, 1890–1930* (Urbana: University of Illinois Press, 1986), chs. 1 and 2.

3. At the time of Utah's entrance into the union, a bargain was struck so that there would always be one Mormon and one non-Mormon senator. From 1902 to 1932, Mormon Apostle Reed Smoot sat in the U.S. Senate.

4. Richard Nixon received 54.81 percent of Utah's popular vote in 1960, and John F. Kennedy got 45.17 percent. See the U.S. Election Atlas, http://uselectionatlas.org/RESULTS/data.php?year=1960&datatype=national&def=1&f=0&off=0&elect=0.

5. Both the Texas State Library and Archives Commission in Austin and the LDS Church History Library in Salt Lake City contain files of letters between Lyndon Johnson and David O. McKay. See also Gregory Prince and Wm. Robert Wright, *David O. McKay and the Rise of Modern Mormonism* (Salt Lake City: University of Utah Press, 2005), 70.

6. Douglas D. Alder, "The German-Speaking Immigration to Utah, 1850–1950" (Master's thesis, University of Utah, 1950), 115.

7. Garth L. Mangum and Bruce D. Blumell, *The Mormons' War on Poverty: A History of LDS Welfare 1830–1990*, Publications in Mormon Studies (Salt Lake City: University of Utah Press, 1993), 76–78.

8. Thomas G. Alexander, "From War to Depression," ch. 25 in Richard D. Poll, ed., *Utah's History* (Provo, Utah: Brigham Young University Press, 1978), 463–67.

9. Mangum and Blumell, *The Mormons' War on Poverty*, 95.

10. "Heber J. Grant and FDR," *The Millennial Star*, October 18, 2007, http://www.millennialstar.org/heber-j-grant-and-fdr/.

11. Note the check mark on 1936 in the figures above. This mark indicates that church members were instructed how to vote in this election, the only time church leaders have ever given church member direct instructions about how to vote.

12. For the national results of the 1936 presidential election, see http://uselectionatlas.org/RESULTS/national.php?year=1936. For the 1936 presidential election results from the state of Utah, see http://uselectionatlas.org/RESULTS/data.php?year=1936&datatype=national&def=1&f=0&off=0&elect=0.

13. John F. Bluth and Wayne K. Hinton, "The Great Depression," ch. 26 in Poll, ed., *Utah's History*, 482.

14. Mangum and Blumell, *The Mormons' War on Poverty*, 97, 111–12.

15. Mangum and Blumell, *The Mormons' War on Poverty*, 119 ff.

16. Glen L. Rudd, *Pure Religion: The Story of Church Welfare Since 1930* (Salt Lake City: Deseret Book, 1995), 45.

17. Bluth and Hinton, "The Great Depression," 488–89.

18. Jan Shipps, "The Scattering of the Gathering and the Gathering of the Scattered," ch. 13 in *Sojourner in the Promised Land: Forty Years Among the Mormons* (Urbana: University of Illinois Press, 2000), 258–78.

19. Shipps, "From Satyr to Saint: American Perceptions of the Mormons, 1860–1960," ch. 2 in ibid., 68–69, 99.

20. Correspondence between McMurrin and the *Coronet* editors is found in the McMurrin correspondence in the University of Utah Special Collections.

21. Sheri L. Dew, *Ezra Taft Benson: A Biography* (Salt Lake City: Deseret Book Company, 1987), passim.

22. In the 1964 presidential election, 54.86 percent of Utah voters chose the Democratic incumbent, Lyndon Johnson, over Republican Barry Goldwater, who received 45.14 percent of the vote. See the U.S. Election Atlas at http://uselectionatlas.org/RESULTS/state.php?fips=49&year=1964.

23. Prince and Wright, *David O. McKay and the Rise of Modern Mormonism*, 286–95.

24. In 1936, Benson did additional graduate study at the University of California, Berkeley, but he did not earn a doctorate.

25. Prince and Wright, *David O. McKay and the Rise of Modern Mormonism*, 307–310.

26. Conversation with Leonard Arrington at the annual meeting of the Western History Association in the fall of 1977.

27. *Sermons and Writings of President Ezra Taft Benson* (Salt Lake City: The Church of Jesus Christ of Latter-day Saints, 2003).

6 Testimony and Theology

The Mormon Struggle with America's Civil Religion

Russell Arben Fox

Mitt Romney's defeat in the 2012 presidential election brought to an end, at least tentatively, a long period of intense media scrutiny of the Church of Jesus Christ of Latter-day Saints,[1] of which Romney was a lifelong member and a lay congregational leader. Much of this scrutiny was premised upon the oddness or "outsiderness" of the Mormon faith in America, and it generated some real anxiety among many members of the church: namely, over how, in response to such attention, to make sense of—or how to defend, or how to transcend—Mormonism's apparent separateness from the dominant religious presumptions and expectations at work in American political discourse. While various historical, social, and cultural factors can help explain that anxiety, one factor that should not be ignored, and which this chapter aims to explore, is the political (or perhaps more accurately, the *rhetorical*) consequences of Mormon theology.

Now it is of course true that the millenarian[2] and theocratic[3] worldviews of the nineteenth-century LDS Church are more than one hundred years gone—and even those periods themselves may not have been quite as authoritarian as both the church's critics and defenders might choose to believe.[4] Thus one could assume that now, in the twenty-first century, there is no reason why Mormons' theological beliefs should not be seen as fitting easily into America's liberal civil religion. Indeed, as Nathan Oman has argued, "we now have twice as much experience with [post-theocratic] Mormonism as we have with post-Vatican II Catholicism," and "given historical experience . . . it's ridiculous to imagine a believing Catholic like Joe Biden as part of a subversive Roman agenda," thereby implying that similar theological concerns about Mormon candidates should also be put to rest.[5]

I don't disagree with the common sense of this argument. Yet it elides Mormonism's problematic relationship with one of the crucial components of America's dominant, if implicit, civil religious presumptions—namely, the question of revelation, and how that relates to one's embrace of, or rejection of, America's pluralistic civil order itself. The real issue to unpack is how Mormons *communicate* with each other about what they hold to be revealed truths, and how their theological construction of that idea, whether implicit or explicit, often appears to undermine their political participation in broader civil discourse within the American public sphere. But first, let's establish some basic terms.

America's Civil Religion

As mentioned above, a common theme in nearly all the reportage that accompanied the "Mormon Moment" of the 2012 election cycle was that Mormons were theological outsiders to the mainstream of American political life. This could be considered an odd concern: in a nation with strong (though admittedly always contested) First Amendment guarantees and no established church, what would it matter what any one group's particular religious theology was? Nonetheless, an awareness of that focus was widespread; Romney himself touched on it in his speech "Faith in America," which he gave at Texas A&M University during his first run for the Republican nomination back in 2007. There he insisted that "while differences in theology exist between the churches in America, we share a common creed of moral convictions."[6] Most saw this speech primarily in terms of Romney's desire to find acceptance with the conservative Christian (mostly evangelical Protestant and Catholic) faction within the Republican coalition, but there is more to the story than that; there is the matter of the general discomfort with Mormonism and Mormon beliefs which nonetheless remains widespread in American discourse.[7] This obviously challenges the liberal conviction that modern democratic politics in the United States should be "conducted as much as possible in an idiom of metaphysical neutrality, taking no position for or against God—or for or against . . . what He might or might not want from human beings"[8]—but it remains a fact nonetheless. Is it surprising? Not to those who study the role of civil religion in American life, it isn't.

To a degree "civil religion" is a catch-all term, one which touches in various ways upon the many intersections of religious belief, religious organizations, and routine civil life in modern democratic societies. The canonical depiction of America's fairly liberal understanding of civil religion is probably the one developed by Robert Bellah more than forty years ago.[9] Drawing upon the writings of the American Founders, Alexis de Tocqueville, Abraham Lincoln, John F. Kennedy, and many others, Bellah posited the existence of a moral sensibility that depends upon biblical archetypes and references, and which is undeniably Judeo-Christian, but far more ethical than theological—the Ten Commandments and the Sermon on the Mount, rather than the Temple of Jerusalem or Christ on the Cross. Bellah himself later backed away from a strong reliance upon civil religion as a way of explaining American history or diagnosing its behavior; instead, he came to speak of how the American religious ideal is best conceived as a wholly internalized, noninstitutionalized one.[10] However, his original formulation remains the way most of those Americans not paid professionally to think about such issues probably situate religion in American public life: in a highly religious but basically free, individualistic, and diverse society, certain religious bodies and institutions are valued for their ethical traditions, but generally not for their theological roots. This assumption easily fits alongside survey data that reveal an America which, whatever its level of popular religious piety, often appears to take a "post-denominational" and flexible attitude toward spirituality.[11]

But in practice, such an emphasis upon ethical presumptions (and, as Romney put it in 2007, "moral convictions") does not and probably never could entirely escape the question of the theological *form* these presumptions and convictions take, if only because civil understandings need to have some sort of established articulation if they are to endure.[12] If it were otherwise, sectarian arguments—about placing monuments to the Ten Commandments in government buildings, or funding scholarships which can be used for religious schools, or inscribing the words "In God We Trust" on our currency—wouldn't be so constant. Perhaps it is an inevitable facet of human nature to want to understand the actions of individuals as embedded in some sort of collective, established, morally (and often religiously) substantive—that is, "truthful"—cultural order. In other words, a broadly affirmed civil religion demands elaboration and codification, even if at the same time we seem reluctant to grant or even resist the legal extremities of such, and even if the venues for expressing that codification vary and grow more diverse over time.[13] The political theorist Graham Walker suggested that, given these realities, perhaps "some form of religious establishment is inexorable."[14] Or, as Eldon Eisenach more extensively made the same observation, "American national identity was shaped . . . through a series of voluntary national religious establishments. . . . [And h]istorically, there has never been a voluntary national religious establishment without a national political theology to give it point, purpose, and direction."[15] The liberal civil religion of American history and American politics today may not have overt partisan or sectarian overtones, but it cannot wholly avoid theological ones, which means it is not so deeply liberal after all.

We may chart through the decades the form that this kind of "nonestablished religious establishment" has taken in America. For example, Catholicism slowly journeyed throughout the twentieth century toward acceptance into what Martin Marty called the "public church" that sustains our civil religion;[16] in a different and more oblique way, Judaism made a similar journey. The very label "Judeo-Christian" itself indicated a sense of establishment which nominally prioritized the act of belief over its particular content—but perhaps only so long as the act of belief itself occurred within, and was discussed in the context of, an "acceptable" theological context.[17] Is Mormonism making a similar journey, or can it? Given the possibility that, as Damon Linker has recently argued, "not all theological assumptions are equally compatible with the political order of the United States," the importance of such questions—to Mormon candidates like Mitt Romney as well as to Mormons at large —is undeniable.[18]

Mormon Revelation and Civil Religion

Nothing challenges the liberal notion of civil religion like revelation, and Mormonism is the revelatory religion *par excellence*, beginning with Joseph Smith's claim to have been actually commissioned by God Himself to found a specific religious movement, purportedly at that particular place and at that foreordained time. The legacy of that commission has continued on down to the present moment, where it is a literal article of faith among Mormons that God will reveal His instructions to the leaders of the church, who are sustained as "prophets, seers, and revelators." Logically, a religion like Mormonism—one whose foundation includes the interruption of quotidian life with new scripture and a new apostolic commission, and posits the continuing possibility of further revealed truths that supersede any other form of authoritative discourse—would be of little use in regard to the classic purposes of civil religion. Mormonism's prophets are generally not, almost by definition, understood to be ministers to or supporters of any established civil order, if only because they attend to an exclusive order which is not mandated or maintained by any earthly power. Of course, the prophetic revelation of a higher order of things was present from the very beginnings of the Jewish and Christian religions, but by the time the Western world arrived at the notions of civil society that still reign today, incorporating the ideas of individual conscience and popular sovereignty, most religious movements had been separated (or had separated themselves) from the theocratic implications of that distant revelation, and as a result had been, one might say, "civilized."[19] So here a question could be asked: has Mormon revelation been civilized? The near-antinomian opposition that existed between the early LDS Church and both America's federal government as well as its pluralistic popular culture could be taken of evidence that such a civilizing was necessary.[20]

But again, perhaps that is unfair. Of course, one could insist upon viewing Mormonism solely through a nineteenth-century lens, with Joseph Smith speaking of "theodemocracy" and Brigham Young leading an estranged and persecuted people to the desert to establish the Kingdom of God on earth. But this ignores the deep influence that the American polity had on some of the leading figures of the early church,[21] as well as the many complications and compromises that came along with the conflicts of that era.[22] Most of all, what those pondering the place of the Mormon theology of revelation within America's civil religion need to attend to is what happened to *end* that tension between the Mormon theocracy and a hostile American government. Specifically, the LDS Church changed; moreover, it changed in accordance with what its leaders affirmed as a revelation from God. Which means that, as Frederick Mark Gedicks put it, the Mormon God "does not always demand faithfulness over survival."[23] So perhaps Mormon revelation—not just the teachings and practices of the mostly patriotic and politically conservative body of Mormon believers in America today, but the actual doctrine of revelation itself—is amenable to providing ethical and moral support to America's civil society, with no taste of theocracy to complicate matters.

At this point, we could poke our heads outside of this historical and theoretical argument and look at actual evidence: is the literal support for civil society itself among Mormons—the participation, the volunteering, the law-abidingness, the solidarity and mutual sociability—actually there? Or do Mormon teachings about revelation, suggesting the availability of higher, more direct, less debatable and more exclusive routes to truth, nonetheless seem a factor in keeping Mormons away from civil action itself? The data crunched by Robert Putnam and David Campbell fairly conclusively demonstrate that the common stereotype about religion and good works is true: members of religious communities donate more to charity, contribute more to public works, and generally are more civicly active than those of a more secular bent. Mormons are by no means outliers in these conclusions.[24] But these researchers also point out Mormons' exceptionally high levels of affirmation in response to questions about the absolute truth of their church and moral beliefs—and their correlated high levels of religious exclusion and homogeneity, which many would argue can only have negative consequences for their ability to contribute to America's pluralistic civil society.[25] Such exclusiveness is, of course, hardly unknown in American religious life—one can only imagine how Putnam and Campbell's scales would have been affected had they been able to recover data on such questions from Old Order Amish communities. But then, Americans have never seen a member of an Old Order Amish community become a presidential candidate from a major political party. So even if Linker's conclusion that "Mormonism will remain a theologically unstable . . . politically perilous religion" is overwrought,[26] perhaps Mormons do need to ponder the politically narrowing potential of their theology revelation—particularly, how it shapes how they even talk about it.

Receiving and Speaking Revelation

The worship and faith life of most Mormons is not, on the surface, all that different from that of many other Christians, especially those of a conservative Protestant stripe. And yet profound disagreements seem almost endemic to any evangelical-Mormon dialogue. The reason for this, according to Terryl Givens, is that Mormon worship and faith life takes "its particular cast" from an "underlying cosmology" not shared by mainstream Christianity.[27] Other writers besides Givens have studied the distinctiveness of Mormonism's ontology of revelation, but as his analysis helps us understand the civil significance of this theological point, let us follow his consideration of the issue.

Givens draws upon the work of Avery Dulles[28] to identify three different modes of revelation that have played a role in the historical development of Christianity: "revelation as doctrine" (or "revelation as scriptural content," in the sense of God's communication with humankind being "propositional" or "conceptual"), "revelation as history" (in the sense of the "self-disclosure . . . [of] God's historically significant activity"), and "revelation as inner experience." Givens argues that the third mode, which "holds out the promise of a paradigm in which God communicates particular truths to the individual," has over the centuries been diluted into a subsidiary confirmation of the first two.[29] That is, though "traces of a more literal definition [of revelation] stubbornly persist," most discussion of revelation in the Christian tradition has made revelation out to be primarily a "feeling" of its own "sufficiency." This view stipulates that through the Bible and through history, we have already been given "all we need to know."[30] Givens attributes this intellectual development to several factors, but the one he finds most telling is what he calls the modern "theological resistance to anything tending toward anthropomorphism"; the result is that the concreteness of received revelations (such as are depicted throughout the Old Testament, with specific commandments given and responses made, with observable results) generally becomes "metaphorized into . . . more nebulous concepts of revelation."[31] The consequences of this development for Christian and Judaic interactions with civil society are clear; as Lilla argued, this theological movement away from dialogic immediacy and instead toward inspiration capable of subjective evaluation and debate helped religious believers find "a way of separating claims to revelation from [their] thinking about the common political good."[32]

However, it is not clear exactly how a similar development could be worked out in regard to Mormonism's theology of revelation. Within that faith, Givens argues, the Book of Mormon's artifactual presence is *itself* the revelation that matters most. Probably most members of the LDS Church would have only a rudimentary understanding of Givens's theoretical point here, but they would, in all likelihood, be able to grasp it nonetheless. He is talking about how Joseph Smith's prophetic commission, and much of Mormons' evangelization ever since, is tied up not in a particular teaching but a particular *thing*: the Book of Mormon, Smith's greatest and most central revelation, and the one that looms largest in Mormons' own discourse about the truth claims of their faith. Givens employs a framework developed by the literary theorist Mikhail Bakhtin to pursue this distinction further. A revelation like the Book of Mormon becomes perhaps the ultimate example of *authoritative discourse* as opposed to *persuasive discourse*, in that the text is not amenable to any "criteria of persuasiveness" which would place it in some sort of larger interpretive or theological-poetical continuum. Its social and spiritual presence for Mormons is "sharply demarcated, compact, and inert"; it simply *is*, a text to be wrestled with—or, one might say, it is its own evidence, its own testimony.[33] The scriptural text incarnates Smith's "authoritativeness" as one who did what he did through endowment rather than effort (for mere human efforts, of course, can be replicated, criticized, debated and improved upon, while Smith's work, by definition, cannot be: it is disconcertingly singular, as even some of Smith's enemies have long noted).[34] Which suggests that any civil instantiation of the faith of Mormons will have little to do with finding authority in Mormon ethical precepts, and relating them to other parallel authoritative articulations throughout America's public church (which is what other churches in American history have done, such as through the abolitionist or Social Gospel or civil rights movements); on the contrary, it would have to involve finding some common expression of this specific authoritative facticity.

Yet putting such exclusive theological truth claims or "facts" first in a discussion of a religion's contributions to civil society is exactly what, over the decades, America's Judeo-Christian civil religion has moved away from. According to Givens, regarding the Book of Mormon, "the reality of the plates and their angelic messenger . . . not the cogency of Nephi's writing, was the point";[35] in terms of civil discourse in a pluralistic society, that's a difficult claim to know how to express. This difficulty is compounded even further by the fact that Mormons' articulation of their reception of this revelation partakes of Old Testament–style concreteness: they read *this* book, and by so doing received a revelation of *its* truthfulness. The idea, as Givens further explains, is that the reader of the Book of Mormon gains access to truth by entering into a dialogic relationship with God's purposes, embodied in a concrete artifact (the Book of Mormon itself), and manifest through quotidian experience (namely, reading it). What is learned from the book about God's commands, much less ethics and politics, is secondary to an experience with the *truth* of the book entirely, and that is something that obviously can only really be shared with others who have also read the book (or at least are part of a community which accepts that reading as a fundamentally truthful act). As Givens sums up, knowing that the particular claims of the Book of Mormon are true is "clearly not the point"; rather, "knowing they are knowable is."[36]

What is the political significance of appreciating this conception of the Mormon theology of revelation, with its unique emphasis upon the broad possibility among the members of the church of accepting oneself as having received, through an encounter with the Book of Mormon, some exclusive, artifactual, revealed knowledge, whatever it may be? Its significance, insofar as civil religion is concerned, is in the aforementioned dialogicity of this knowledge; it arises through encounters, through interactions, through personal investment in a given quotidian thing in common among those in the know—most particularly (though not exclusively), those who have read the Book of Mormon. Hence, one might say that Mormons do *not* fundamentally hold to a revelation of true knowledge that sets them apart from the discourse of civil society. However, they *do* hold to a model of communal discourse, a sharing and assuming of civilly inaccessible truth claims that emerge from greatly varied yet all ultimately similar encounters with facts, with things. First and foremost among these things is a new book of scripture—which is itself, by its very existence, a revelation of truth.

Testimony and Theology

Is the significance of this insight observable in the lives of American Mormons negotiating their place in public life? Well, consider what many Mormon observers have noted: that members of the LDS Church draw a great deal of the strength of their social activity from the fellowshipping experiences which occur as part of their regular collective interactions with one another. Putnam and Campbell documented this in their study of American religions, observing that "no religion group in America feels warmer toward their own group than Mormons." They have no clear explanation for this high level of "in-group attachment," except to propose that, for a variety of reasons, "Mormons ... are a religious group that resembles an ethnicity."[37] Givens's analysis of the dynamics of Mormon revelation suggests that we ought to consider Mormonism's high levels of collective attachment and activity—with all its positive results in terms of certain types of civic behavior—to be the product of a theological variable as well. It may be that Mormons associate with, support, and think highly of each other at least in part because they recognize the fact of revelation through constant dialogue with one another around common artifacts and practices. In Mormonism's quest for and sensitivity to dialogic exchange and affirmation and recognition, there is a subtle theological driver that not only replicates the in-group affections of an ethnicity, but sometimes even surpasses it. Putnam and Campbell's research, for example, suggests that Mormon levels of homogeneity and confident "true belief" within their community is equal to or even greater than those of Jews or black Protestants.[38]

Consider something every churchgoing Mormon would be familiar with: "testimony meetings." Faithful Mormons routinely—indeed, once a month, like clockwork—participate in a ritual of confession, expression, and affirmation, in which they repeat and internalize the dialogue of revelation. This usually occurs with explicit reference to the core theological teachings of the LDS Church, particularly the truthfulness of the Book of Mormon and the prophetic authority of priesthood leadership, but sometimes in reference to any number of other facts of ordinary life which happen to present occasions for revelatory insight: that is, for a sense of knowledge regarding God and His love for humankind. Within the Mormon community, the centrality of this ritual is mostly unquestioned, its theological significance probably overlooked by most, and its civil harmlessness (or indeed, given the frequency with which politically conservative American Mormons testify of the providence of the American nation, its civil benefits) no doubt basically assumed. But it may be Mormonism's tendency to express its theological claims through—indeed, to *identify* its theological claims with—a circumscribed dialogic context which sets Mormons so much apart from America's liberal civil religion.

Frederick Gedicks made the observation that, in a liberal society, "There may be a certain discourtesy . . . in expressing broadly and publically [sic] that [one's religious beliefs] are universally applicable and absolutely true."[39] Surely most intelligent Mormons know this; the problematic issue I am focusing on is not rudeness. Mitt Romney acknowledged such in his "Faith in America" speech: "where the affairs of our nation are concerned, it's usually a sound rule to focus on . . . the great moral principles that urge us all on a common course."[40] The rub here is that "common course"—how is that course charted, elaborated, and expressed? Not through theological argument and doctrinally demonstrating one's civil religion bona fides, at least not primarily. Indeed, Gedicks makes the argument that Romney's attempt to assert such (with his insistence that "I believe that Jesus Christ is the Son of God and the Savior of mankind" while acknowledging that Mormon "beliefs about Christ may not all be the same as those of other faiths") puts him in an "impossible situation," simultaneously insisting the Mormon faith belongs within the Judeo-Christian mainstream while also begging for liberal toleration.[41] Rather, the articulation of the common course of America's post-denominational (yet theologically haunted) religious establishment comes through a shared ecumenical context—through becoming a part of the aforementioned "public church." But when much of ordinary Mormon practice is organized around theologically inculcated in-group affirmations of the truthfulness of the Mormon faith, this becomes difficult. For example, a larger number of Mormons declare that their religion is true and all others false than any other religious group in America,[42] and many Mormons dialogically perceive obedience to central church directions and the resulting social homogeneity and exclusion such obedience engenders—despite its often negative social consequences—as a *further* revelation of that truth.

This is not to say that ecumenical dialogic work is impossible for the Mormons; on the contrary, there are many independent examples of such engagement throughout the church, and over the past twenty-five years many developments have either encouraged such ecumenism (whether liberal or merely strategic), or at least have presented ecumenism as a viable direction for the church as a whole.[43] But such civil engagement must overcome the twin obstacles of testimony and Correlation—the former being the aforementioned ritual sharing and mutual affirmation of a mostly exclusive conversation about everyday experiences with divine truth, the latter being a centralizing of church organizations, administration, and practices that began in earnest in the mid-twentieth century and continues today, and which must loom large in any accurate account of contemporary Mormon identity.[44] This merging of testimony-bearing with the enclosed, often top-down imperatives of correlation has resulted in what the historian Philip Barlow has called the "sacralized corporate sensibility" of the church today.[45] In Armand Mauss's view, Correlation has been a major vehicle in turning monthly repeated testimonial affirmations like "there is only one true church" into "recurrent slogans with intimations of prophetic infallibility,"[46] and its success in making Mormons a highly obedient, authority-responsive people has been noted by social scientists.[47] This is not to deny the benefits or even the necessity of something like the process of Correlation to the LDS Church's development, but it is necessary to acknowledge that Correlation and centralization now partake of a particular theocratic sensibility that the Mormon theology of revelation once, a hundred years ago, pointed toward more explicitly. Mormons today really do—in a manner that is theologically distinct from that of any other non-communitarian and non-isolationist Christian church in America—display a large degree of group-think, taking mid-twentieth-century models of "mainstream corporate respectability" and transliterating them into an assumed and regularly reaffirmed pattern of expressing experiences with dialogic revelation.[48]

Ultimately, Damon Linker was wrong when he argued that Mormonism sits uncomfortably within the liberal order because it "appears to lack the intellectual or spiritual resources to [civilly] challenge a declaration of the prophet . . . regardless of how theologically, morally, or politically radical that declaration may be."[49] Theocratic fears of that sort are simply out of place here. But what is *not* out of place is concern about the political fate of a church that, for reasons both theological and organizational, has perhaps unintentionally echoed elements of its older exclusive sensibility through its very way of talking about its faith. As a result it finds itself failing to establish the same sort of toleration-generating civil bridges that America's Christian mainstream mostly has among its own churches.[50] Mormons surely have the expressions of Judeo-Christian religious faith necessary for admittance to America's civil religion, but can they work out a theology that would enable them to authoritatively express that faith in a civil way, to say nothing of finding the organizational space to adapt to such pluralistic expressive forms?

Conclusion

It is entirely possible that, for all the various complications that America's civil religion poses for the LDS Church today, Mormonism will find its way into it all the same, given time. After all, Catholicism did. So perhaps Mitt Romney—and other Mormon candidates and movements and voters—will be able at some future point to reflect upon their church's slow but, from their future perspective, predictable transformation into a religious partner with whatever kind of establishment will obtain in this yet-to-emerge America. In the meantime, though, the faithful Mormon might conclude that the situation is quite dispiriting, and think that the better route is to wish for civil religion to decline in importance entirely, hopefully pushing all its attendant confusions over testimony and theology further away from the center of political discussion in America. This is the position taken by Frederick Gedicks; invoking John Rawls, Gedicks calls for his fellow Mormons to take as their model, not a church with teachings about truth directly applicable to the moral disputes of the day, but rather a "modest, even humble search for personal truth [which] enriches the individual without doing violence."[51] This is obviously a respectable path to choose.

For my part, though, I suspect establishments of one manner or another will invariably, and probably should, endure; consequently I take some hope from the fact that, however theologically or organizationally unusual its present situation, the Mormon response to the current cultural situation in America is following patterns that suggest a familiar sociological path. Consider the larger picture. There was a time when America's religious establishment felt little need to draw explicit lines, because the American people themselves were traditional enough and grounded enough in their local communities to avoid crossing such lines in the first place. Such was the social environment of much of America a half century ago, during what might be considered the height of America's mainline civil religion. The relative decline of that cultural establishment over the past decades has had many causes, but its primary result has been intense struggle over the meaning and bounds of the communities in which we live, including our national community. Mormons, no less than any other religious group, have become caught up in that struggle. The LDS Church no longer approaches that struggle theocratically, as its own divisive struggles with our de facto national establishment—as well as its older theological tendency to invest revelatory concreteness in specific political structures and positions—have mostly come to an end. What is at work in what both critics and supporters perceive as an energized and politically awakened LDS Church thus is, for better or worse, basically just another instance of religiously based social activism, of the sort that has been often seen throughout America's democratic history.[52] A civil religious establishment has moral meaning to it, and that moral meaning is wanted, and worth fighting over. Hence, Mormons will likely continue to stumble forward, perhaps discovering a language to get around their theology when it comes to engaging with other members of America's public church. Or perhaps America's civil religion will itself change in a Rawlsian direction, particularly as churches which theologically and ecclesiastically embody that religious understanding continue to lose support among a younger generation of Americans,[53] thus loosening further the ways in which America's comprehensive ethical faith might be acceptably expressed, especially in connection with truth claims. Either way, the contestation both within and surrounding Mormonism regarding the question of how it may, or if it can, express a place for itself in America's civil religious space will continue.

Philip Barlow, reflecting on the transformations the LDS Church has gone through, wondered what kind of "spiritual diet" can be provided by a "corporate, consolidated, simplified, international church."[54] It is a church whose truth claims remain emphatic and yet embedded in an everyday discursivity, easily exportable but not particularly inclusive or available for the sort of civil exchanges and theological pairings that have characterized America's public church. Borrowing from Barlow's analysis, I suspect that in the wake of the intense media scrutiny that attended the "Mormon Moment" of 2011–2012, a new transformation of Mormonism is both inevitable and under way—and who knows? Perhaps it will turn out that Mitt Romney, the failed presidential candidate, will turn out to have been its appointed midwife.

Notes

1. For a prominent example, see the June 5, 2011, cover story of *Newsweek*, "Mormons Rock!" Recovered from www.thedailybeast.com/newsweek/2011/06/05/mormons-rock.html.

2. Grant Underwood, *The Millenarian World of Early Mormonism* (Urbana: University of Illinois Press, 1993).

3. See David L. Bigler, *Forgotten Kingdom: The Mormon Theocracy in the American West, 1847–1896* (Logan: Utah State University Press, 1998)—and also an important and corrective review of the above by Eric A. Eliason, "'An Awful Tale of Blood': Theocracy, Intervention, and the *Forgotten Kingdom*," *FARMS Review of Books* 12.1 (2000).

4. Matthew Bowman suggests some of these caveats in *The Mormon People: The Making of an American Faith* (New York: Random House, 2012). See also R. Collin Mangrum, "Mormonism, Philosophical Liberalism, and the Constitution," *BYU Studies* 27.3 (Summer 1987).

5. Recovered from www.nydailynews.com/opinion/mormon-plot-wasn-t-article-1.1014874.

6. Transcript recovered from www.npr.org/templates/story/story.php?storyId=16969460.

7. Poll responses continue to suggest that Mormonism causes broad discomfort amongst a small but significant portion of the electorate. See, for example, this 2011 Gallup poll, recovered from www.gallup.com/poll/148100/hesitant-support-mormon-2012.aspx.

8. Damon Linker, *The Religious Test: Why We Must Question the Beliefs of Our Leaders* (New York: Norton, 2010), 145.

9. Robert N. Bellah, "Civil Religion in America," *Dædalus: Journal of the American Academy of Arts and Sciences* 96.1 (Winter 1967): 1–21.

10. Bellah, *The Broken Covenant: American Civil Religion in Time of Trial* (San Francisco: Harper Books, 1984), 142 and passim.

11. See Frederick Mark Gedicks, "Spirituality, Fundamentalism, Liberty: Religion at the End of Modernity," *DePaul Law Review* 55 (2005): 1216–18; and Christian Smith, *Soul Searching: The Religious and Spiritual Lives of American Teenagers* and *Souls in Transition: The Religious and Spiritual Lives of Emerging Adults* (New York: Oxford University Press, 2005 and 2009).

12. Robert Putnam and David Campbell, in a magisterial survey of the extent and the implications of religious belief and practice in America today, comment with surprise upon the fact that "most Americans have reasonably firm and consistent views" on such theological questions as the nature and requirements of salvation: "we did not expect that nearly half a millennium [after the European religious wars of the sixteenth and seventeenth centuries] . . . most Americans would have stable views on such seemingly arcane theological issues, but they do." Putnam and Campbell, *American Grace: How Religion Divides and Unites Us* (New York: Simon and Schuster, 2010), 467.

13. Robert Wuthnow, "Religious Diversity in a 'Christian Nation': American Identity and American Democracy," in Thomas Banchoff, ed., *Democracy and the New Religious Pluralism* (New York: Oxford University Press, 2007), 151–70.

14. Graham Walker, "Illusionary Pluralism, Inexorable Establishment," in Nancy L. Rosenblum, ed., *Obligations of Citizenship and Demands of Faith: Religious Accommodation in Pluralist Democracies* (Princeton: Princeton University Press, 2000), 111.

15. Eldon J. Eisenach, *The Next Religious Establishment: National Identity and Political Theology in Post-Protestant America* (Lanham, MD: Rowman & Littlefield, 2000), 6.

16. Martin E. Marty, *The Public Church: Mainline–Evangelical–Catholic* (New York: Crossroad, 1981).

17. Will Herberg, *Protestant, Catholic, Jew: An Essay in American Religious Sociology* (Garden City, NY: Doubleday, 1955), 98; see also Peter L. Berger, *The Sacred Canopy* (New York: Anchor Books, 1969), and Frederick Mark Gedicks, "Truth and Consequences: Mitt Romney, Proposition 8, and Public Reason," *Alabama Law Review* 61 (2010): 346 and passim.

18. Linker, *The Religious Test*, 13.

19. There are many historical treatments of this centuries-long process; Mark Lilla's account of what he calls "The Great Separation" is a particularly thoughtful and persuasive one. See Lilla, *The Stillborn God: Religion, Politics, and the Modern West* (New York: Knopf, 2007).

20. For various takes on this conflict at different moments during the history of the early church, see David L. Bigler and Will Bagley, *The Mormon Rebellion: America's First Civil War, 1857–1858* (Norman: University of Oklahoma Press, 2011); Terryl L. Givens, *The Viper on the Hearth: Mormons, Myths, and the Construction of Heresy* (Oxford: Oxford University Press, 1997); Richard T. Hughes, "Soaring

with the Gods: Early Mormonism and the Eclipse of Religious Pluralism," in Eric A. Eliason, ed., *Mormons and Mormonism: An Introduction to an American World Religion* (Urbana: University of Illinois Press, 2001); and Marvin S. Hill, *Quest for Refuge: The Mormon Flight from American Pluralism* (Salt Lake City: Signature Books, 1989).

21. Consider, for example, the liberal, even Madisonian assumptions at work in claimed revelations within the Doctrine and Covenants itself. See Rodney K. Smith, "James Madison, John Witherspoon, and Oliver Cowdery: The First Amendment and the 134th Section of the Doctrine and Covenants," *BYU Law Review* (2003): 891–940.

22. See Leonard J. Arrington, Feramoz Y. Fox, and Dean L. May, *Building the City of God: Community and Cooperation Among the Mormons*, 2d ed. (Urbana: University of Illinois Press, 1976); Sarah Barringer Gordon, *The Mormon Question: Polygamy and Constitutional Conflict in Nineteenth-Century America* (Chapel Hill: University of North Carolina Press, 2002); and B. Carmon Hardy, *Solemn Covenant: The Mormon Polygamous Passage* (Urbana: University of Illinois Press, 1992).

23. Gedicks, "The Integrity of Survival: A Mormon Response to Stanley Hauerwas," *DePaul Law Review* 42 (1992): 171.

24. Putnam and Campbell, *American Grace*, 443–92.

25. Ibid., 519–47.

26. Linker, *The Religious Test*, 83.

27. Terryl Givens, *By the Hand of Mormon: The American Scripture That Launched a New World Religion* (Oxford: Oxford University Press, 2002), 210.

28. Avery Dulles, S.J., *Models of Revelation* (New York: Doubleday, 1983).

29. Givens, *By the Hand of Mormon*, 210–11.

30. Ibid., 212, 214.

31. Ibid., 215.

32. Lilla, *The Stillborn God*, 90.

33. Givens, *By the Hand of Mormon*, 81. Givens quotes Mikhail Bakhtin from "Discourse in the Novel," *The Dialogical Imagination: Four Essays*, ed. Michael Holquist (Austin: University of Texas Press, 1981), 42.

34. I think here of Fawn Brodie's wondering expression of amazement that Smith attempted to get away with "found[ing] a new religion in the age of printing." See Brodie, *No Man Knows My History: The Life of Joseph Smith*, 2d ed. (New York: Vintage, 1995), vii.

35. Givens, *By the Hand of Mormon*, 85.

36. Givens, *By the Hand of Mormon*, 228.

37. Putnam and Campbell, *American Grace*, 503–504.

38. Ibid., 525–26, 545–46.

39. Gedicks, "Truth and Consequences," 353.

40. Recovered from www.npr.org/templates/story/story.php?storyId=16969460.

41. Gedicks, "Truth and Consequences," 364.

42. Putnam and Campbell, *American Grace*, 545–46.

43. See Armand L. Mauss, "Rethinking Retrenchment: Course Corrections in the Ongoing Campaign for Respectability," *Dialogue: A Journal of Mormon Thought* 44.3 (Winter 2011): 1–42; and Frederick Mark Gedicks, "Mormonism in Western Society: Three Futures," *Dialogue* 44.3 (Winter 2011): 144–62.

44. Matthew Bowman gives a thoughtful and thorough (and, I think, somewhat too positive) account of correlation in *The Mormon People*, 184–215.

45. Philip L. Barlow, "Shifting Ground and the Third Transformation of Mormonism," in Peter W. Williams, ed., *Perspectives on American Religion and Culture* (Malden, MA: Blackwell, 1999), 150 and passim.

46. Mauss, "Rethinking Retrenchment," 20.

47. See, for example, Rick Phillips, "Religious Market Share and Mormon Church Activity," *Sociology of Religion* 59.2 (1998): 117–30.

48. Warner P. Woodworth, "Brave New Bureaucracy," *Dialogue* 20.3 (Fall 1987): 34 and passim; Roger Terry, "Competing Values within the Restored Church: An Organizational Analysis," cited by Mauss, "Rethinking Retrenchment," 3.

49. Linker, *The Religious Test*, 83.

50. Putnam and Campbell, *American Grace*, 534.

51. Gedicks, "Truth and Consequences," 371.

52. I discuss church actions, from such national ones as the fight over Proposition 8 in California, to local ones involving property claims in Salt Lake City, in the essay "The Church and the Public Square(s)," recovered here: http://squaretwo.org/Sq2ArticleFoxUtahPolitics.html.

53. Putnam and Campbell, *American Grace*, 120–32.

54. Barlow, "Shifting Ground and the Third Transformation of Mormonism," 152.

> *And inasmuch as ye shall keep my commandments, ye shall prosper, and shall be led to a land of promise; yea, even a land which I have prepared for you; yea, a land which is choice above all other lands.*
> —The Book of Mormon prophet Nephi, recording a revelation from the Lord (circa 600 BCE; 1 Nephi 2:20)

7 Chosen Land, Chosen People

Religious and American Exceptionalism Among the Mormons

Philip L. Barlow

Members of the Church of Jesus Christ of Latter-day Saints—the Mormons—have long harbored the notion that America is a special place.[1] The specialness of this place, populated by a chosen people for a singular destiny, is a controlling premise and motif of the Book of Mormon. Following the perspective of their founding prophet, Joseph Smith, contemporary Mormons tend to construe the United States Constitution as an inspired document. For the past three-quarters of a century, American Saints have been viewed as dependably patriotic and are often recruited for sensitive government work, such as within the FBI. American exceptionalism seems a feature of Mormonism's DNA.

The role the United States plays in Mormon thought and culture, however, is more complex than at first appears. Coming to terms with this still-unfolding role requires pairing "American exceptionalism" with "religious exceptionalism" as they function in the Mormon mind. In each of these two spheres there inheres an originally dominant exceptionalist gene and a contrasting recessive gene that challenges exceptionalist assurance. Moreover, the proportional influence of these genes has shifted over time; in both cases the influence of the recessive gene is stronger than formerly. All this means that American exceptionalism, while not unusual, manifests in ways that are strong, mild, absent, or even inverted in individual Latter-day Saints. Across time and space, this is true also in portions of Mormon society. Predicting how this legacy might influence any individual Mormon's perspective on national policy is problematic.

Religious Exceptionalism: Dominant and Recessive Genes

To discern the ambiguous character of American exceptionalism in Mormon culture, it helps first to consider Mormonism's claims of religious uniqueness, which, taken as a whole, are similarly ambiguous. The dominant gene in this sphere, especially during the movement's first 150 years, was a pronounced religious exceptionalism. In 1820, the teenage Joseph Smith was driven to prayer in quest of forgiveness of sin. He was also motivated by confusion at the cacophony of religious competition in a nation newly shorn of established churches. Which of all the existing denominations and sects was correct? In one account of his first vision, written in 1838 and later canonized, the boy encountered Deity, who instructed that he must join none of the churches, "for they were all wrong; and the Personage who addressed me said that all their creeds were an abomination in his sight; that those professors were all corrupt" (Joseph Smith History 1:18–19).[2] Smith subsequently received, at the hands of angels, an exclusive priesthood, whose restoration to the earth was necessitated by a general apostasy over the centuries from the once-pure Christian church.

With this authority, Smith organized the Church of Christ, which the Lord declared to be, Smith reported in 1831, "the only true and living church upon the face of the whole earth with which I the Lord am well pleased" (Doctrine and Covenants [hereafter abbreviated D&C] 1:30). This single line of scripture has assumed a life of its own among many Latter-day Saints, who express their faith to their own congregations by the phrase, "I know the church is true." Other Christians who convert to Mormonism are required to receive a new baptism by proper LDS authority. Because the Mormon view of heaven is a relational rather than a merely individual affair, only those married or "sealed" to each other by appropriate priesthood authority are seen as heirs of the highest realm in the hereafter (D&C 76; 131:1–3; 132:15–16). Also restored were spiritual gifts, such as healing and prophecy, and ancient, pure doctrines.

Today, these claims to be the restored and uniquely true church retain majority status in Mormon discourse. Many Mormons are apt to respect honorable traditions and wisdom in other faiths, but think of them as incomplete, subject to correction, refinement, or completion in a Mormon context bolstered by living prophets and divine authority.

A recessive Mormon gene, however, dilutes and challenges this self-understanding. Believing Mormons treasure truths they hold as distinctive and sacred, but Mormon prophets make no claim to a monopoly on truth itself. The Book of Mormon insists that God is God to all of His children. One of the book's preeminent figures, Nephi, condemned an exclusivist confidence too constricted to value God's word wherever it surfaces. "Know ye not that there are more nations than one?" he asks.

> Know ye not that I, the Lord your God, have created all men, and that I remember those who are upon the isles of the sea; and that I rule in the heavens above and in the earth beneath; and I bring forth my word unto the children of men, yea, even upon all the nations of the earth? . . . I command all men, both in the east and in the west, and in the north, and in the south, and in the islands of the sea, that they shall write the words which I speak. . . . I shall speak unto the Jews . . . and I shall also speak unto the Nephites . . . and I shall also speak unto all nations of the earth. (2 Nephi 29:7,11,12)

A later Book of Mormon prophet, Alma, similarly decried the religious conceit of a sectarian tribe called Zoramites:

> Now the place was called by [the Zoramites] Rameumptom, which, being interpreted, is the holy stand. Now, from this stand they did offer up, every man, the self-same prayer. . . . We thank thee, O God, for we are a chosen people unto thee, while others shall perish. (Alma 31:22, 28)

As against this narcissistic arrogance, the mature Joseph Smith in 1842 adapted the language of the biblical Paul while couching a passage now canonized for Latter-day Saints as part of the culminating Thirteenth Article of Faith: "If there is anything virtuous, lovely, or of good report, or praiseworthy, we seek after these things." Rather than being a threat to the Mormon gospel, virtuous and lovely things, whatever their immediate source, are to be embraced as a part of Mormonism. Smith's successor, Brigham Young, taught similarly:

> You say you belong to the Presbyterians; it is no matter if you have got the truth. Are you a Calvinist, or a Wesleyan? It is no matter . . . that truth is "Mormonism," it is my property. Are you a Quaker? It is no matter. . . . Are you a Catholic, and have got the truth? That is my doctrine, and I will not quarrel about it. "Well," says one. "I am a Jew; I guess I can get up a quarrel with you." No, you cannot. I shall not contend with you, for the Jews have got true principles, and they possess no truth but what belongs to "Mormonism"; for there is *not a truth on earth or in heaven, that is not embraced in "Mormonism."* Another steps forward and says, "I am a Pagan; I think you will not agree with me." Yes I will, as far as you follow the path of truth.[3]

Moreover, to be a "chosen" people does not necessarily mean, in Mormon scripture, to be superior; it can mean simply to be chosen for a role or task. There are exceptions, but as Jesus put it baldly to those he thought hypocrites hiding behind their heritage as "chosen people": "Think not to say within yourselves, We have Abraham to [as] our father: for I say unto you, that God is able of these stones to raise up children unto Abraham" (Matthew 3:9).[4] Joseph Smith never retreated from claims that his movement boasted fresh revelation, distinctive truths, and exclusive authority for his religious mission. Nor was he above criticizing other faiths. Yet his Mormonism also entailed forthrightly learning and borrowing from them, and indeed from any source of truth whatsoever. He also recorded revelations wherein the Lord alluded to "holy men that ye know not of" whom the Lord had "reserved unto [him]self," suggesting that the saved and righteous were not exclusive to the Mormons (D&C 49:8).

Thus the Mormon impulse to religious exceptionalism has a history that dates to its beginnings; it thrives even today. But a discernible and more inclusive countercurrent dates to Mormon beginnings as well, and has deepened in the most recent generation as the Saints have grown internationally and in cultural stature, having more meaningful and informed dealings with a wider world. The dominant and recessive genes comprising the church's relative religious exceptionalism has a parallel in, and sheds light on, its views of American exceptionalism.

American Exceptionalism

Not until Ronald Reagan's 1980s did the term "American exceptionalism" approximate the meaning expressed by contemporary (especially Republican) presidential candidates. The *concept* of an American space providentially set apart from ordinary places, however, has roots preceding the formation of the United States, preceding even the mass migration of Europeans to the New World. John Winthrop's famous 1630 address aboard the *Arbella* in effect renewed the Abrahamic covenant between God and a chosen people brought to a chosen land with divine expectations upon them. The ordained mission of this incipient Puritan community was to be as a "city upon a hill," claimed Winthrop. This "errand into the wilderness" must become a light shining abroad to the nations, forming "a model of Christian charity" and order, signaling to the world that God's hand was upon New England.[5]

So chosen was this land that, a century later, Jonathan Edwards discerned it as the likely future place of Christ's second coming. The subsequent American century saw the rise of a new, experimental, different sort of nation: a democratic United States possessed of an exuberant sense of freedom and innocence and possibility, partially ensconced in its Declaration of Independence and its Constitution.[6] Here was a "new order for the ages" *(Novus ordo seclorum)* superintended by God *(Annuit cœptis)*, as the reverse side of the Great Seal of the United States cast it in 1782 and as dollar bills since 1935 proclaim.[7] Less formally, the United States was to become a "redeemer nation," intoxicated with both civic and religious millenarian expectations and aspirations. The nineteenth century also witnessed the conquest of the continent—the fulfillment of an allegedly providential destiny of annexation and growth that seemed "manifest" to so many non-Native occupants. Despite his brooding ways and his untraditional religion, Abraham Lincoln described the embattled United States and the freedom it promised to all as "the last, best hope of earth."[8]

The idea, then, of America as a unique land and nation with a unique mission and destiny held sway long before and during the rise of Mormonism. During the last thirty years, U.S. politicians and cultural analysts have adopted the specific term "American exceptionalism"—which in popular parlance has come to suggest that the United States is not only distinct from, but superior to, other countries; it is the natural leader of the free world. References to this term in print media increased from two in 1980 to almost 3,000 in 2011.[9]

Dominant and Recessive Traits in Mormon Versions of American Exceptionalism

The rise of Mormonism added to the historical stream designating America as chosen. Even before the church was organized in 1830, the newly published Book of Mormon gave the nation its most sustained tract supporting exceptionalism. The book purports to be a modern translation of an ancient record, inscribed on metal tablets. Reprising the Hebrew Bible's predominant motifs of covenant, exodus, entry to a promised land, and striving for righteousness, the narrative tells of a Jewish family's God-directed departure from a hardened, corrupted Israel about to fall to Babylon and into exile (circa 587 BCE). Lehi, the visionary patriarch of this family, was led across the seas to a land God had prepared for them. "Notwithstanding our afflictions," he would say,

> we have obtained a land of promise, a land which is choice above all other lands; a land which the Lord God hath covenanted with me should be a land for the inheritance of my seed. Yea, the Lord hath covenanted this land unto me, and to my children forever, and also all those who should be led out of other countries by the hand of the Lord.... Wherefore, this land is consecrated unto him whom he shall bring. And if it so be that they shall serve him according to the commandments which he hath given, it shall be a land of liberty unto them; wherefore, they shall never be brought down into captivity. (2 Nephi 1: 6–7)

Prophecies in the unfolding story seem to identify this land as what would, two millennia later, become known as America. They allude to the new land's future, to the joys and travails of Lehi's erring descendants, whose fortunes during the subsequent millennium would hinge on their fidelity to their covenant with God in the land of promise. The prophecies further speak of the eventual arrival of Gentiles who would, by God's might, emerge from their own captivity and be lifted in the new world above all other nations. The prophets preached righteousness and warned of the demise of the people if faithlessness and sin should abound. There were to be "no kings upon the land" (1 Nephi 2, 13, 22; 2 Nephi 10:11).

But, as in the original Israel, kings did come, and often enough along with them came sin and tribal corruption. The people "dwindled in unbelief." Civil war eventually exterminated one faction of the civilization, while their conquerors turned degenerate. One message of the Book of Mormon is that a special burden is placed on the inhabitants of this chosen land to obey God's commandments, to remain faithful, to maintain a just and merciful society. Should faith dissolve and iniquity flourish, "cursed shall be the land for their sakes" (2 Nephi 1:7, 10; Ether 13:3; *passim* in the Book of Mormon).

The gold plates on which this record was etched were abridged by the ancient warrior-editor, Mormon, and buried by his son in the fifth century CE in what became upstate New York. By supernatural assistance, the record came to light again through Mormonism's founding prophet, Joseph Smith, who translated the work. The resultant Book of Mormon launched a new religious movement, bestowed upon it a nickname, and set it apart as a distinctive brand of Christianity. In the eyes of believers, it also bequeathed to the new American Republic a powerful sense of providential oversight.

Outside of the Book of Mormon, Joseph Smith reiterated and augmented these themes of America's special calling. He added that the millennial New Jerusalem is to be built upon the American continent.[10] He reported the Lord as saying, in the context of antebellum America, that "it is not right that any man should be in bondage one to another. And for this purpose have I established the Constitution of this land, by the hands of wise men whom I raised up unto this very purpose, and redeemed the land by the shedding of blood" (D&C 101:79–80).

More recent Mormon leaders have extended these teachings. In an era of communist threat, Ezra Taft Benson, Dwight Eisenhower's Secretary of Agriculture and later president of the LDS Church, went so far as to speak of America as "the Lord's base of operations."[11] J. Reuben Clark, erstwhile U.S. Undersecretary of State, later ambassador to Mexico, and eventual prominent member of the LDS Church's First Presidency, championed beliefs taught from his infancy: that "the U.S. Constitution [is] inspired and that the free institutions which it creates and perpetuates are God-given." "I am," he said, "a member of that class which has a firm and unshakable determination to guard our institutions and our Constitution at all cost; that believes that ours is the greatest and best government upon the face of the earth."[12]

Mormonism was born in the United States only a generation following the birth of the nation itself. The religion's infancy was harbored in the nation's adolescence; both took form together. Early Mormonism naturally appropriated, as well as contributed to, diverse American ideas and values, including an orientation to the nation's place in past and future history. The religion treasured its motherland. Despite international growth since World War II, the church's administrative headquarters remain in Salt Lake City. During most of its history, American exceptionalism has enjoyed high station in the Mormon genome.

But the genome includes other genes; Mormonism is complex. In parallel with its ambiguous claims of religious exceptionalism, a recessive gene increasingly challenges believers' sense of a privileged America. In the Book of Mormon, America is a land of promise . . . until it's not. Once the migrating Jews are established in their new promised land, the narrative tells of recurrent departures of disparate subgroups from peoples and lands grown decadent in affluence, arrogance, social injustice, and lust for war (1 Nephi 22:3–5; 2 Nephi 5:5; 2 Nephi 10: 19–22; Omni 1:14–17; Mosiah 23:1–20; Helaman 8:21; 3 Nephi 15:19; Ether 1:38, 42–43; 2:9–10, 12). There appear in the record, over centuries, an impressive series of promised lands and peoples who succeed or fail to live into their chosen roles. These who fail become *un*chosen. Indeed, the overarching prophetic promise of the Book of Mormon, tragically fulfilled in the end, is as much a threat as anything: a threat of demise and destruction if the people should lose their moral fiber and forsake their God. And, as with claims of religious elitism, Americans as "a chosen people" and America as a "promised land" can mean "selected for a role" rather than "spiritually superior."

Furthermore, a central preoccupation of Mormonism for the past forty years, amid its vast international growth, has been how to shed its American presumptions and function in and honor the diverse cultures of the world. This is an incomplete process, but it has been more than a century since LDS authorities urged converts to gather to Utah, once thought of as the Mormon "Zion." Instead, converts are encouraged to build Zion in their home cultures. Not since 1996 have most Mormons lived in the United States, and the gap is widening. Mormon growth predominates not in the United States, much less in Europe, but in such areas as Africa and in South and Central America; these people are proud of their own cultures, their lands full of promise. In the near future, there will be more Portuguese- and Spanish-speaking Saints than English-speaking ones.

Moreover, the very notion of a "promised land" as a single location begins to blur upon careful study of Mormon scripture and history. For example, nineteenth-century Mormons assumed that the Book of Mormon explained the origins of North American Native Americans, who were construed as wild descendants of the peoples portrayed in the Book of Mormon. Faced with a paucity of anthropological and archaeological evidence to make such a case in the modern era, sophisticated though controversial arguments have been marshaled in recent decades by Mormon scholars at Brigham Young University and elsewhere that the civilizations described in the Book of Mormon actually were contained within a geography of only a few hundred square miles in Mesoamerica or South America. To the considerable extent that the modern Mormon faithful subscribe to these theories, however, it would seem to draw into question notions such as those of Apostle Ezra Taft Benson that the United States is "The Lord's base of operations."

Such elements as these reflect a recessive gene in Mormon awareness, undercutting simple and monolithic assessments of Mormon notions of American elitism.

Mitt Romney: A Case Study

The 2012 candidacy of Mitt Romney for the U.S. presidency exemplifies the error of presuming that general Mormon notions of American exceptionalism dictate the perspectives of any particular Mormon candidate for high office. Candidate Mitt Romney argued that President Obama's alleged lack of belief in American exceptionalism was leading the nation to decline, and that this danger should have defined the 2012 election: "We have a president now who thinks America is just another nation," said Romney, "just another nation with a flag."[13] "President Obama seems to think that we're going to have a global century, an Asian century."[14]

Romney's proposed foreign policy contrasted sharply: "I would be guided by an overwhelming conviction that this century must be an American century, where America has the strongest values, the strongest economy, and the strongest military. An American century means a century where America leads the free world and the free world leads the entire world."[15] Unlike President Obama, Romney proclaimed, "I will never apologize for the United States of America."[16]

There was room in Romney's vision of the coming century for Providence: "This is a time where America has got to return to principles that will keep us the hope of the earth and the shining city on the hill. That light from that shining city has dimmed over the last three years, and I will help restore it."[17] "God did not create this country to be a nation of followers. America is not destined to be one of several equally balanced global powers. America must lead the world, or someone else will."[18]

During both the 2008 and 2012 campaigns, voters wanted to know—and various critics insinuated through rhetorical questions that they did know—how a President Romney's religion would affect his judgment. Now is it possible, even if only unconsciously, that Romney's view of America's proper role in history was and is tinged with his Mormon sensibilities? And had Romney been elected, might those sensibilities have colored his judgment in crafting foreign policy? Yes, of course, it *is* possible. Just as it is possible that President Obama's religion—or his parents' divorce, or his Hawaiian background, or his experience in law school—have informed the way that he thinks. But the limitations on this observation are many and severe; the contours of any such influence are difficult to discern. No more than with Obama's religion could Romney's faith be responsibly used to confidently assess, much less to predict, his prospective policy outlook.

One limitation is the difficulty of psychoanalyzing anyone, let alone a mass analysis performed on a public figure, based on press reports, television glimpses, or superficial and often distorted impressions of his religion.

A second difficulty is that, as we have noted, American exceptionalism has deep roots antedating Mormonism. If a Mormon current influenced Romney's position, it was likely an eddy in a wider historical stream. Other Republican candidates in the 2008 and 2012 campaigns professed strong versions of national exceptionalism, with or without citing God.

A third problem is that Romney was and is a complex figure, and Mormonism is but one strand of his background. His trumpet of exceptionalism might derive from his personal competitive drive, his faith in capitalism, or his secular patriotism as readily as from his religion.

A fourth reason for caution in assigning a controlling religious influence to Romney's thinking is that Mormonism is itself complex, as we have glimpsed previously. Its notions of American exceptionalism are ambiguous and evolving, bearing dominant and recessive genes. What any single Mormon politician might deliberately or unconsciously extract from this complex religious heritage, as it applies to practical political policy, is neither obvious nor inevitable. Mormons are not made from cookie-cutters. The mere presence on the recent national political stage of such Mormons as Orrin Hatch, Jon Huntsman, and Harry Reid should help to make the point.

These limitations do not eliminate the possibility of Romney's Mormonism affecting his mind and character; doubtless they do. But neither do they lend themselves to facile assignment of Mormon thinking as a causal agent in Romney's or other Mormons' political judgment.

Conclusion: Romney and Obama

As a final point, we should note that the incumbent candidate, Barack Obama, despite his critics, also spoke of American exceptionalism. His version was not based on the nation's military prowess or economic dominance. Americans, said the president, "have a core set of values that are enshrined in our Constitution, in our body of law, in our democratic practices, in our belief in free speech and equality, that, though imperfect, are exceptional." The United States was to be a nation whose true strength came from "the enduring power of our ideals: democracy, liberty, opportunity, and unyielding hope"; and, above all, a place of ceaseless innovation and an abiding sense that "anything is possible." "I believe in American exceptionalism," declared the president, "just as I suspect that the Brits believe in British exceptionalism and the Greeks believe in Greek exceptionalism."[19]

We live in a dangerous world. The contrasting assessments proffered by Obama and Romney concerning the sources of American exceptionalism had, and retain, competing strengths and dangers; they merited debate in 2012 and afterward. It remains worth noting that one could extract from Mormon history, culture, and scripture reasons for supporting *either* man's understanding of what makes the nation special. Religion may inform, but it does not presage, a candidate's political choices.

NOTES

1. The author thanks Shaina Robbins and Andrew Izatt for research assistance, and Chase Kirkham for assistance with research and annotation. An earlier

version of this article was originally published in *The Review of Faith & International Affairs* 10.2 (Summer 2012): 51–58, as part of a special issue on the theme of "Religion and American Exceptionalism." It is reprinted by permission of the Institute for Global Engagement. *The Review of Faith & International Affairs* is available at www.tandfonline.com/rfia.

2. The Joseph Smith History is contained in the Pearl of Great Price, the fourth of the four Mormon "standard works" of scripture. The others are the Bible, The Book of Mormon, and the Doctrine and Covenants (D&C).

3. Brigham Young, *Journal of Discourses* 1:244 (July 24, 1853); accessed online at http://jod.mrm.org/1/233.

4. One exception is found in Joseph Smith's Book of Abraham in the Pearl of Great Price. Chapter 3 of the Book of Abraham recounts a vision the biblical patriarch Abraham beheld of individuals chosen by God in a pre-earth life to be rulers while in mortality. God chose these rulers because they were "good" and "noble and great"; this suggests to believers that some pre-mortal individuals were chosen and superior.

5. John Winthrop, "A Model of Christian Charity," *Norton Anthology of American Literature: Shorter Fourth Edition* (New York: Norton, 1995), 101–112; Perry Miller, *Errand into the Wilderness* (Cambridge: Harvard University Press, 1956).

6. R. W. B. Lewis, *The American Adam: Innocence, Tragedy, and Tradition in the Nineteenth Century* (Chicago: University of Chicago Press, 1955).

7. Charles Thomson provided an official explanation of the final version he gave to the Great Seal, noting that "the Eye" over the pyramid and the phrase Annuit Cœptis allude to "the many signal interpositions of providence in favour of the American cause." *Journals of the Continental Congress*, quoted in http://greatseal.com/mottoes/coeptis.html.

8. Abraham Lincoln, "Last Best Hope of Earth: Annual Message to Congress, December 1, 1862," *Abraham Lincoln: A Documentary Portrait through His Speeches and Writings*, ed. Don E. Fehrenbacher (Stanford, CA: Stanford University Press, 1964), 202–209.

9. Jerome Karabel, "'American Exceptionalism' and the Battle for the Presidency," *Huffington Post*, December 22, 2011; accessed online at www.huffingtonpost.com/jerome-karabel/american-exceptionalism-obama-gingrich_b_1161800.html.

10. Tenth Article of Faith, The Pearl of Great Price.

11. Ezra Taft Benson, "The Lord's Base of Operations," *Conference Report* (April 1962), 103–6.

12. D. Michael Quinn, *Elder Statesman: A Biography of J. Reuben Clark* (Salt Lake City: Signature Books, 2002), 255.

13. Karabel, "'American Exceptionalism' and the Battle for the Presidency."

14. Michael A. Cohen, "Foreign Policy: Politics Stops at the Water's Edge," National Public Radio commentary, November 28, 2011, accessed online at www.npr.org/2011/11/28/142842453/foreign-policy-politics-stops-at-the-waters-edge.

15. Charles Lane, "The Candidates and Foreign Policy," *World Affairs Journal* (January–February 2012), accessed online at www.worldaffairsjournal.org/article/candidates-and-foreign-policy.

16. Ruth Marcus, "The Consistently Inconsistent Mitt Romney," *Washington Post*, November 10, 2011, accessed online at www.washingtonpost.com/opinions/the-consistently-inconsistent-mitt-romney/2011/11/10/gIQAANas9M_story.html.

17. "Full Transcript: ABC News Iowa Republican Debate," December 11, 2011, accessed online at http://abcnews.go.com/Politics/full-transcript-abc-news-iowa-republican-debate/story?id=15134849.

18. Associated Press, "Romney: God Wants U.S. to Lead, Not Follow," accessed online at www.foxnews.com/politics/2011/10/07/romney-god-wants-us-to-lead-not-follow/.

19. Karabel, "'American Exceptionalism' and the Battle for the Presidency."

8   Like Father, Unlike Son

*The Governors Romney, the Kennedy
Paradigm, and the Mormon Question*

Randall Balmer

On December 6, 2007, less than a month before the Iowa precinct caucuses, the first electoral test of the 2008 presidential campaign, the former governor of Massachusetts, an aspirant for the Republican presidential nomination, strode to the lectern at the George Bush Presidential Library in College Station, Texas. The forty-first president (the library's namesake) had just introduced the candidate, whose wife sat in the front row with four of the couple's five sons.[1]

Ever since the Romney campaign had announced, several days earlier, the candidate's intention to address the issue of his Mormon faith, the media had referred to the impending event as Romney's "JFK speech," a reference to John Kennedy's address to a group of several hundred Protestant ministers at the Rice Hotel on September 12, 1960, just ninety miles south of College Station, in Houston. On the face of it, the circumstances surrounding the two speeches were not dissimilar. Only once before, in 1928, had a Roman Catholic been a major-party nominee for president, and Alfred E. Smith, the governor of New York and the Democratic nominee, lost decisively to Herbert Hoover amid widespread fears, fanned in part by a recrudescence of the Ku Klux Klan, that any Roman Catholic in the Oval Office would do the bidding of the pope in governing the United States of America. According to popular lore, when the results were tallied on election night, Smith sent a one-word telegram to the Vatican: "Unpack."

Despite the fact that Roman Catholics in America had made huge strides to vindicate their patriotism by fighting in World War II (in many cases against nations from which their families had only recently emigrated), the junior senator from Massachusetts was fully aware of lingering anti-Catholicism as he prepared to run for the Democratic nomination in 1960. Just eleven years earlier, Beacon Press in Boston had published a book titled *American Freedom and Catholic Power*, which argued the incompatibility of Roman Catholicism with American democracy. This was not a new argument; nativists had been making that case since the nineteenth century. What set this book apart, however, was that its author was not some nativist crank; he was a Congregationalist minister, an alumnus of the University of Michigan and Union Theological Seminary who had studied at both Columbia and Harvard.

The popularity of *American Freedom and Catholic Power*—eleven printings in as many months—signaled to Kennedy and his campaign that his Roman Catholic faith could be an impediment to his quest for the presidency. Kennedy's defeat of Hubert Humphrey, the Democratic senator from Minnesota, in May's primary balloting in West Virginia, an overwhelmingly Protestant state, provided some measure of confidence that his faith would no longer be an issue. But that relief proved temporary. Billy Graham, equivocating on an earlier promise to remain neutral during the general election, convened a group of Protestant leaders in Montreux, Switzerland, on August 18, 1960, to discuss ways to deny Kennedy's election in November. A subsequent, larger gathering of Protestant ministers at the Mayflower Hotel in Washington on September 7 finally convinced Kennedy that he needed to address what was widely known as the "religious issue" directly.[2]

Similarly, Mitt Romney also faced questions about his faith in the run-up to the 2008 Republican primaries. As a member of the Church of Jesus Christ of Latter-day Saints, Romney, in the opinion of many voters, stood outside the mainstream of religious life in the United States. Ever since the emergence of the Religious Right in the late 1970s, moreover, politically conservative evangelicals had formed the backbone of the Republican Party, much the way labor unions once did for the Democratic Party. Because one of the strongholds of the Religious Right was in Iowa, site of the first test of the primary season, Romney needed to curry favor with those voters and allay their fears.

On August 2, 2007, during an especially contentious interview with Jan Mickelson, a conservative talk-show host on WHO-Radio in Des Moines, Romney tried to brush off questions about his faith. "I'm not going to have a conversation about what my church views are," Romney protested on the air. During the commercial breaks and after the interview concluded, the conversation became heated. "You're trying to tell me that I'm not a faithful Mormon," the candidate told Mickelson. "I'm not running to talk about Mormonism." Mickelson sought to placate Romney, expressing the wish that he would return for more "quality time" on the air. "No, I don't like coming on the air and having you go after my church and me," Romney shot back. "I'm not running as a Mormon, and I get a little tired of coming on a show like yours and having it all about Mormon."[3]

By late 2007, however, Romney's efforts to deflect questions about his faith had failed to quell suspicions. As the Mickelson interview indicated, Romney's strategy had been to avoid talking about his faith whenever possible. His stock responses on the campaign trail consisted of declaring that he was "not a theologian" and that "I don't speak for my church." Later in the campaign, he protested that he was running to be commander-in-chief, not pastor-in-chief. But the questions persisted, especially as Iowa voters began to consider another contender for the Republican nomination, Mike Huckabee, the former governor of Arkansas and an ordained Baptist minister, whose religious sympathies struck evangelical voters in Iowa as far less exotic than Romney's Mormonism.

Similar to the Kennedy campaign forty-eight years earlier, the Romney camp had debated at length the wisdom of publicly engaging the issue of the candidate's faith. In 1960, Kennedy advisers Archibald Cox and John Kenneth Galbraith pushed the senator to take on the issue. For Romney, Huckabee's surge in the polls settled the matter, and so, on a warm Texas day in December, when the temperature climbed into the low seventies, Romney, like Kennedy before him, prepared to address the religion question.

With ten flags and the presidential seal behind him, Romney opened his remarks with an encomium to George H. W. Bush, who had introduced him. Romney noted that, nearly half a century earlier, "another candidate from Massachusetts explained that he was an American running for president, not a Catholic running for president," and he briefly echoed Kennedy's argument that a candidate "should not be elected because of his faith nor should he be rejected because of his faith."[4]

But the similarities between Romney and Kennedy ended there. Whereas Kennedy had declared that he believed "in an America where the separation of church and state is absolute," Romney, in an apparent overture to the Religious Right, temporized. "We should acknowledge the Creator as did the Founders—in ceremony and word," Romney said. "He should remain on our currency, in our pledge, in the teaching of our history, and during the holiday season, nativity scenes and menorahs should be welcome in our public places." He attacked those who "seek to remove from the public domain any acknowledgment of God," and he accused unnamed entities of acting "as if they are intent on establishing a new religion in America—the religion of secularism."[5]

Another difference between the Romney and Kennedy speeches was the venue. Romney addressed the religion question in the safety of a friendly environment, at the library of a likeminded politician (even though Bush had not formally endorsed Romney) and before an audience of family members, campaign workers, invited guests, and the press. For Kennedy, on the other hand, members of the Greater Houston Ministerial Association could hardly be considered sympathetic. Whereas Romney took no questions following his speech in College Station, Kennedy fielded queries, many of them hostile, from members of the audience and concluded by saying, "I don't want anyone to think, because they interrogate me on this important question, that I regard that as unfair or unreasonable or that somebody who is concerned about the matter is prejudiced or bigoted."[6]

Finally, perhaps the most important difference between the Romney and Kennedy speeches lay in each candidate's references to his own faith. Whereas Kennedy repeatedly referred to his Roman Catholic identity, Romney mentioned the word "Mormon" only once, preferring to use terms like "my church" and "my religion."

However instructive a comparison of the Kennedy and Romney speeches might be, the comparison of Mitt Romney's handling of his faith with that of his father, George, is even more compelling. George Romney, also a Mormon, was also a governor, the governor of Michigan, when he pursued the 1968 Republican presidential nomination.[7]

George Wilcken Romney's great-grandfather had helped to build the Mormon Temple in Nauvoo, Illinois, and headed west with Brigham Young to the Great Salt Lake Basin following Joseph Smith's murder in 1844. Romney's forebears were polygamists who sought refuge in northern Mexico after the United States government pressured Mormons to abandon plural marriage, with the Edmunds Act of 1882 and the Edmunds-Tucker Act of 1887. Born in Chihuahua, Mexico, in 1907, George Romney grew up in several states before settling with his family in Salt Lake City, Utah. The family struggled during the Great Depression; Romney attended several colleges but never graduated. After serving a mission to Great Britain for the Church of Jesus Christ of Latter-day Saints and a stint on Capitol Hill in Washington, Romney headed to Detroit in 1939 to become manager of the Automobile Manufacturers Association during World War II. In 1948 he joined Nash-Kelvinator and six years later became chief executive of that company's successor, American Motors Corporation, where he emerged as an early advocate for smaller, more fuel-efficient automobiles.[8]

Romney parlayed his success as a businessman into politics. He headed an effort to call for a state constitutional convention, won election to that convention, and served as a vice president of the convention during its proceedings in 1961–62. Having declared himself a Republican, Romney (who hailed from a long line of conservative Republicans) quickly began to attract notice as a potential candidate for office. Although he briefly considered running for the United States Senate in 1960, he ran instead for governor of Michigan two years later, but only after, according to *Time* magazine, he "fasted for 24 hours in prayerful consideration." Romney's narrow victory over the Democratic incumbent (50.9 percent of the popular vote) ended fourteen straight years of Democratic administrations in the state; Romney was the only Republican that year to win statewide office.[9]

While some in the national media had speculated that the Church of Jesus Christ of Latter-day Saints' refusal to ordain men of color to the priesthood (a ban not overturned until 1978) would limit Romney's political prospects, that concern proved to be no hindrance to Romney, even in a state with a large African American population. In addition, his opponent in 1962, John B. Swainson, the incumbent governor, had been reared in the Reorganized Church of Jesus Christ of Latter Day Saints (now Community of Christ), a fact that, despite the differences between the two branches of Mormonism, would have blunted the issue. On the matter of race, Romney, in fact, had already opposed segregation, and his record as governor burnished his credentials as a champion of civil rights (at least until the Detroit riots in 1967). One of the Republicans who took a keen interest in the Michigan governor and his political prospects was Dwight Eisenhower; the former president served as a political mentor.[10]

In anticipation of the 1964 campaign season, John Kennedy, contemplating his own bid for reelection, remarked that, "The one fellow I don't want to run against is Romney." The role Romney played at the 1964 Republican National Convention, however, was not nominee but rather critic of the hard-right policies of the Republican Party and its nominee, Barry Goldwater. In a speech before the National Press Club earlier that year, Romney had warned that "a party representing one or a few narrow interests cannot indefinitely survive in this country," a not-so-subtle jab at Goldwater, and in June Romney declared that Goldwater had "voiced public views that do not square with the principles for which the Republican party stands on the basis of its past record and heritage." Therefore, the governor concluded, "I will do everything within my power to keep him from becoming the party's presidential candidate." On his way to the Republican convention in San Francisco, George Romney stopped in Salt Lake City to ask his uncle, Vernon Romney, head of the Utah delegation, to back the Michigan governor's resolutions in support of civil rights and against extremism. Vernon Romney refused. In the end, Romney was so distressed by Goldwater's nomination that he declined to endorse the Republican candidate for president in 1964; his own curious nomenclature was that he would "accept, but not endorse" his party's nominee.[11]

Romney himself, however, bucking the Lyndon Johnson Democratic landslide, won reelection as governor in 1964 (40 percent of Johnson voters in Michigan also voted for Romney) and again in 1966. A poll immediately after the November 1966 election showed Romney beating Johnson, 54 percent to 46 percent, in a hypothetical matchup for the presidency in 1968. As the primary season for the 1968 election rolled around, Romney's name appeared at or near the top of everyone's list of potential Republican nominees. By 1967 he had established a solid résumé as well as a campaign apparatus, and with the flagging popularity of the incumbent president together with the fact that the Republicans had no presumptive nominee, Romney's prospects for 1968 looked promising. J. Willard Marriott, hotel magnate (and Mitt Romney's namesake), headed fundraising efforts for Romney's campaign.[12]

Both Mitt and George Romney served as stake presidents (roughly the equivalent of a lay bishop) for the Church of Jesus Christ of Latter-day Saints. Unlike his son, however, George Romney rarely shied away from talking publicly about his faith. "My religion is my most precious possession," the elder Romney, still a private citizen, wrote in a *Detroit Free Press* article in 1959. "It teaches me the purpose of life and answers life's greatest questions: Where we come from, Why we are here, and Where we are going. It provides me with yardsticks for life based upon eternal values." Romney also affirmed the Mormon teaching that the Constitution is a "Divinely Inspired Document." In the course of his baccalaureate address at Brigham Young University later that same year, Romney said, "Whatever success I have had is primarily the result of my church training."[13]

In the run-up to 1968, the press touched lightly on George Romney's Mormonism. "To understand George, you must first of all understand that he is a Mormon," a friend of the governor told the *New York Times Magazine*. "He is a deeply religious person who has a great belief in the individual and the family. For him, each person is a distinct personality and child of God." Most of the coverage, aside from the so-called "Negro question," was benign, consisting primarily of observations about Romney's ascetic habits—no alcohol, tobacco, or caffeine—and about his perceived self-righteousness. As for the "Negro question," most journalists who brought up the topic dutifully reported Romney's rejoinder that such talk unfairly "injects my religious beliefs into the campaign" and that he should be judged by his record on civil rights, a record that most observers agreed was sympathetic. Stewart Alsop, commenting in the *Saturday Evening Post*, wrote, "The appearance of the man, the impression he gives, the earnestness, sincerity and just plain goodness which Romney fairly exudes, are vital assets."[14]

What happened? The standard interpretation holds that Romney's presidential prospects crashed suddenly when he declared that he had been "brainwashed" about Vietnam. Romney, like Nixon, his principal rival for the Republican nomination, had been inconsistent about his position on the Vietnam War. Romney had strongly endorsed the war in 1965, but by 1967 he referred to the conflict as a "tragic" mistake. In a television interview with Lou Gordon on Detroit's WKBD on August 31, 1967, Romney was asked why he had, until recently, supported the war, even well beyond his visit to Vietnam in November 1965. "When I came back from Viet Nam," the governor said, "I had just had the greatest brainwashing that anybody can get when you go over to Viet Nam."[15]

The pundits and the politicians pounced. Eugene McCarthy, the Democratic senator from Minnesota and a candidate for the Democratic presidential nomination, remarked that, in the case of Romney, brainwashing was not necessary; "a light rinse would have been sufficient." Robert T.

Stafford, Republican member of Congress from Vermont, said that, "If you're running for the presidency, you are supposed to have too much on the ball to be brainwashed." The *Detroit News*, long a Romney supporter, urged Romney to withdraw from the race in favor of Nelson A. Rockefeller, and the *Chicago Daily News*, also well disposed to the Michigan governor, wondered if the United States "can afford as its leader a man who, whatever his positive virtues, is subject to being cozened, flimflammed and taken into camp." Romney's poll numbers fell dramatically.[16]

While Romney was trying to contain the damage from his "brainwashing" remark—he initially refused to back down—Nixon was busy securing delegates in advance of the first primary. In addition, as Romney floundered, Rockefeller, who had previously championed Romney's candidacy, declared his own willingness to accept a draft to become the Republican nominee. On the eve of the New Hampshire primary, a poll warned that Nixon's support was six times that of Romney, and so on February 28, 1968, before a single vote was cast, Romney withdrew from consideration for the Republican presidential nomination.

Even more than four decades later, there is some historiographical debate about what derailed Romney's candidacy. In a 1971 article in *BYU Studies*, Dennis L. Lythgoe, a columnist for the *Deseret News* and a professor of history at Bridgewater State University, contended that George Romney's "religion proved to be a handicap and had a profound impact on the campaign's outcome." Lythgoe, however, provided no evidence—no polling data, no quotations to support his conclusions, only assertions to the effect that Romney's candidacy was hobbled by "the somewhat abstract concept that he was 'too good to be true.'" In their analysis of George Romney as part of their survey of Mormon candidates for the presidency, Newell G. Bringhurst and Craig L. Foster echo Lythgoe's assessment that Romney's Mormonism crippled his candidacy but similarly fail to provide corroborating evidence. The evidence they cite is Lythgoe's article and a passing comment in T. George Harris's authorized biography of Romney—written and published in 1967, a year *before* the 1968 campaign.[17]

An alternative view, advanced most comprehensively by Andrew L. Johns in the spring 2000 fascicle of the *Michigan Historical Review*, is that Romney's candidacy faltered not because of his faith but because he had so vigorously challenged the Republican political establishment in 1964. Romney's refusal to endorse Goldwater's candidacy together with the rightward drift of the Republican Party effectively jettisoned his chances. Romney's stand on civil rights and his growing opposition to the Vietnam War placed him at odds with other Republicans and made it unlikely that the party would turn to him as its nominee.[18]

Indeed, what is so utterly striking about George Romney's quest for the Republican nomination in 1968 is that the political impact of his Mormon faith ranged somewhere between negligible and nonexistent. Although such a conclusion veers perilously close to reasoning from absence, there is no evidence that voters rejected—or were prepared to reject—his candidacy on account of his faith. Nor did Romney face any pressure to deliver a "JFK speech" to dispel suspicions about his allegiances.

Part of this may have been due to the candidate's strategic handling of the matter. Romney carefully sought to inoculate himself against those whose suspicions of Mormonism might prejudice their views of the candidate. Speaking before the Salt Lake City Ministerial Association on February 20, 1967, for example, Romney assured these non-Mormon clerics of his commitment to the "vital necessity" of the First Amendment and the separation of church and state. On the "Negro question," Romney reiterated that he had "fought for civil rights for a long time and I will continue to do so." The church hierarchy also sought to defuse what might have been an issue, namely Romney's independence from ecclesiastical authorities. David O. McKay, president of the Church of Jesus Christ of Latter-day Saints, assured the *Los Angeles Times* that the church would never "try to enforce its will on the members who hold national office."[19]

When Romney did talk about faith, he did so in the bromides and platitudes that have become commonplace on the campaign trail. "The churches of our land have a vital role to play in shaping our future," Romney told students and faculty at Concordia Lutheran College in Ann Arbor, Michigan, on July 23, 1966. "Faith in God, added to knowledge, produces understanding," the governor concluded. "And the loss of faith in God produces confusion of values, moral decline, and social disintegration."[20]

Deep into Tom Wicker's "News Analysis" piece in the *New York Times*, published the day after Romney's withdrawal, Wicker referred to the governor's faith only obliquely and in passing. "Mr. Romney's decision to withdraw confounded those who had thought his Mormon religious background would not permit him to 'quit' so soon," he wrote. The conventional wisdom about Romney's failure, Wicker reported, was that

Romney was not "knowledgeable enough about national or foreign policy issues" and that his personal bearing was "too intense to be sympathetic."[21]

If George Romney's quest for the Republican presidential nomination foundered on factors other than his religious affiliation, the question remains why Mitt Romney felt obliged publicly to address his Mormon faith in advance of the 2008 presidential primaries when his father encountered no such pressure forty years earlier. Here it becomes necessary to step back from a narrow consideration of the two Romneys and take in the larger sweep of American presidential politics since 1960. Many Americans still imbibed deep suspicions of Roman Catholicism in 1960; the popularity of *American Freedom and Catholic Power* provides merely one index of those misgivings. A Gallup poll in 1959 found that 25 percent of Americans would not support a Roman Catholic for president.[22]

Although Kennedy's progress through the primaries steadily whittled down that number, he still faced formidable opposition to his candidacy because of his religion. Following the gathering of Protestant ministers at the Mayflower Hotel on September 7, the Kennedy campaign recognized the imperative to address the issue directly. On the weekend of September 9–10, Kennedy and Ted Sorenson, his aide and speechwriter, huddled in Los Angles to write the address that he would deliver on Tuesday evening, September 12, to the ministers in Houston.

That speech, widely regarded as a classic articulation of a candidate's faith and its relevance to the First Amendment and to public service, effectively instructed voters to disregard a candidate's religion when they entered the voting booth. Although Kennedy's arguments may not have swayed many votes inside the Rice Hotel's ballroom, where his audience was overwhelmingly Protestant, the campaign regarded the speech as so successful that it broadcast excerpts of it more broadly as advertisements for the Kennedy-Johnson ticket.

Kennedy's argument that he was "not the Catholic candidate for president" but rather "the Democratic Party's candidate for president, who happens also to be a Catholic" assuaged the reservations of enough voters to propel him to the White House in the closest presidential election of the twentieth century. More important, Kennedy's argument cast a long shadow over presidential politics. For more than a decade, including the 1968 presidential primaries and election, American voters evinced very little interest in the religious affiliations of presidential candidates.[23]

Kennedy's successor, Lyndon Johnson, for example, is often thought—erroneously—to be a Baptist; Johnson, in fact, was a member of the Disciples of Christ, an apparent consequence of an adolescent rebellion against his devout Baptist mother. Richard Nixon was reared a Quaker in Whittier, California, but voters knew little about his religious views—and apparently cared even less. George S. McGovern, United States senator from South Dakota and Nixon's Democratic challenger in 1972, was the son of a Methodist minister and had actually studied for the ministry at Garrett Evangelical Theological Seminary before going on for a PhD in history and a career in public service. McGovern's faith, however, did not play any appreciable role in the 1972 campaign.[24]

George Romney's run for the Republican presidential nomination in 1968, then, took place amid the "Kennedy paradigm" of voter indifference to a candidate's faith. It simply was not an issue in the minds of most voters, certainly not an issue important enough to warrant a candidate devoting an entire speech to explaining his religious sympathies and affiliations. Romney, in fact, was so indebted to the Kennedy paradigm that he echoed some of Kennedy's arguments, whether consciously or not. Just as Kennedy had implored the Houston ministers to judge him not on the basis of "select quotations out of context from statements of Catholic church leaders" but rather "on the basis of fourteen years in the Congress" and on his opposition to "an ambassador to the Vatican" and "unconstitutional aid to public schools," so too Romney, responding to Mormonism's refusal to ordain men of color, asked voters to judge him on his record of civil rights. "If my church prevented me from working to eliminate social justice and racial discrimination, as I have worked for 25 years," Romney told a gathering of ministers, "I would not belong." He asked instead "to be judged on the basis of my record and the actions that speak louder than words."[25]

What changed? What happened to the Kennedy paradigm? In a word: Nixon. The mendacity of Richard Nixon, the Watergate scandal, and the culture of corruption that infested the Nixon White House persuaded Americans that they needed to pay more careful attention to matters like character and probity. The victorious candidate in the ensuing presidential election, a Southern Baptist Sunday-school teacher, perfectly embodied those qualities. It would be impossible to imagine Jimmy Carter, a little-known one-term governor of Georgia becoming president had it not been for Richard Nixon; ever since, voters have expected their presidential candidates to talk about their faith.

Some have done so more fluently than others. For a variety of complex reasons, the same evangelicals who helped elect Carter in 1976 turned dramatically against him four years later in favor of a man who rarely attended church but who spoke the language of piety. George H. W. Bush, an Episcopalian, was not always comfortable talking about his faith, but his path to the White House was made easier because his Democratic opponent, Michael S. Dukakis, although ostensibly Greek Orthodox, was widely viewed as a secularist. Bill Clinton, whom novelist Toni Morrison called America's "first black president," was rarely more at ease than when he was behind the pulpit of an African American church, and George W. Bush openly traded on his identity as an evangelical and spoke frequently about his religious conversions. The kerfuffle over the incendiary rhetoric of Jeremiah Wright, Barack Obama's pastor in Chicago, prompted the Democratic candidate to speak candidly about his faith during the course of the 2008 presidential campaign.

Ever since Carter introduced the language of religion and piety into presidential politics in the mid-1970s, Americans have come to expect that aspirants to the White House will talk about their faith. In the United States, for better or worse, religion functions as a proxy for morality, and ever since Nixon, voters want to know whether their presidential candidates are good, moral, upright people.

One test for morality is religious affiliation and how comfortable and conversant a candidate is in talking about his faith. George Romney, pursuing the presidency during the Kennedy paradigm of voter indifference to a candidate's religious affiliation, faced no expectations or pressures to do so, even though Romney, on several occasions, volunteered information about his faith. Mitt Romney, his son, ran for president during a very different historical moment, a time when voters expected some discourse, however superficial, about faith. Mitt Romney's refusal to engage that conversation—whether from fears of ridicule for his Mormon beliefs or of alienating the evangelicals of the Religious Right, the core constituency of the Republican Party—played a not inconsiderable role in determining his political fortunes.

Pundits and historians sifting through ashes of the 2012 presidential election have much to consider. The conventional wisdom, at this writing, is that the Obama campaign, riding the tide of at least a modest economic recovery, was much better organized and was able, with sophisticated metrics and superior technology, to target and to motivate specific groups of voters sympathetic to the incumbent Democratic president. The corollary narrative is Mitt Romney's ham-handedness in dealing with ordinary voters—his plutocratic style, his awkward and insensitive comments, and his remarks (to wealthy donors) that 47 percent of Americans were "dependent upon government, who believe that they are victims." The candidate added: "I'll never convince them that they should take personal responsibility and care for their lives."

All of those considerations doubtless played a role in the outcome of the 2012 election, an election that Romney, by all accounts, thought he would win. Any calculus in evaluating the election, however, should include Romney's handling of his Mormon faith, or, more specifically, his refusal to address the matter as many candidates before him—Kennedy, Carter, Obama, or even his own father, George Romney—were willing to do. All of those candidates for the presidency, albeit at different times and in different historical contexts, spoke candidly and forthrightly about their faith, refusing the subterfuges of "I'm not a theologian" and "I don't speak for my church."

With the luxury of hindsight, we can only guess what might have transpired had Mitt Romney declared at some point in his nearly decade-long quest for the presidency something like the following: "Yes, I'm a Mormon. My family has been Mormon for generations, and I refuse to abjure my faith for political gain. The Church of Jesus Christ of Latter-day Saints sustains me and reminds me of my responsibility for others. I recognize that not all Americans will agree with the tenets of my faith, but I respectfully remind them of Article VI of the Constitution, which prohibits any religious test for office. I also remind my fellow Americans of our long, though imperfect, tradition of respect for the rights of minorities." Mitt Romney might even have quoted his father, who said about his faith: "It teaches me the purpose of life and answers life's greatest questions: Where we come from, Why we are here, and Where we are going. It provides me with yardsticks for life based upon eternal values."[26]

We'll never know whether such a statement might have changed the outcome of the 2012 election, but Americans generally prefer candor to subterfuge. The history of the United States, moreover, is the story of Americans coming around, sooner or later, to embrace the principles encoded into their charter documents, including freedom of religious expression and respect for minorities. For some Americans, especially for African Americans and women, that embrace of equality has come far too belatedly, but Americans have a history of rising to their better selves.

So too with the presidency. The last half century has witnessed the election of a Roman Catholic and an African American to the nation's highest office. A woman came tantalizingly close to winning the nomination of a major party, and a Jew was that party's vice presidential nominee eight years earlier.

Could Mitt Romney have broken though the "Mormon barrier" to win the White House? Again, we can't know; counterfactual speculation may be a useful analytical tool, but it offers no certain answers. One thing, however, is certain: Had Mitt Romney been willing to talk about his faith on the campaign trail, he would at the very least have made it easier for the next Mormon who pursues national office.

NOTES

1. Among the many media accounts of the speech, see Michael Luo, "Romney, Eye on Evangelicals, Defends His Faith," *New York Times*, December 7, 2007, A1; Linda Feldman, "Romney Moves to Allay Mormon Concerns Directly," *Christian Science Monitor*, December 7, 2007, 1; John Ibbitson, "Religious Faith, Democratic Freedom and Mitt Romney's Flagging Campaign," *Toronto Globe and Mail*, December 7, 2007, A1. For a text of the speech, see Newell G. Bringhurst and Craig L. Foster, *The Mormon Quest for the Presidency: From Joseph Smith to Mitt Romney and Jon Huntsman* (Independence, MO: John Whitmer Books, 2011), appendix D.

2. Graham wrote directly to Kennedy on August 10, eight days before the Montreux gathering, assuring the senator that he would not "raise the religious issue publicly during the presidential campaign." Letter, Billy Graham to John F. Kennedy, August 10, 1960 ("Religion" folder, Pre-Presidential Papers, Senate Files, box 550, John F. Kennedy Library).

3. Michael Luo, "Romney Defends His Faith," *New York Times*, August 4, 2007; Jake Tapper, "Romney Defends His Religion," ABC News website, August 5, 2007, accessed June 8, 2012.

4. Transcripts of Romney's speech are widely available, including "Transcript: Mitt Romney's Faith Speech," NPR.org, accessed June 8, 2012.

5. Kennedy's speech to the Houston ministers has been widely reprinted and anthologized. One source is Randall Balmer, *God in the White House: How Faith Shaped the Presidency from John F. Kennedy to George W. Bush* (San Francisco: HarperOne, 2008), 175–80; quotation on 176.

6. Gladwin Hill, "Reaction of Ministers," *New York Times*, September 14, 1960 (Transcript, September 12, 1960, "Religion" folder, Pre-Presidential Papers, 1960 Campaign, box 1049, John F. Kennedy Library).

7. The parallels between father and son are endless. In early 1962, when George Romney was gearing up to run for governor, *Newsweek* remarked that "If Central Casting were to pick the ideal Presidential Candidate, Romney would be it"—a sentiment repeated many times about his son ("Dark Horse: Off and Running," *Newsweek*, February 19, 1962, 23). When campaigning for governor in 1962,

George Romney, the former president of American Motors, often remarked that he was "an unemployed businessman looking for a new job," a statement strikingly similar to Mitt Romney's widely reported jest to unemployed workers in Florida that he too was unemployed. Finally, George Romney called for the breakup of General Motors; his son opposed a federal bailout to GM when it was facing bankruptcy. See D. Duane Angel, *Romney: A Political Biography* (New York: Exposition Press, 1967), 189, 204; Jeff Zeleny, "Romney: 'I'm Also Unemployed,'" *New York Times*, June 16, 2011.

8. For biographical details, see (among other sources) Bringhurst and Foster, *Mormon Quest for the Presidency*, ch. 2.

9. "Fresh Face in an Open Field," *Time*, February 16, 1962, 22. On Romney family politics, see T. George Harris, *Romney's Way: A Man and an Idea* (Englewood Cliffs, NJ: Prentice-Hall), 1967), ch. 2.

10. The fear about the LDS priesthood ban on people of color was articulated even in George Romney's campaign biography; see Angel, *Romney*, 232–33.

11. George Romney, quoted in Angel, *Romney*, 104, 105, 109; Benjamin Wallace-Wells, "George Romney for President, 1968," *New York*, May 20, 2012; Harris, *Romney's Way*, 14.

12. Angel, *Romney*, 174; Bringhurst and Foster, *Mormon Quest for the Presidency*, 62, 64.

13. George Romney, "A Yardstick to Measure Life's Values," *Detroit Free Press*, February 15, 1959; George Romney, *The Concerns of a Citizen* (New York: Putnam's, 1968), 282.

14. David R. Jones, "This Republican for 1968?" *New York Times Magazine*, February 28, 1965, 28; Romney, *Concerns of a Citizen*, 280; Steward Alsop, "It's Like Running Against God," *Saturday Evening Post*, October 22, 1966, 20. For an analysis of press coverage of Romney's Mormonism, see Dennis L. Lythgoe, "The 1968 Presidential Decline of George Romney: Mormonism or Politics?" *BYU Studies* 11 (Spring 1971): 219–40. Lythgoe seems to detect a religious bias against Romney and Mormonism that (in my judgment) is not borne out by the sources he cites. Lythgoe concludes, without corroborating evidence, that voters were "uneasy about electing a man as religious as Romney" and that "Romney's religion proved to be a handicap and had a profound effect on the campaign's outcome" (ibid., 238, 239). Andrew L. Johns also challenges Lythgoe's conclusions; Johns, "Achilles' Heel: The Vietnam War and George Romney's Bid for the Presidency, 1967 to 1968," *Michigan Historical Review* 26 (Spring 2000): 1–29.

15. "The Brainwashed Candidate," *Time*, September 15, 1967, 26.

16. Ibid. Tom Wicker would later describe Romney's brainwashing comment as "a shattering political gaffe from which he never really recovered." Tom Wicker, "Impact of Romney Move," *New York Times*, February 29, 1968.

17. Bringhurst and Foster, *Mormon Quest for the Presidency*, 72.

18. Johns, "Achilles' Heel."

19. Bringhurst and Foster, *Mormon Quest for the Presidency*, 66; Dan L. Tharpp, "Mormons See Romney in Race on His Own," *Los Angeles Times*, November 27, 1966.

20. From speech reprinted in Bringhurst and Foster, *Mormon Quest for the Presidency*, 349, 352.

21. Wicker, "Impact of Romney Move."

22. Lydia Saad, "In U.S., 22% Are Hesitant to Support a Mormon in 2012," June 20, 2011, www.gallup.com/poll/148100/hesitant-support-mormon-2012.aspx. Accessed July 29, 2012.

23. John F. Kennedy, quoted in Balmer, *God in the White House*, 179. I have developed this argument in greater detail in *God in the White House*.

24. An anecdote: When I was interviewing H. R. (Bob) Haldeman, Nixon's chief of staff, for a documentary on Billy Graham at Haldeman's home in Santa Barbara, California, in 1992, I asked if the Nixon reelection campaign in 1972 was at all fearful that McGovern's seminary background might erode Nixon's popularity among evangelical voters. Haldeman professed not to know that McGovern had attended seminary or that he had once considered becoming a minister.

25. Kennedy, quoted in Balmer, *God in the White House*, 179; George Romney, quoted in Harris, *Romney's Way*, 206.

26. George Romney, "A Yardstick to Measure Life's Values," *Detroit Free Press*, February 15, 1959.

PART III

Into the Twenty-first Century

9   A Politically Peculiar People

How Mormons Moved into and Then out of the Political Mainstream

David E. Campbell, Christopher F. Karpowitz, and J. Quin Monson

In recent years, American Mormons, or members of the Church of Jesus Christ of Latter-day Saints, have become known as one of the most reliable components of the Republican coalition of social and economic conservatives.[1] But Mormons have not always been so reliably Republican, and as we will show, even today they do not march in lockstep with their fellow partisans. The partisan politics of American Mormons have undergone a dramatic transformation from a position of conflict and separation during the mid-nineteenth century, to a position of conformity and accommodation with American political norms during the late nineteenth and early twentieth centuries, to a position predominantly aligned with social conservatism and the Republican Party in the late twentieth and early-twenty-first centuries. This dramatic movement from a position completely outside the political mainstream to incorporation within the national party system and, further, to a core constituency of the Republican Party should not blind us to the fact that Mormons remain politically distinctive. The realignment in Mormon political behavior has not, for example, meant complete adoption of the issue attitudes of white evangelical Protestants, another religious group that has become reliably Republican.[2] Despite the fact that the two groups are stalwarts in the same partisan coalition, their positions on several important issues are distinct.

Compared to their partisan bedfellows, American Mormons are still a somewhat peculiar people. Perhaps they are not as peculiar as they once were, but peculiar nonetheless.

This chapter describes the unique political attitudes and voting behavior of ordinary American Mormons, with special, though not exclusive, focus on those in the intermountain West. The arc of our story is that Mormons went from being highly peculiar in the era before and just after Utah statehood to conformity with national political trends through much of the twentieth century.[3] Over roughly the last thirty years, however, Mormons have once again become peculiar when compared to the nation as a whole. They are staunchly Republican and largely conservative, and thus appear to share their peculiarity with other stalwart constituencies of the Republicans' coalition, particularly white evangelical Protestants. Yet a close analysis of Mormons' attitudes reveals that they are distinctive, aligning with neither evangelicals nor any other religious group.

We begin by tracing briefly the significant shift in LDS partisan allegiances that occurred during the twentieth century, then turn our attention to the current political identity of American Mormons across a full range of social and political issues. We conclude by discussing the normative consequences of Mormons' perceived partisan homogeneity, suggesting that it masks their political distinctiveness—to the detriment of democratic dialogue within Mormonism, and the politics of the nation writ large.

The Transformation of Mormon Partisanship

To understand the changing partisanship of American Mormons, and the possibility for change in the future, it is helpful to look back in history. The LDS Church has roots in the Eastern and Midwestern United States, but with the exodus from Nauvoo, Illinois, in 1846 and the travel of Mormon pioneers to Utah under Brigham Young beginning in 1847, the church has been headquartered in Utah. Any historical narrative of Mormon political behavior necessarily intersects with the predominance of Mormons in Utah politics, and a brief review of Mormon political behavior in the context of Utah political history is essential to understanding American Mormon political behavior more broadly.

Utah's quest for statehood began shortly after the arrival of the first Mormon pioneers in 1846 but was futile until the church officially shed the practice of polygamy in 1890 and increased conformity to national political norms, including a strong Utah presence for both national political parties.[4] The political opposition to polygamy at the national level was led by the newly formed Republican Party, which paired polygamy and slavery as the "twin relics of barbarism" in its 1856 party platform. In the early 1890s, as Utah prepared for yet another statehood bid, church leaders urged Mormons to "nationalize" their politics by disbanding their local, largely Mormon political party (the "People's Party") and aligning with one of the two major parties.[5] Given the vehemence of Republican opposition to polygamy, many Mormons turned to the Democrats.[6] In the election of 1896, for example, Utahns—like most of the Western states—gave their overwhelming (87 percent) support to the populist Democrat William Jennings Bryan.

One way to illustrate the evolution of Mormon political allegiance over time is to examine Utah voting patterns in presidential elections compared to national trends and see how different or similar Utah is from the rest of the country. Ideally, we would report voting patterns of Mormons and not simply residents of Utah, as not all Utahns are Mormons and not all Mormons live in Utah. However, such data do not exist for times past. We therefore discuss evidence of how Mormons have voted over time by reporting on the presidential vote in Utah—an imperfect proxy, but informative nonetheless.[7] Having been settled by Mormons, Utah's population was and is predominantly LDS. While the precise percentage of Mormons in the state's population has fluctuated modestly over time, during its history the proportion of Utah that is LDS has ranged between about 60 and 70 percent.[8]

We begin by comparing the presidential vote in Utah to the rest of the nation, which reveals when Utah has and has not mirrored national voting trends. More precisely, figure 9.1 presents the absolute value of the difference between the Utah and the national popular vote for the winner of each U.S. presidential election between 1896 and 2008. The farther each data point is from zero, the greater the difference between Utah and the national popular vote in that presidential election. The success of Mormon efforts to integrate into the national party system can be seen, at least in part, by the extent to which heavily Mormon Utah mirrored national political trends throughout much of the twentieth century.

The election of 1896 represents Utah's first vote after statehood. William McKinley won the election, taking 51 percent of the national vote. Yet he only won 17.3 percent of the vote in Utah—a substantial difference of

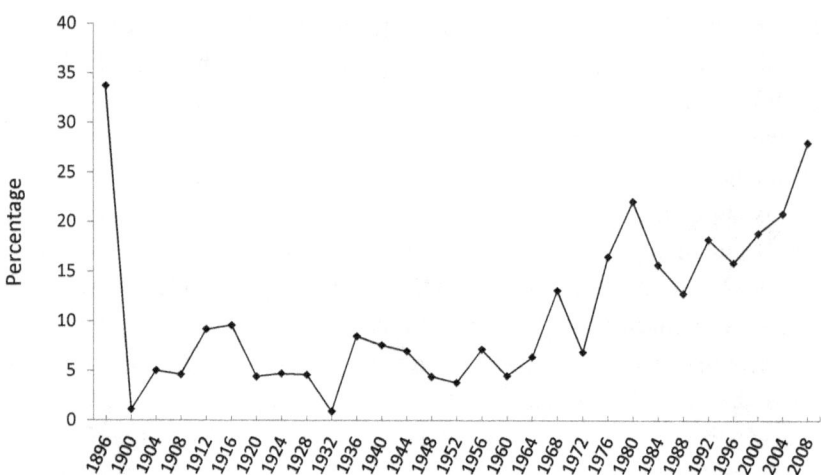

FIGURE 9.1 Utah moves into, then out of, the political mainstream: Percentage voting for the presidential election winner. Absolute value of Utah popular vote minus the national popular vote. *Source*: Faith Matters 2011 Survey.

37.3 percentage points. This dramatic departure from the closely contested national outcome is not so unusual, however, when considering the regional differences in the appeals of the two candidates. The election featured a sharp divide between the rural and agricultural South, Midwest, and West, where voters tended to vote for Bryan, and the comparatively more populous and urban states of the upper Midwest and East Coast, which went for the Republican McKinley. Bryan's economic populism, such as his intense opposition to the gold standard, was especially compelling to cash-strapped farmers and others who lived outside the nation's major urban areas. Religiously, many Mormons were likely wary of Bryan's brand of fundamentalist Protestantism, but even warier of the Republicans' antagonism toward Mormons. However, in spite of the idiosyncratic factors affecting the Mormon vote, Utah's support for the populist Democrat was similar to neighboring states. The entire region went heavily for Bryan.

Political scientists sometimes call the election of 1896 a "critical" or "realigning" election because it ushered in a new era of Republican dominance in national politics.[9] By 1900, McKinley was an incumbent president running on the strength of a significantly revived economy and the success of the Spanish-American War. This dramatically altered national political landscape can also be seen in Utah. With McKinley and Bryan again on the ballot in 1900, the difference between Utah and the national vote diminished to a single percentage point. Though the neighboring states of Nevada, Idaho, and Colorado stayed with Bryan, Utah followed the national trend almost exactly—and this despite the Republicans' recent history of antipathy toward Mormons and polygamy (see chapter 3).

Beginning in 1900, then, Utah stood in the national political mainstream. For essentially the next seven decades, the difference between Utah and the national vote for presidential election winners is relatively small (holding steady in single digits). Not until 1968 did Utah deviate substantially from the national average, when the state's support for Richard Nixon exceeded the national average by 13.1 percentage points. The 1968 divergence is deceiving, however, since it can be explained by the presence of third-party candidate George Wallace on the ballot. A Southerner, Wallace drained conservatives' votes from Nixon in many states, but had little appeal in Utah.[10] Given the heavy Republican presence in Utah today, it is striking to note that during the New Deal era, Utah was a reliably Democratic state in presidential elections. In the landmark election of 1932, Utah mirrored the national election results almost exactly, and in the elections of 1936, 1940, 1944, and 1948, differences between the state and the national partisan outcomes emerge because Utah voted *more* Democratic than the nation as a whole.

Healthy party competition—including significant Democratic success—continued in Utah from the 1950s to the early 1970s, with the state mirroring national trends by voting for the winner of the national election in almost every case. The only exception to national outcomes is the election of 1960, when Utah leaned slightly toward Nixon over Kennedy. Four years later, however, Utah supported the Democrat Lyndon Johnson over Republican challenger Barry Goldwater. Though Johnson's victory margin in Utah was not quite as great as in his landslide national victory, he still took the state by a solid ten percentage points. During this period, Utah's elected officials also included a healthy dose of Democrats, including Democratic control of the state legislature during the 1970s and Democratic governors Calvin Rampton and Scott Matheson throughout the 1960s and 1970s. All of this comports nicely with the data in figure 9.1, which suggests that many more Mormons were supporting Democratic candidates in the 1960s and 1970s than one might expect if simply (and naively) extrapolating backward from the current political climate.

Again we stress that this comparison of Utah to the rest of the nation is meant to be suggestive only, as these election-by-election snapshots do not capture the changing demographics of the state and other political factors. Our point is only that there is evidence consistent with the claim that through much of the twentieth century, Mormons voted much like the rest of the nation. In other words, in this era Mormons' politics—at least as roughly indicated by Utah election returns—were not terribly peculiar.

Further evidence that, at least in the late 1960s, Mormons were not politically peculiar can be found in data collected by Armand Mauss in 1967 and 1968.[11] Mauss conducted surveys of Mormons in two cities, Salt Lake City and San Francisco, in which he asked a variety of questions about their political, social, and religious attitudes. To our knowledge, these were the first large-scale, scientifically valid, and publicly available surveys of Mormon attitudes. While the sample is not necessarily representative of all Mormons everywhere, the results do reflect well the attitudes of LDS Church members in the late 1960s in two urban centers. Since the data are derived from surveys of individuals, they provide a check on our interpretation of the state-level returns. Our confidence in the conclusions we have drawn from the state-level results is strengthened, as they are consistent with Mauss's conclusions.

As with the aggregate Utah voting data, the story that emerges is not one of overwhelming conservatism. Indeed, Mauss contends that whatever the common stereotypes might have been, the best descriptors of Mormon attitudes at the end of the 1960s were "moderate" and "mainstream."[12] Only between 18 and 21 percent of Mormons in the sample described themselves as "conservative Republicans."[13] The modal category was "moderate Republicans" (39 percent in Salt Lake and 34 percent in San Francisco), though Mauss notes that levels of attachment to the Republican Party among Mormons were probably not higher than in the West generally.[14] In addition, a significant percentage of Mormons aligned with the Democrats. In Salt Lake City, for example, more than 20 percent identified as liberal or moderate Democrats—easily balancing those who said they were conservative Republicans. When independents are added, nearly 40 percent of Mormons in the Salt Lake sample identified as something other than Republican.

With respect to issues, too, Mauss finds that Mormons in the late 1960s were far more moderate than conservative. He constructed an index of domestic policy conservatism, made up of questions about labor unions, medical care for the aged, internal communism, the threat of socialism, and the House Un-American Activities Committee (popularly, HUAC). He reports that only one-quarter of Salt Lake City Mormons and only 10 percent of San Francisco Mormons scored as highly conservative on this issue scale.[15] In matters of foreign policy, a scale made up of questions about the United Nations, China, and Vietnam, Mormons in the sample were even less conservative, with only 6 percent of Salt Lake City Mormons and 2 percent of San Francisco Mormons rating as highly conservative on the scale. As Mauss interpreted the foreign policy data, Mormons could best be described as "doves," not "hawks." As late as 1968, then, it appears that healthy percentages of Mormons could be found in either party, and Mormons adopted generally moderate stands on many of the most salient issues of the day.[16]

The Return of Peculiarity

The era of mainstream moderation and the roughly even division of Mormons between the two parties did not last. As figure 9.1 demonstrates, the 1976 presidential election marked the beginning of Utah's unusually, even peculiarly, strong allegiance to the Republican Party. In 1972, Utah voted overwhelmingly for Nixon, but so did the rest of the country. Whereas Nixon captured nearly 68 percent of the vote in Utah, he also took almost 61 percent of the vote nationally. Then in 1976 the country swung back toward the Democrats and elected Jimmy Carter. Utahns, however, did not budge, with more than 62 percent of voters preferring the Republican Gerald Ford. Between 1972 and 1976, the difference between the Utah and national proportions of the vote more than doubles, jumping from under seven to more than sixteen percentage points. As much of the rest of the country recoiled from Watergate and the bitter end of the Nixon administration, Utah remained staunchly in the Republican fold—the pattern that has continued ever since.

Indeed, from 1972 until today, no Democrat has received more than one-third of the votes in Utah in any presidential election. During the Reagan era, Republicans' hold on Utah solidified—and with an intensity that far outstrips national trends. In 1980 and 1984, Reagan received more than 70 percent of Utah's votes. Even Reagan's landslide victory in 1984, when he received nearly 60 percent of the vote nationally, is eclipsed by his showing in Utah, where almost three-quarters of voters cast their ballots for him. In the 1990s, Utahns roundly rejected the Clinton presidency (he never received more than 33 percent of the vote), and the closely contested elections of 2000 and 2004 were anything but competitive in Utah, with

George W. Bush winning handily. In 2008, only 34 percent of Utahns voted for Barack Obama.

The classification of Mormons as among the most solid members of the Republican coalition in recent years is also supported by individual-level data from the Utah Colleges Exit Poll (UCEP) conducted by the Center for the Study of Elections and Democracy at Brigham Young University.[17] As exit polls, they consist of surveys administered to voters as they leave their polling place. The UCEP began in 1982 so it is not easy to pinpoint precisely when the Republican shift occurred, but by the 1984 presidential election 82 percent of Utah Mormons who turned out at the polls voted for Ronald Reagan. Furthermore, 68 percent self-identified as Republicans. Following the time trend in figure 9.1, the support among Mormons for the Republican candidate was 86 percent for George W. Bush in 2004, and 76 percent for John McCain in 2008. In 2010, 77 percent of Utah Mormons identified as a Republican.

The movement of Mormons into the Republican camp includes two important catalysts: first, the evolving positions of the national parties on emerging social issues (such as abortion, feminism, and homosexuality); second, an emphasis by LDS Church leaders on these and other conservative social issues. Political scientists have catalogued the stark changes that have occurred in the American party system since the mid-1960s.[18] Whereas both major political parties in the 1950s and 1960s included conservative, liberal, and moderate wings, today both the Democrats and Republicans are much more sharply defined by ideology. The Republican Party increasingly came to emphasize social issues like opposition to abortion and gay rights, and to use religious symbolism and rhetoric, while the Democratic Party simultaneously moved to the left on these issues.[19] Like other socially conservative groups—evangelicals and conservative Catholics especially—Mormons responded to these changes by embracing the Republican Party.

As the two parties reconfigured themselves in the 1970s and 1980s, with Republicans staking out conservative claims and Democrats becoming more liberal on social issues, Mormons gravitated toward the Republican Party. This was in part because the party's platform on prominent social issues mirrored the pronouncements of LDS church leaders. For example, in the 1970s the LDS Church was instrumental in defeating the Equal Rights Amendment,[20] while in the 1990s the church worked in a number of states to oppose same-sex marriage.[21] Mormons are especially responsive to such pronouncements: LDS voting and attitudinal patterns tend to follow close behind when church leaders make clearly unified and public political statements.[22] During the late twentieth century, such official pronouncements and other statements by church leaders about social issues had important partisan consequences not because church leaders were explicitly urging members to join one party over the other, but because when church leaders spoke out, they were doing so in a political world where certain issues were clearly the province of one party.

Mormons' Politics Today

We have briefly sketched the basic storyline of partisan change that occurred during the twentieth century. Members of the Church of Jesus Christ of Latter-day Saints underwent a remarkable series of transformations—starting as an isolated group that functioned well outside the mainstream party system, then adopting that party system nearly wholesale, voting consistently for the national winner (whether Democrat or Republican), and holding moderate political positions on the issues. The last stage of the transformation is a late-twentieth-century movement noticeably to the right, as politically active Mormons became a staunchly reliable element of the Republican base. The changes in Mormon political behavior did not occur in isolation. They were largely responses to the evolution of the parties themselves over time, with the parties moving in directions that made the Republicans a comfortable home for many Mormons.

But where does that leave Mormons today? Are they now indistinguishable in their political attitudes from other members of the Republican conservative coalition, or do they retain vestiges of their distinctive political storyline? How, for example, do they compare to other elements of the present-day Republican base, such as evangelical Protestants?

Prima facie, there are reasons to think that Mormons and evangelical Protestants do not share much political common ground. They differ theologically, sociologically, and even geographically. Yet, as described above, they are similar politically. With the formation of the Republican Party's ecumenical "coalition of the religious," by which religious voters of many different traditions have banded together, Mormons and evangelicals have been partisan allies.[23] Because they are larger numerically, evangelicals get more press as the base of the GOP. Yet Mormons are actually more reliably conservative and Republican.[24] Can Mormons therefore be characterized as "just like evangelicals, but even more so?"

To answer that question, our analysis proceeds by comparing Mormons to evangelical Protestants, as well as members of other major religious traditions in America. In addition to evangelicals, these include mainline Protestants, Catholics, Jews, Black Protestants, and people who have no religious affiliation (the "nones"). These are the seven largest religious traditions in the contemporary United States.[25] The data are taken from the 2011 Faith Matters survey, a nationally representative survey of 2,646 Americans.[26]

We turn first to party identification. As shown in figure 9.2, Mormons are more likely to be Republican than the rest of the population. Sixty-three percent of Mormons identify as Republicans.[27] This compares to 53 percent of evangelicals and 52 percent of mainline Protestants, the two groups with the next highest level of GOP support.

Mormons are also the most likely to favor traditional gender roles. The Faith Matters survey asked respondents their view on the following statement:

> It is much better for everyone involved if the man is the achiever outside the home and the woman takes care of the home and family.

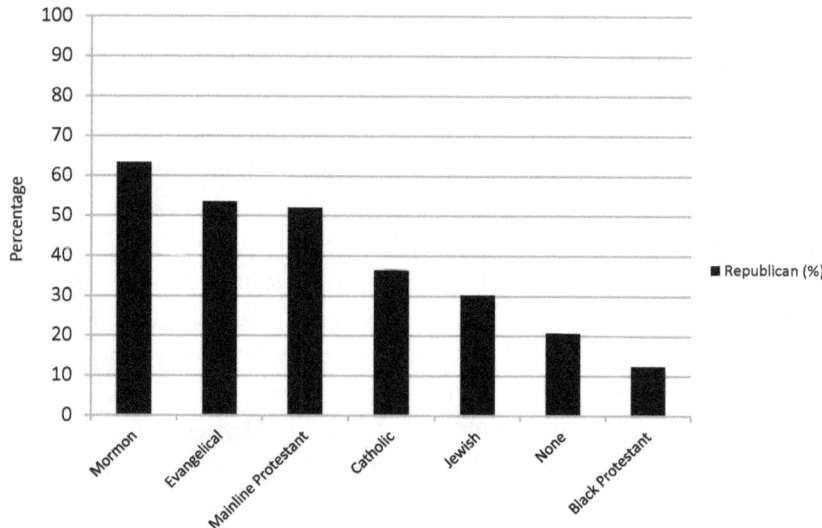

FIGURE 9.2 Mormons and the GOP: A match made in heaven? *Source*: Faith Matters 2011 Survey.

Sixty-eight percent of Mormons agree that women should stay home, a far greater proportion than any other religious group. For example, only 45 percent of evangelicals agree. In the population as a whole, 30 percent believe that it is best for men to be breadwinners and women to be homemakers.

Mormons are just as distinctively conservative on the question of how best to help the poor. When asked which should play a bigger role in helping the poor, 72 percent choose individuals and private charities over government support for the disadvantaged. This is much higher than the three groups that are tied for the next highest level of support for charity over state-provided assistance. Half of all evangelicals, mainline Protestants, and Jews favor private over public assistance. Forty-one percent of the overall population favor private over public help for the poor.

It is not surprising that Mormons have such distinctive views on both gender roles and welfare, as these are issues that pertain to contemporary LDS teachings. The LDS Church idealizes the traditional family structure and has established an extensive church-run welfare program designed to keep church members from relying on the dole (see chapter 5).

While Mormons are clearly conservative, on some issues that conservatism comes with nuance. We see this in their attitudes on the two issues that have defined the "culture wars"—abortion and same-sex marriage. Figure 9.3 displays the results from a question on the Faith Matters survey that asks respondents to choose among four views on abortion:

(1) By law, abortion should never be permitted
(2) The law should permit abortion only in case of rape, incest, or when the woman's life is in danger
(3) The law should permit abortion for reasons other than rape, incest, or danger to the woman's life, but only after the need for the abortion has been clearly established
(4) By law, a woman should always be able to obtain an abortion as a matter of personal choice.

When we combine options 1 and 2—either outright opposition to abortion, or approval in relatively rare circumstances—Mormons look like evangelicals and Catholics. Fifty-eight percent of both Mormons and evangelicals take one of these two positions, while 53 percent of Catholics do as well. However, Mormons are far more likely to approve of abortion in the cases

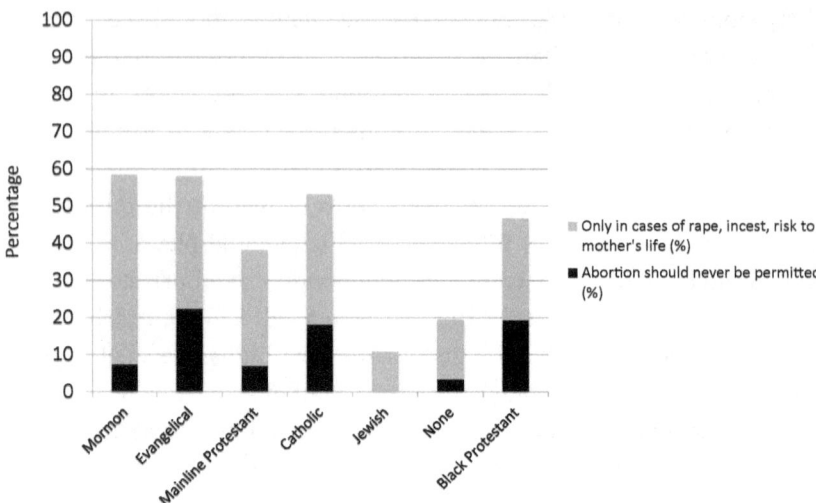

FIGURE 9.3 Mormons are the most likely to approve of abortion only in cases of rape, incest, and risk to the mother's life. *Source*: Faith Matters 2011 Survey.

of rape, incest, or jeopardy to the mother's life (but not in other situations). Fifty-one percent of Mormons select this option, significantly greater than any other religious group (36 percent of evangelicals and 35 percent of Catholics have this view). Here we have a clear case where Mormons' political attitudes are closely aligned with the teachings and policy of their church. The LDS Church generally forbids abortion, but permits exceptions for these three situations.

It is important to note that, in contrast to other religious leaders associated with social conservatism (notably evangelicals and Catholics), LDS officials have not focused much attention on abortion. Tellingly, abortion is rarely mentioned in the public discourse of Mormon leaders. Neither has it been a political priority of the LDS Church. For example, lds.org, the official website of the LDS Church, states that "The Church has not favored or opposed legislative proposals or public demonstrations concerning abortion."[28] Nonetheless, the current LDS policy on abortion has been in place for over thirty years, thus providing most Mormons an opportunity to become aware of it.

The issue of abortion provides an excellent example of our argument that Mormons' opinions differ from evangelicals'. Even though abortion is the central issue on the socially conservative agenda that has defined the contemporary Republican Party, Mormons and evangelicals do not see eye-to-eye on it. Mormons largely adhere to the precepts of their church, staking out a more moderate approach that allows for abortion in some circumstances, a position that distinguishes them from evangelicals.

Mormons exhibit a similar strain of relative moderation on same-sex marriage, the political issue on which Mormons have been most visible in recent years. The Faith Matters survey provided three options for the legal status of same-sex couples.

(1) They should be allowed legally to marry
(2) They should be allowed legally to form civil unions, but not marry
(3) They should not be allowed to obtain legal recognition of their relationships

As displayed in figure 9.4, in keeping with their reputation as opponents of gay marriage, only 13 percent of Mormons believe that people of the same sex should be able to wed. However, the remaining 87 percent are split nearly down the middle between those who oppose all legal recognition for same-sex relationships and those who would permit civil unions. In fact, across all religious groups, Mormons are the most likely to approve of civil unions.[29]

Why do so many Mormons support civil unions for homosexuals? It is not because the LDS Church actively promotes this position on the issue.

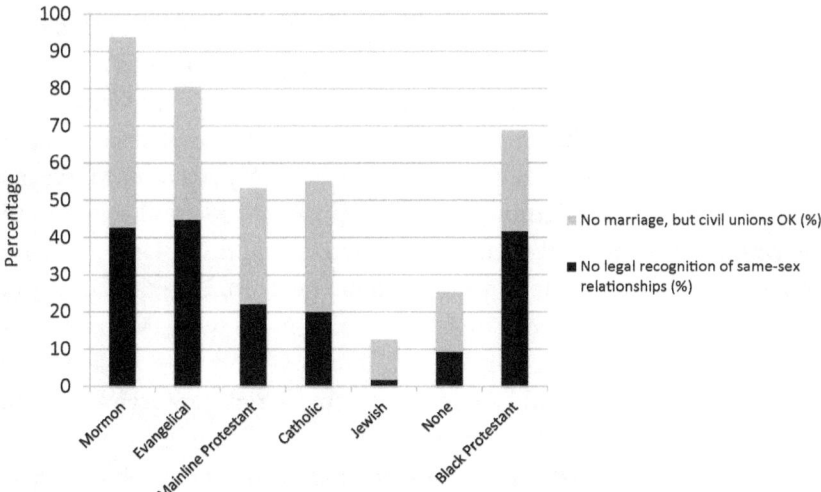

FIGURE 9.4 Mormons oppose gay marriage, but are the most likely to approve of civil unions for same-sex couples. *Source*: Faith Matters 2011 Survey.

Rather, we suspect that it reflects the fact that the church has targeted its opposition specifically to same-sex *marriage*, and not homosexual rights per se. In 2015, the church even publicly announced its general support for laws prohibiting discrimination based on sexual orientation, while balancing its position by simultaneously calling for "religious freedom protections." While this announcement caught many pundits by surprise, it is consistent with the LDS Church's endorsement in 2009 of a municipal statute in Salt Lake City outlawing discrimination against gays and lesbians in housing and employment (albeit one with an exemption for religious organizations).[30]

While abortion and same-sex marriage reflect a nuanced version of conservatism, on at least two other issues Mormons diverge more sharply from conservative orthodoxy. One is the priority they place on civil liberties and privacy over security. When asked, "which do you think is more important: protecting your civil liberties and privacy from being invaded, or protecting your safety and surroundings from terrorism?," 58 percent of Mormons say protecting their civil liberties and privacy. This compares to the virtual three-way tie between evangelicals (40 percent), mainline Protestants (39 percent), and Catholics (38 percent). On this question, Mormons look like two of the most politically liberal groups in the population, Jews (also 58 percent) and "nones" (65 percent). We suspect that this item picks up on a libertarian streak among Mormons, perhaps a vestige of Mormons' historical memory of hostility from the federal and state governments in the nineteenth century.

The final issue on which Mormons stand out is immigration, as they are more accepting of immigrants than most other Americans, particularly in contrast to evangelicals. The Faith Matters survey gave respondents the option of saying that immigration should be increased, decreased, or kept the same as it is. As shown in figure 9.5, 26 percent of Mormons would like to see more immigration. That may not seem like a lot until Mormons are compared with other religious traditions. Only Jews are more likely to favor greater immigration (29 percent). By contrast, only 12 percent of evangelicals favor more immigration. Likewise, Mormons are also on the low end of favoring less immigration—only Jews are less likely to say that America should decrease the number of new arrivals in the country.

We hypothesize that the high proportion of Mormons who serve as missionaries in other countries fosters an empathetic perspective on illegal immigrants. Indeed, the LDS Church has a large missionary pres-

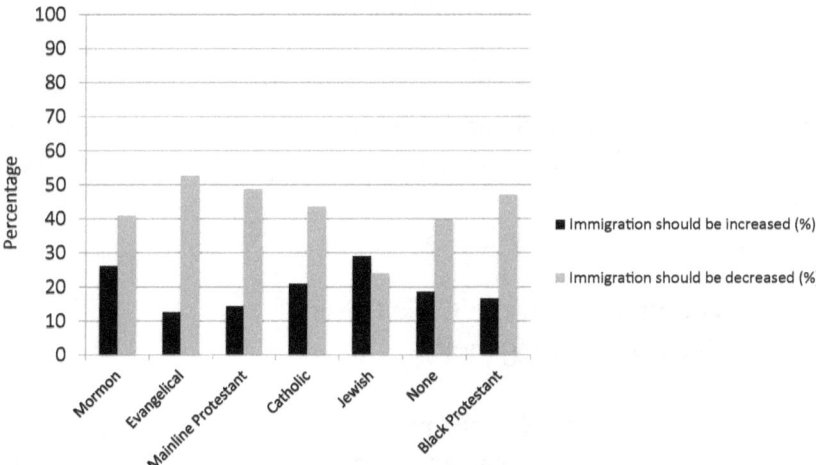

FIGURE 9.5 Compared to most other religious traditions, Mormons favor immigration. *Source*: Faith Matters 2011 Survey.

ence in Latin America, the source of most undocumented workers in the United States. Many Mormons, therefore, have seen firsthand the abject poverty that compels migrants to enter the United States illegally. Furthermore, the church's own policy is to turn a blind eye toward people who are in the United States illegally[31]—the church will baptize them, call them on missions, and even have them serve as church leaders.[32] LDS leaders have consistently been a voice of compassion regarding immigration. A notable example is the message of emeritus church general authority Elder Marlin Jensen, who has urged lawmakers to consider illegal immigrants as "God's children" and to "slow down, step back and carefully study and assess the implications and human costs involved" in legislation designed to curb illegal immigration.[33] More recently, the church has taken a vocal stand for moderate immigration reforms that balance a law-and-order mentality against compassion for immigrants and a strong desire for policies that keep families together. These stances moved public opinion among conservative Utah Mormons in a more moderate direction.[34]

Taken together, these data warn against the overly simple conflation of Mormons with other segments of the Republican Religious Right. For example, Mormons and evangelicals may appear politically simpatico, but it would be wrong to infer that these two groups are always in sync. They differ, and do so in ways that go beyond a single continuum of being more or less conservative. Rather than more or less, they are better described as simply being conservative in different ways. Both groups are heavily Republican and predominantly conservative, but have different opinions on a number of issues that define both today's Republican Party and the conservative movement. Some differences are more pronounced than others, but as a whole they add up to the conclusion that Mormons are a politically peculiar people.

Peculiarity and the Civic Costs of Partisan Homogeneity

Mormons are politically peculiar in two respects. First, when compared to the general population, they are far more Republican and conservative—although this has not always been the case. For most of the twentieth century, Mormons were squarely in the national mainstream of American politics. Second, even within the Republican coalition, they remain peculiar. On many issues they are distinct from evangelical Protestants, the group that—on the surface at least—would appear to be their culturally conservative compatriots.

The differences between Mormons and evangelicals remind us that religious beliefs and experiences matter, and can shape political attitudes in distinctive ways. To look only at the commonality in the party identification of evangelicals and Mormons obscures their policy differences. Nowhere is this clearer than on abortion, which Mormons are far more likely to permit in the cases of rape, incest, and when the mother's health is in jeopardy. More generally, observers of religion and politics should remember that Mormons' attitudes are not identical to other members of the Republicans' culturally conservative coalition, and should not be treated as though they are. Candidates for office should also remember this lesson. Whether Mormons are seeking evangelical support or evangelicals are seeking Mormon support, politicians would be wise to take note of how these two groups differ.

Our concern here, however, lies less in what our results might suggest for politicians, and more in their implications for rank-and-file Mormons. Should Mormons be concerned that, as a group, they overwhelmingly favor one party over another? The current situation is an echo of the past, as the Mormons have a history of political uniformity—although in the past, that uniformity was not necessarily tied to one national party. In the 1830s, one impetus for mob violence against Mormons in Missouri was their bloc voting.[35] Further, as we describe above, Mormons' political homogeneity in the late 1800s was an obstacle to Utah's statehood. To demonstrate that Mormons could align with the politics of the day, LDS leaders explicitly encouraged Mormons to affiliate with one or the other of America's two national parties.[36]

Today, the problem with the appearance of Mormon political uniformity is not the opposition it might engender from foes of the LDS Church. Rather, it is the missed opportunity for Mormons' distinctive voice to be heard in national politics. Mormons are the quintessential example of a group that has been "captured" by a party, and thus taken for granted. When a voting bloc is overwhelmingly identified with one party and seen as having no other place to go, neither party has an incentive to listen to it. In a closely divided electorate, even small voting blocs earn the attention of politicians seeking their support—if they have reason to believe that such attention might sway votes. Unwavering loyalty to one party means that the Mormon electorate is unlikely to garner much attention during political campaigns, even in politically competitive environments where Mormons are heavily concentrated.

Mormon political homogeneity not only keeps Mormons from exerting much influence on national politics, it also has implications within the Mormon community. We are especially concerned about ways in which partisan uniformity leads to lost opportunities for healthy civic and political dialogue among church members. Within Mormonism, it is likely that distinctive voices—particularly those expressing opinions contrary to Republican orthodoxy—will feel uncomfortable in expressing those views or even when emboldened will find it difficult to be heard by their fellow Mormons. The political discourse of Mormons themselves is thus impoverished. When partisan attachments are overwhelmingly homogeneous and social norms within congregations clearly favor one party, church members lose opportunities to benefit from constructive political debate and disagreement—a basic element of healthy deliberation and robust democratic citizenship. We stress that ours is not a partisan statement; we would be equally concerned if Mormons so overwhelmingly identified as Democrats.

There are hints that LDS leaders are again concerned about Mormons' partisan near-uniformity, and seek to increase political diversity among the rank-and-file membership. During Mitt Romney's presidential campaigns, the church took pains to reiterate its political neutrality. At church-owned Brigham Young University, a campus where protest is rare and carefully controlled by university officials,[37] in 2007 the university permitted students to protest Vice President Dick Cheney when he spoke at the university's graduation ceremony.[38] Harry Reid, Senate majority leader and a Mormon, has also spoken at BYU and pointedly declared that "I am a Democrat because I am a Mormon, not in spite of it."[39] The aforementioned Marlin K. Jensen—a church leader and a self-identified Democrat—has also spoken at some length about the need for greater political diversity within the LDS Church. In a far-reaching interview with the *Salt Lake Tribune*, he discussed his own Democratic Party affiliation and lamented the nearly monolithic partisan preference of American Mormons. "I think we regret more than anything that there would become a church party and a non-church party. That would be the last thing we would want to have happen."[40]

While meaningful, these actions by the LDS Church hardly mean that Mormons are poised to become like Catholics, and split their vote between the parties.[41] Once formed, partisan attachments can be difficult to change, especially when reinforced by an overwhelming majority of coreligionists. Elder Jensen spoke his cautionary words well over a decade ago and, in the ensuing years, little appears to have changed. Mormons are as Republican now as then—probably even more so. And, Harry Reid notwithstanding, it seems unlikely that there will be any significant increase in partisan diversity among Mormons anytime soon. If some movement away from the Republicans is to be found, it is likely to occur when the statements of church leaders about political and social issues emphasize positions that are not clearly owned by the Republican Party. Of the issues we have reviewed here, immigration comes closest to that description, though LDS leaders have not emphasized the issue in sermons or church publications.

Without an increase in partisan diversity, we see little prospect for Mormons' political peculiarity to garner much attention. As long as Mormons are thought to be overwhelmingly supportive of one party over another, we fear that the distinctiveness of their voices on particular issues will not be heard—either inside Mormonism or out.

NOTES

1. John C. Green, *The Faith Factor: How Religion Influences American Elections* (Westport, CT: Greenwood, 2007); Geoffrey Layman, *The Great Divide: Religious and Cultural Conflict in American Party Politics* (New York: Columbia University Press, 2001).

2. Many readers will recognize our description of Mormons as a "peculiar people" which is taken from the Bible. "But ye are a chosen generation, a royal priesthood, an holy nation, a peculiar people" (1 Peter 2:9). See also Deuteronomy 7:6 and 14:2. Mormons often use this term to describe themselves. For more on the use of this expression, and many of the other themes covered in this chapter, see David E Campbell, John C. Green, and J. Quin Monson, *Seeking the Promised Land: Mormons and American Politics* (Cambridge: Cambridge University Press, 2014).

3. For a discussion of Mormon assimilation more generally over roughly the same period, see Armand L. Mauss, *The Angel and the Beehive: The Mormon Struggle with Assimilation* (Urbana: University of Illinois Press, 1994). For a thorough treatment of the political context in which Mormonism was situated during the early years of the twentieth century, see Kathleen Flake, *The Politics of American Religious Identity: The Seating of Senator Reed Smoot, Mormon Apostle* (Chapel Hill: University of North Carolina Press, 2004).

4. Thomas G. Alexander, *Mormonism in Transition: A History of the Latter-day Saints, 1890–1930* (Urbana: University of Illinois Press, 1986), ch. 2; Edward Leo Lyman, *Political Deliverance: The Mormon Quest for Utah Statehood* (Urbana: University of Illinois Press, 1986), ch. 6.

5. Roger M. Barrus, "Political History," in *Encyclopedia of Mormonism*, ed. Daniel H. Ludlow (New York: Macmillan, 1992); Alexander, *Mormonism in Transition*; Lyman, *Political Deliverance*.

6. Sarah Barringer Gordon, *The Mormon Question: Polygamy and Constitutional Conflict in Nineteenth-Century America* (Chapel Hill: University of North Carolina Press, 2002).

7. In future work we will pursue more sophisticated analysis, using the appropriate statistical methodology to overcome the "ecological fallacy"—the impossibility of inferring individual-level behavior from aggregate-level data. For an example of how this can be done, see David E. Campbell and J. Quin Monson, "Following the Leader? Mormon Voting on Ballot Propositions," *Journal for the Scientific Study of Religion* 42.4 (December 1, 2003): 605–619.

8. Richard Douglas Poll et al., eds., *Utah's History* (1978; rpt., Logan: Utah State University Press, 1989), 662–63.

9. Walter Dean Burnham, *Critical Elections and the Mainsprings of American Politics* (New York: Norton, 1970); Walter Dean Burnham, "Periodization Schemes and 'Party Systems': The 'System of 1896' as a Case in Point," *Social Science History* 10.3 (October 1, 1986): 263–314, doi:10.2307/1171128; V. O. Key, "A Theory of Critical Elections," *The Journal of Politics* 17.1 (February 1, 1955): 3–18; James L. Sundquist, *Dynamics of the Party System: Alignment and Realignment of Political Parties in the United States* (Washington, D.C.: Brookings Institution Press, 1983).

10. Nationally, Wallace received 13.4 percent of the vote, compared to the Democrat Hubert Humphrey's 43.4 percent. But Wallace's support was concentrated in the South, so it is not surprising that in Utah he received only 6.4 percent of the vote, whereas the Republican Nixon received a comparatively hefty 56.5 percent.

11. Armand L. Mauss, "Moderation in All Things: Political and Social Outlooks of Modern Urban Mormons," *Dialogue: A Journal of Mormon Thought* 7.1 (1972): 57–69.

12. Mauss, "Moderation in All Things," 57.

13. Unfortunately, the response categories Mauss uses, while based on similar large-scale surveys conducted at the time, are somewhat different from the partisan response categories usually employed by political scientists today. For that reason, comparisons with levels of partisanship we will report later are rough and incomplete.

14. These results are thus limited to practicing Mormons only—800 from Salt Lake City and 179 from San Francisco.

15. These findings are drawn directly from Mauss's 1972 article. They include all Mormons in the sample and are not limited to those who say they are still affiliated with the church. In the Salt Lake City sample, that is the overwhelming majority of the respondents (90 percent), while in San Francisco, it is a lower percentage (62 percent).

16. It is worth restating that our aggregate-level Utah voting pattern analysis does not isolate Utah Mormons and is suggestive but not definitive of Mormon voting patterns. It is possible that a trend toward Republican voting could have already begun during the 1960s or earlier, but it could be masked in the aggregate data analysis by a counter trend among non-Mormons voting increasingly for Democrats.

17. These data are publicly available at http://exitpolldata.byu.edu.

18. Edward G. Carmines and James A. Stimson, *Issue Evolution: Race and the Transformation of American Politics* (Princeton, NJ: Princeton University Press, 1990); Nolan McCarty, Keith T. Poole, and Howard Rosenthal, *Polarized America: The Dance of Ideology and Unequal Riches* (Cambridge: MIT Press, 2008); Morris P. Fiorina, Samuel J. Abrams, and Jeremy Pope, *Culture War?: The Myth of a Polarized America* (New York: Longman, 2011); Christina Wolbrecht, *The Politics of Women's Rights: Parties, Positions, and Change* (Princeton, NJ: Princeton University Press, 2000).

19. Layman, *The Great Divide*; David C. Leege et al., *The Politics of Cultural Differences: Social Change and Voter Mobilization Strategies in the Post–New Deal Period* (Princeton, NJ: Princeton University Press, 2002).

20. Jane J. Mansbridge, *Why We Lost the ERA* (Chicago, IL: University of Chicago Press, 1986); D. Michael Quinn, *The Mormon Hierarchy: Extensions of Power* (Salt Lake City, UT: Signature Books, 1997).

21. David E. Campbell and J. Quin Monson, "Dry Kindling: A Political Profile of American Mormons," in *From Pews to Polling Places: Faith and Politics in the American Religious Mosaic* (Washington, D.C.: Georgetown University Press, 2007), 105–129.

22. Campbell and Monson, "Following the Leader?"

23. Robert D. Putnam and David E. Campbell, *American Grace: How Religion Divides and Unites Us* (New York: Simon and Schuster, 2010).

24. Frank Newport, *Mormons Most Conservative Major Religious Group in U.S.* (Gallup, Inc., January 11, 2010), www.gallup.com/poll/125021/mormons-conservative-major-religious-group.aspx; Pew Forum on Religion and Public Life, *Mormons in America: Certain of Their Beliefs, Uncertain of Their Place in Society*, 2012, www.pewforum.org/mormons-in-america/.

25. For further explanation of and justification for this method of classifying American religions, see Brian Steensland et al., "The Measure of American Religion: Toward Improving the State of the Art," *Social Forces* 79.1 (2000): 291–318. For details on how specific denominations are coded, see Putnam and Campbell, *American Grace*.

26. The 2011 Faith Matters survey is a follow-up to the 2006 Faith Matters survey. Of the 2,646 respondents, 1,685 were interviewed in both 2006 and 2011, while the remainder were interviewed in 2011 only. The sample has been weighted to reflect the national population. For more details, see the epilogue to the paperback edition of Putnam and Campbell, *American Grace*.

There are forty-nine Mormons, 809 evangelical Protestants, 342 mainline Protestants, 574 Catholics, forty-five Jews, 230 Black Protestants, and 490 "nones" in the sample. While the sample size for Mormons in the 2011 survey is relatively small, in part due to panel attrition, we chose to use the 2011 Faith Matters data because it allows us to discuss a broader range of issues. The results reported here for abortion, gay marriage, and party identification are all very consistent with larger Mormon samples in the 2006, 2008, and 2010 Cooperative Congressional Election Study surveys (results available from the authors) as well as the Pew Forum on Religion and Public Life data. There are also eighty-nine respondents who fall into the catch-all category of "other non-Christian," which includes everything from Muslims to Buddhists to Sikhs. Since its constituent religious groups differ substantially, and no single group is large enough for valid analysis, we have omitted the groups in this category from the discussion.

27. These numbers include people who initially say that they are independent but lean toward the Republican Party.

28. This is in contrast with the heavy involvement of the church to defeat the Equal Rights Amendment and repeated efforts to affect the debate over gay marriage at both the national and state level. For more details, see Mansbridge, *Why We Lost the ERA*; Quinn, *The Mormon Hierarchy*; Campbell and Monson, "Dry Kindling: A Political Profile of American Mormons."

29. Notably, these percentages are consistent with 2010 data among Utah Mormons that demonstrate a large shift away from no legal recognition toward favoring civil unions. More recent data suggest this trend is continuing, see Kelly D. Patterson, *Public Opinion on Gay Marriage in Utah*, 2012; http://utahdatapoints.com/2012/07/public-opinion-on-gay-marriage-in-utah/.

30. Laurie Goodstein, "Mormons Seek Golden Mean Between Gay Rights and Religious Beliefs," *New York Times*, January 27, 2015, www.nytimes.com/2015/01/28/us/mormons-seek-golden-mean-between-gay-rights-and-religious-beliefs.html?_r=0; Matt Canham, Derek P. Jensen, and Rosemary Winters, "Salt

Lake City Adopts Pro-gay Statutes—with LDS Church Support," *Salt Lake Tribune*, November 10, 2009, http://archive.sltrib.com/article.php?id=13758070&itype=NGPSID.

31. Peggy Fletcher Stack, "LDS Church Takes Public Stance on Immigration Legislation," *Salt Lake Tribune*, March 17, 2011, www.sltrib.com/sltrib/home/51439173-76/bills-burton-church-immigration.html.csp.

32. The online newsroom of the LDS Church's website says the following about its policy toward undocumented church members: "The First Presidency has for many years taught that undocumented status should not by itself prevent an otherwise worthy Church member from entering the temple or being ordained to the priesthood. Bishops are in the best position to make appropriate judgments as to Church privileges. Meanwhile, Church members should avoid making judgments about fellow members in their congregations." Available at: www.mormonnewsroom.org/article/avoiding-being-judgmental-immigration (accessed October 23, 2012).

33. Matthew LaPlante, "LDS Church Asks Lawmakers to Weigh Morality, Ethics in Immigration Reform," *Salt Lake Tribune*, February 14, 2008.

34. J. Quin Monson and Jordan Stauss, *Did the Utah Compact Actually Change Attitudes About Immigration?* (Utahdatapoints.com, April 20, 2011), http://utahdatapoints.com/2011/04/did-the-utah-compact-actually-change-attitudes-about-immigration/.

35. Leonard J. Arrington and Davis Bitton, *The Mormon Experience: A History of the Latter-day Saints* (Urbana: University of Illinois Press, 1992).

36. Barrus, "Political History"; Lyman, *Political Deliverance*.

37. Bryan Waterman and Brian Kagel, *The Lord's University: Freedom and Authority at BYU* (Salt Lake City, UT: Signature Books, 1998).

38. Martin Stolz, "Rare Protests at Brigham Young Over Planned Cheney Appearance," *New York Times*, April 10, 2007.

39. Tad Walch, "Reid Gets Warm Reaction at BYU," *Deseret Morning News*, October 10, 2007.

40. Marlin K. Jensen, "To Have a Robust, Multi-Party System: Transcript of *Salt Lake Tribune* Interview with Elder Marlin K. Jensen," *Sunstone* (August 1998).

41. J. Matthew Wilson, "The Changing Catholic Voter: Comparing Responses to John F. Kennedy in 1960 and John Kerry in 2004," in *A Matter of Faith: Religion in the 2004 Presidential Election* (Washington, D.C.: Brookings Institution Press, 2007), 163-79.

10 "Twice-told Tale"

Telling Two Histories of Mormon-Black Relations During the 2012 Presidential Election

Max Perry Mueller

Setting the Stage

In 2012, on the long road to the Republican nomination for president of the United States, Mitt Romney's much-debated "Mormon Problem"—perhaps his main impediment to the nomination in 2008—became less of a problem among the conservative, white evangelicals on whose support he built his presidential hopes. In large measure, this was due to the Romney campaign's very successful rebranding of their candidate.

For most of the campaign, Romney and his strategists assiduously—some would say doggedly—sidestepped almost all connections between Romney and his faith. From Romney and his surrogates, there was scant mention of the candidate's many years as leader of his Mormon community in Belmont, Massachusetts. For that matter, there was little talk of Romney's one term as Massachusetts' governor. Instead, the Romney campaign presented their candidate as a successful businessman: a turn-around specialist who made millions for himself and for his partners at Bain Capital, and saved the 2002 Salt Lake City Winter Olympics from budget overruns and scandal. In the fall of 2011, when the *Washington Post* and the Pew Research Center surveyed Americans about the one word that came to mind when they thought of Mitt Romney, by far the most popular response was "Mormon." A year later in 2012, the most popular responses were "honest," "businessman," and "rich." "Mormon" fell out of the top ten.[1]

It was only at the Republican National Convention in Tampa that Romney appeared to participate in the "Mormon Moment"—a moment that he, in large measure, created. With the nomination officially in hand, Romney invited some of his fellow Mormons from Belmont to take the convention stage and talk about Mitt the "pastor" who, as Romney's longtime friend Grant Bennett described, "spent thousands of hours over many years serving [his] church." Bennett said Romney's religious stewardship of the Mormons of Belmont took the form of leadership by example: "[Mitt] taught [his congregation] faith in God, personal integrity, self-reliance and service to our fellow men."[2]

In 2012, many Americans grew more comfortable with the idea of a Mormon president, perhaps because Romney worked hard to show that while Mormon theology might differ from America's mainstream Christianities, the "moral values" of Romney's faith (pro-life, anti–gay marriage, pro-personal responsibility) were in sync with those held by many conservative American evangelicals and Catholics. Yet one issue of Mormonism—or perhaps more fairly, of Mormonism's past—remained a sticking point to a fuller integration of the Church of Jesus Christ of Latter-day Saints into the American religious mainstream: Mormonism's "black problem."

For over 140 years, the LDS Church forbade blacks from full church membership. For most of this time, leading church officials justified the exclusion by asserting that blacks were, by dint of their African lineage, spiritually inferior to all other races, especially white Europeans. In the nineteenth century, Brigham Young (1801–1877) shared a belief, common to many American religious communities, especially defenders of African chattel slavery, that blacks were the permanently cursed descendants of the antiheroes Cain and Ham. "The seed of Ham, which is the seed of Cain descending through Ham, will, according to the curse put upon him, serve his brethren," Young taught in 1855, three years after Utah became the first western American territory to legalize slavery.[3]

In the twentieth century, LDS leaders like Church Historian and President Joseph Fielding Smith (1876–1972) made famous a theology unique to Mormonism: that blacks' spiritual iniquity extended back even before biblical times. In a premortal existence, Smith taught, God's spirit children had proven their aptitude, and based on their merits and talents, God selected the "choice spirits to come through the better grades of nations." Smith believed that the choicest spirits who came into mortal existence in white bodies should be kept "segregate[ed] from other races," especially the least favored spirits who were born into black bodies.[4] These racial theologies meant that, for most of the LDS Church's history, black men could not hold the Mormon priesthood, the essential sacred authority conferred upon almost every Mormon male. And black couples could not participate in marriage "sealings" in Mormon temples, a ritual that Mormons believe unites families together for eternity.[5]

On June 9, 1978, then-LDS Church president Spencer W. Kimball (1895–1985) announced that, after years of praying for such a change, members of the First Presidency and the Quorum of the Twelve Apostles had received a revelation lifting the restriction on full church membership for people of African descent. "The long promised day has come," wrote Kimball. "Every faithful, worthy man in the Church may receive the holy priesthood with the power to exercise its divine authority, and enjoy with his loved ones every blessing that flows there from, including the blessings of the temple."[6] While black women weren't specifically mentioned, the "priesthood revelation," as it is commonly known, also meant changes for the handful of black women church members. They could now enter the temple for sacred rituals, serve as missionaries for the church, and serve in leadership positions in the women's auxiliary group, the Relief Society.

Vetting Mitt, Vetting Mormonism's "Black Problem"

For many Mormons alive when the priesthood revelation was announced, June 9, 1978, became a moment frozen in time. A generation of LDS Church members can recall precisely where they were when they heard the news that the church had changed its policy toward people of African descent. For example, during a 2007 appearance on *Meet the Press*, Mitt Romney tearfully recounted his reaction to the news of the revelation. "I was driving home ... from law school. ... I heard it on the radio and pulled over and literally wept."

Yet while the 1978 revelation was a watershed moment in Mormon history—only comparable to the 1890 "Manifesto" officially ending the Mormon practice of plural marriage—why has the debate about Mormonism and race continued? The main reason for this is the LDS Church hierarchy's reluctance to fully repudiate the positions of its past leaders. Instead, today's Mormon apostles have followed the tack established by President Kimball, to "let [the revelation] stand on its own."[7] In February 2012, a *Washington Post* article quoted a popular Brigham Young University (BYU) professor, Randy Bott, defending the priesthood ban as the will of God.[8] Yet the LDS Church's response was to explain away racist declarations made by Bott, as well as the church's deceased prophets, as merely personal speculation. Though it is doubtful that LDS Church presidents Brigham Young and Joseph F. Smith saw their statements as less than authoritative, a day after the *Post* story was published, the LDS Church released an official statement declaring that "personal statements [made in the past by church leaders] do not represent Church doctrine."[9] This approach to the voluminous record of Mormon leaders' explicit theological justifications for the priesthood ban follows a well-established strategy: distance the contemporary church from pronouncements of past leaders without explicitly condemning those prophets as actually wrong on the issue of black church membership.

For decades, scholars, pundits, and critics of the LDS Church filled the void created by the church's reticence on the history of the exclusion of blacks from full church membership. This was especially true during the 2012 presidential race when part of the process of America's vetting of Mitt Romney was an unprecedented scrutiny of his religion. In particular, the image of a devout Mormon trying to unseat America's first black president led to questions about Romney's responsibility to address his church's "black problem." At the *Huffington Post,* biblical scholar Obery M. Hendricks insisted that he does not "believe in religious litmus tests of any kind. . . . Yet, I must admit that there is something about Mitt Romney's religion that I find deeply troubling." Most troubling for Hendricks was the "keystone" for the Latter-day Saint movement: the Book of Mormon itself. For Mormons, the often spoken phrase "I believe that the Book of Mormon is true" is part of the litany of truth claims that forms the unofficial LDS confession of faith, the Mormon equivalent to the Islamic Shahada. Beginning his article with a dismissal of religious litmus tests, Hendricks, an African American, ended it with an open letter to Romney, demanding that he "disavow the portions of your holy book that so sorely denigrate the humanity of me, my loved ones and all people of black African descent."[10] According to Hendricks, for Romney to be president of "all Americans," he must disavow some of the Book of Mormon's truth claims. He must, in essence, apostatize.

At the *New York Times,* Lee Seigel proposed what is, at first glance, a counterintuitive argument. Four years after much of the nation celebrated the election of America's first African American president, Seigel posited that Romney's whiteness "is the one quality that has subtly fueled his candidacy thus far and could well put him over the top in the fall."[11] For Seigel, this whiteness is not about actual phenotype. It "telegraphs"; it *signifies* the "cultural alternative to America's first black president. It is a whiteness grounded in a retro vision of the country, one of white picket fences and stay-at-home moms and fathers unashamed of working hard for corporate America."[12]

Seigel locates the incubator of Romney's whiteness in the LDS Church, which Seigel asserts is the strongest "bastion of pre-civil-right-America whiteness." In Seigel's view, white evangelicals can call Mormonism a cult. They can also thank God that the LDS Church denied full black membership until 1978, safeguarding "white American culture" so that it can be restored—to use LDS theological parlance—in November 2012, in the latter days of white American exceptionalism.[13]

I contributed to the "vetting" of Mormonism and race. In the *New Republic,* I tried to situate the history of Mormon racial exclusion as a conflict between the two major impulses of Mormon identity: a particularistic doctrine that favors certain ethnic groups over others, and a universalizing call to teach the gospel to everyone everywhere. I hoped to show that the modern church has emphasized Mormon universalism over racial particularity. For almost twenty-five years after the announcement that the church would end its ban on the priesthood, church leaders in Salt Lake did not repudiate the troubling statements of their predecessors, despite calls from Mormons and non-Mormons to do so. This silence from the top meant that some black Mormons continued to be the targets of racial slurs and epithets, in ward meetinghouses and even in Mormon temples.[14]

In December 2013, the LDS Church began the process of filling this void left by the current leaders' reluctance to distance themselves from the views of their predecessors when it published a new essay titled "Race and the Priesthood" on its Gospel Topics website, an official LDS resource for historical and theological issues. The essay was the church's longest history lesson to date on its complex relationship with people of African descent, and included dozens of footnotes citing a generation's worth of scholarship on the subject.[15]

In it, the church pointed out that the ban was established during a time in American history when racism and race-based segregation and oppression were rampant in American culture. In other words, the church acknowledged that the ban was historical and not an eternal "commandment from the Lord," which had been its official policy for much of the twentieth century.[16] Past Mormon leaders, from Brigham Young to Joseph Fielding Smith, were men of their times. And today's LDS Church officially "disavows the theories advanced in the past that black skin is a sign of divine disfavor or curse . . . or that blacks are or people of any other race or ethnicity are inferior in any way to anyone else."[17] The LDS Church hopes that this new Gospel Topics statement will allow Mormons to come to terms with what they understand as the incongruity between their church's missionary mandate to bring the Mormon-specific gospel to, as the Book of Mormon declares, "all nations, kindreds, tongues, and people," and the church's long-held antiblack beliefs and policies. The new statement also serves as a ready-made response when critics inevitably connect "racist" and "Mormon Church" in the same sentence.

Mormonism and Race: A "Twice-Told Tale"

Media criticism—or the church's efforts to respond to it—is not the central discipline that informs my essay. Instead, I wish to engage in the narration of history—or, more precisely, the narration of *histories*, especially more complicated, multivalent histories about the black Mormon past than those presented in the 2012 presidential election cycle.

The history of the LDS Church's practice of and politicking for racial exclusion has always been *well known*—or at least, to borrow self-consciously from the history of African American slave narratives, this history is an "oft-told tale."[18] But it is a tale rarely told well or accurately. There are at least two histories of the LDS Church and its relationship with African Americans—even two pre-1978 histories. One is of racial exclusion. The other history—almost never told—is one of Mormon empathy, even kinship, with African Americans (a kinship that was, in some instances, mutually expressed), created out of a shared past of persecution by "white" or "gentile" America. This kinship included the shared experience of a failure of the American constitutional system to protect basic civil liberties.[19] The second history is not a rebuttal of the first. Instead, it is a parallel history that emerges from a different set of assumptions about Mormons and their church. This one oft-told tale becomes "twice-told."[20]

The rest of this chapter narrates both of these histories by focusing on four aspects of the history of Mormon-black relations: the content of the Book of Mormon; Joseph Smith and abolition; nineteenth-century slavery in Utah territory; and the civil rights era.[21] Each of the four aspects of the history of Mormon racial exclusion will be followed by a telling of the same or similar aspect from the perspective of the history of Mormon racial inclusion, or at least empathy. These histories, I believe, are needed to better contextualize the "Mormon Moment" created, in large part, by the 2012 presidential race. I also hope to show that the 2012 contest between Mitt Romney and Barack Obama was not simply a "Mormon Moment"; it was also a "Black Moment" in American political and religious history.

The Book of Mormon: White Supremacy and Universal Gospel

Obery Hendricks is correct that any discussion of Mormonism and African Americans must begin with the Book of Mormon itself. But Hendricks's version of racialism in the Book of Mormon unjustly flattens this text, this American scripture, to one single note of white supremacy. The Book of Mormon is in fact, as Jared Farmer has described it, "complicated, multivoiced, and prophetic."[22]

The Book of Mormon is the story of one family of ancient Israelites, exiled in the New World, which splits into two rival and racialized factions. The fair-skinned "Nephites," whose historians and prophets keep the records that would become the Book of Mormon, portray their degenerate cousins, the "Lamanites," as wicked and unrighteous, constantly at war with the God-fearing (though fallible) Nephites. Within the first generations of these ancient Israelites' arrival in America, the Lamanites' degeneracy is so profound that God intervenes and curses them with dark skin. As the Jerusalem-born Nephi declares, "For behold, they [Lamanites] had hardened their hearts against him, that they had become like unto a flint." God hopes that such a demarcation will prevent confusion—and mating—between those who are his righteous followers and those of inequity and spiritual unworthiness. Nephi continues, "As they [the Nephites] were white, and exceedingly fair and delightsome, that they might not be enticing unto my people the Lord God did cause a skin of blackness to come upon them [the Lamanites]" (2 Nephi 5:21).

It is important to note that the Book of Mormon's pre-Columbian American history contains neither "black" Africans nor "white" Europeans. In the end of the Book of Mormon's narrative, the white-skinned Nephites are slaughtered by the dark-skinned Lamanites who, the Book of Mormon claims, become the Native Americans, "a dark, and loathsome, and a filthy people" (1 Nephi 12:23) who would be scattered to the four corners of America and spend the next millennium living as savage heathens, constantly at war with each other.[23] Yet because Americans have, since at least the founding of the Republic, understood race as a black/white binary, readers of the Book of Mormon have often understood the Nephites to signify white Europeans, while Lamanites serve as stand-ins for dark-skinned people of African descent.[24]

In the Book of Mormon, whiteness is the mark of purity, while darkness is the mark of impiety and unworthiness. This view, that whiteness signifies both civilization and chosenness, influenced the way early Mormons viewed dark-skinned people. Take, for example, the May 1844 "patriarchal blessing" (a sort of spiritual roadmap Mormons receive from church patriarchs) that the early black Mormon convert, Jane Manning James, received from Joseph Smith Jr.'s brother, Hyrum Smith, only a month before the Smith brothers' deaths. According to Hyrum Smith, because James was an African American, she was a descendent of the cursed lineage of "Cainnan [sic] son of Ham." She was not of the royal Israelite lineages of Ephraim, Manasseh, or Jacob, the supposed progenitors of many of the early white latter-day Saints destined to lead the millennial kingdom that the Saints were then attempting to create in Nauvoo, Illinois. In the blessing, Hyrum explained to James that this curse, this "mark upon ... [your] forehead" that God himself placed, only God can remove "and stamp upon you his own linage [sic]." This change of lineage—one that would allow James to be considered a full member of the Mormon sacred community—could only occur "if," Hyrum wrote, James and her kin remained faithful to the gospel, "generation to generation."[25]

Of course, the Book of Mormon also influenced how Mormons saw Native Americans. Particularly in the Utah period, which began with the first wave of Mormons arriving in the Great Salt Lake Basin in 1847, Mormons expended great energies to proselytize and "civilize" Native Americans, including through the marriages of white Mormon men to Native American women (as plural wives). Mormons believed that, once converted to Mormonism and Anglo-American economic conceptions of landownership and agriculturally based permanent settlements, these fallen but soon-to-be-redeemed people would cease to be nomadic, savage, and fratricidal "Indians." They would rediscover their true ontology as "Lamanites" and "many generations shall not pass away among them, save they shall be a white and a delightsome people" (2 Nephi 30:6).[26]

In the twenty-first century, reading that the Book of Mormon claims that "whiteness" is close to "godliness" is disturbing. It was also a problem for an aspiring 2012 presidential candidate who accepted Joseph Smith's assertion that the book is "the most correct of any on earth."[27] But the Book of Mormon does not solely teach an ethic of white "chosenness." It also teaches the possible redemption of all humanity, even those accursed with dark skin. Jane Manning James could work to have the mark of Canaan/Ham removed from her forehead. The patriarchal blessing of Elijah Abel, the most well-known priesthood holder of African descent ordained during Joseph Smith's lifetime, foretold that, in the kingdom to come, he would be "equal to thy brethren, and thy soul [will] be white in eternity and thy robes glittering."[28] In an age when Harvard's Louis Agassiz and other professors of polygenism gave the racist assumptions of the disunity of human origins and the rigidity of racial categories the imprimatur of "science," Mormons were professing the "modern" view that racial categories were mutable and constructed.[29]

"Blackness" signified unworthiness. But blackness as such wasn't always fixed to black bodies. In 1838, Willard Richards, who would become a member of Brigham Young's First Presidency (the highest level of the Mormon hierarchy), described a trustworthy "freed slave" he sent from Richmond to his brother in Boston: "A black skin may cover as white a heart as any other skin, and the black hand may be as neat and clean as the white one, and all the trouble arises from want of familiarity with the two."[30] The reverse held true: in March 1845, Mormon apostle John Taylor's newspaper, the *Nauvoo Neighbor*, declared that "the murderers" of Joseph and Hyrum Smith, who disguised their faces with black paint or mud before assassinating the Smith brothers, "no doubt are sorry that they have white skin." The black masks made their "faces correspond with their hearts." On May 10, 1845, in the Mormons' New York City–based newspaper, the *Prophet*, Apostle Parley P. Pratt called the Smith brothers' killers "artificial black men."[31] In other words, black men and women could become white and worthy through their dedication to the gospel and the performance of good deeds, and white men could become black for their perfidy and anti-Mormon violence.

Certainly, the Book of Mormon's conception of whiteness as the standard to which all people should aspire rightfully makes us squirm. The possibility of attaining—though perhaps seldom realized—what I call a "universal whiteness" for dark-skinned Mormons does not free the Book of Mormon from its racist moorings.³² Yet in an age when leading Christian theologians and leading scientists taught that race was immutable and eternal, it is important to note that, for the Book of Mormon and its earliest believers, whiteness represents both a racial category *and* a signifier of worthiness, which could be applied to all who prove themselves dedicated to the Mormon gospel, even those whose bodies were covered in "black skin."³³

Joseph Smith: Slavery-Apologist and Abolitionist Presidential Candidate

In an April 1836 letter to Mormon missionaries in the South, and printed in the LDS publication *The Messenger & Advocate,* Joseph Smith published a defense of African chattel slavery, one that could have been written by any southern antebellum pro-slavery apologist.³⁴ In the article, Smith excoriated northern "abolitionists" as the instigators of discord among southern slaves. Abolitionists' claims that slavery was against God's will, Smith wrote, prompted "the slave to acts of murder, and the master to vigorous discipline [of the belligerent slaves], rendering both miserable, and unprepared to pursue that course which might otherwise lead them both to a better condition." Citing Genesis 8:25–27, Smith argued that slavery was in fact biblical, enacted by "Noah who was perfect in his generation and walked with God." Noah's prophecy that the progeny of Canaan would serve the more worthy offspring of "Shem" has been fulfilled throughout the "history of the world from this notable event down to this day." Smith argued that if slaves and slave masters lived by the code of paternalistic and Christian mutual obligation (Ephesians 6:5–9), slaves obeying their masters, the masters caring for their slaves, both bondsmen and master would fulfill their biblically mandated duties, and create societies of Christian charity, prosperity, and peace.³⁵

Eight years later, Joseph Smith, the one-time pro-slavery apologist, became the (gradual) abolitionist candidate for president of the United States. Frustrated that the federal government refused to provide special protection to his community when Smith believed the states of Ohio,

Missouri, and Illinois had denied the Mormons their constitutionally guaranteed rights to religious freedom, he decided to run for president himself. Smith opened his presidential platform, *General Smith's Views of the Powers and Policy of the Government of the United States* (Nauvoo: John Taylor, 1844), by declaring that the current leaders of the federal government had abandoned the principles upon which the revolutionary generation founded the Republic. Smith asserted that the Mormon persecutions in Ohio, Missouri, and Illinois had shown that, when it comes to the ideals of the Declaration of Independence—that the government shall protect the God-given rights of "life, liberty and the pursuit of happiness" for "all men"—Mormons need not apply. Smith wrote, "Hundreds of our own kindred have been incarcerated," unjustly detained for practicing their faith. But Smith's persecuted religious minority was second on his list of Americans whom the federal government had failed. The men and women most in need of constitutional reparation were "some two or three millions of people [who] are held as slaves for life, because the spirit in them is covered with a darker skin than ours."[36] African slaves and Mormons were made kin by unlawful bondage and unconstitutional persecution.

Utah: Slavery and Freedom

Under the direction of Brigham Young, in February 1852, Utah's first territorial legislature made slavery legal, though the legislature avoided using the term *slavery*:

> Sect. 1 Be it enacted . . . that any person or persons coming into this Territory, and bringing with them servants justly bound to them, arising from special contract or otherwise, said person or persons shall be entitled to such service or labor by the laws of this Territory.[37]

The connection between Mormons, slavery, and Utah was nothing new. At least three slaves made up the vanguard company that arrived in the Salt Lake Basin on July 24, 1847, celebrated today in Utah as "Pioneer Day." These slaves and Mormon pioneers looked on as Brigham Young declared that Utah was "The Place" where the Mormons would build their kingdom in the desert.

From the outside, the legalization of slavery in Utah meant that the "twin relics of barbarism"—as the 1856 Republican presidential platform called slavery and polygamy—were both in practice in Zion. The introduction of slavery was also noticed—and derided—by a former sympathizer of the Mormons, and the most famous black man in America, Frederick Douglass. In the *North Star* and *The Frederick Douglass Papers*, Douglass had previously printed empathetic reports of the Mormons' expulsion from Illinois. In the late 1840s, Douglass's newspapers make scant mention of the Mormons' unorthodox theology, economic communitarian principles, or family structures. Instead, these reports implied kinship with members of the religious sect, who like African Americans, bonded or free, were often deemed enemies to the peace and prosperity of the white American Republic. Mormons too, like African Americans, were frequent victims of "Judge Lynch's" vigilante violence.[38] Only when Brigham Young moved to legalize slavery in Utah did Douglass's papers make mention of polygamy, equating it, as many antipolygamists did, with the institution of chattel slavery itself.[39]

Yet what the Republicans and Douglass failed to realize is that Utah's slavery was not the same as the "Peculiar Institution" practiced in the South. Certainly Young's decision to legalize slavery had a great deal to do with placating the Mormon slave masters already in Utah, and those he hoped would join the Saints from the South, on the right side of the law. However, more than the "Negro problem" it was the "Indian problem" that led to slavery's legalization in Utah. By regulating slavery, LDS leaders hoped to curb the lucrative trade of Indian slaves along the Old Spanish Trail that passed through the territory.[40] Motivated by Mormons' particular theological view of Indians and compassion for these Indian slaves, mostly women and children captured from weaker tribes, Mormons hoped to buy these Indians into freedom, place them in Mormon homes, or marry them to Mormon men—transforming them from "savages" into civilized Lamanites and making them "white and delightsome."[41]

In the territory's slave statutes, Young and his territorial legislature intended to differentiate slavery in Utah from slavery in the South in two important ways. First, under the threat of a three-year prison sentence, a $500 fine, and the forfeiture of claims on their servants, no "master or mistress [shall have] carnal intercourse with his or her servant or servants." Sleeping with one's slaves was both a storied pastime for southern masters and, of course, a means of increasing one's wealth.[42] Second, the legislature made it "a duty of all masters and mistresses to send their servant or servants to school, no less than eighteen months."[43] This compulsory education in Utah stood in sharp contrast with the southern practice of "compulsory ignorance," in which most states in the antebellum South criminalized formal education for slaves out of fear that education might lead to slave revolts.⁴⁴

Young was no Joseph Smith. During the same legislative session, Young made his position on the inherent distinction between worthy whites and accursed blacks unequivocal: "Any man having one drop of the seed of [Cain] in him cannot hold the Priesthood and if no other Prophet ever spoke it before I will say it now in the name of Jesus Christ I know it is true and others know it." Yet he also made it clear that he deplored slavery: "My own feelings are, that no property can or should be recognized as existing in slaves, wither Indian or African. No person can purchase them without their becoming as free, so far as natural rights are concerned, as persons of any other color."⁴⁵

If slavery had to come to Utah (and Young believed it did, ironically as a means of liberating Indians), it would not be the slavery practiced by the so-called "Christian" gentile slave masters. It would be a more benign, even "Mormon" form of the institution. Or so Young hoped.

The Civil Rights Era: Denial and (Re-)Discovery of a Black Mormon Past

During the civil rights era, protests and denouncements from leading civil rights groups rattled the Brethren. During the 1960s, the NAACP accused members of the LDS hierarchy, many of whom also served in the Utah state legislature, of failing to support civil rights legislation. After the state legislature passed employment and housing protections, the church's priesthood ban itself became the target of the NAACP's protests, which included the threat to picket the LDS Church's semiannual general conference.⁴⁶ In December of 1969—the end of a year during which the church faced boycotts against the athletic teams of BYU—the First Presidency issued an official statement, "On [the] Position of Blacks with The Church and Civil Rights." The statement declared that the LDS Church and its prophets had always "taught that Negroes, while spirit children of a common Father, and the progeny of our earthly parents Adam and Eve, were not to receive the priesthood, for reasons which we believe are known to God, but which He has not made fully known to men."⁴⁷

The LDS Church's leadership was famous for its suspicion of the changing views of race in America. Until his death in 1972, Joseph

Fielding Smith—the most famous articulator of the premortal thesis of black accursedness—continued to publicly defend the immutability of the priesthood restriction. Time and again, he insisted that the practice was consistent with "the teachings of Joseph Smith," and established by "the Lord."[48] According to Joseph Fielding Smith, there had never been black priesthood holders, and thus there had never been a "black Mormon past."

During the 1950s and 1960s, the message from the First Presidency was that black Saints were not only ineligible for the priesthood. The danger that their "cursed blood" might soil the purity of those lineages eligible for the priesthood meant that the LDS Church discouraged interracial marriage. And until 1963, many church leaders supported legalized racial segregation. For example, in 1954, Apostle Mark E. Peterson told BYU students that in their fight for civil rights, blacks were not just after economic and political equality: "The Negro seeks absorption with the white race." Mixing with the Negro, especially marrying the Negro, Peterson argued, "is to forfeit a 'nation of priesthood holders.'" Echoing the patriarchal blessings given to Jane Manning James and Elijah Abel in the 1830s and 1840s, Peterson declared that if "[the Negro] is faithful all his days, he can and will enter the celestial kingdom." Yet Peterson's views on the possibility of full racial redemption were even less progressive than his predecessors' from more than a century before. Early church leaders believed that "race" as a mark of segregation would cease to exist in heaven, with the souls of all Saints—even black ones—becoming "white in eternity." Peterson believed that a black Mormon who did enter the highest levels of heaven would "go there as a servant."[49]

However, not all Mormons agreed with the Brethren when it came to this retrograde view of African Americans' place in American politics, society, and even heaven. Mitt Romney proudly boasts of the pro-civil rights stance of his father, George Romney. In 1962, while running for governor of Michigan, George Romney declared his "political independence" from the LDS Church's position on questions regarding civil rights and black Mormon membership. U.S. Secretary of the Interior Stewart Udall also attempted to stake out an alternative Mormon position when it came to Mormonism and African Americans. In a 1967 letter addressed to the church's First Presidency—and forwarded to the *New York Times*—Udall declared: "The restriction now imposed on Negro fellowship is a social and institutional practice having no real sanction in essential Mormon thought. It is clearly contradictory to our most cherished and spiritual moral ideals," which Udall understood as the potential for a universal brotherhood of all humanity. Udall urged LDS Church president David O. McKay to consider lifting the ban, a practice that Udall believed "demeans our faith, damages the minds of our youth, and undermines the integrity of our Christian Ethic."[50]

The Brethren did not take kindly to getting lectured to, and told Udall so directly.[51] But in some ways, they listened to the growing chorus of Mormons from outside the hierarchy who found the perpetuation of the priesthood ban untenable in a civil rights–era America. This was especially the case because the ban was increasingly justified based solely on the church hierarchy's unquestionable authority to set policy for the entire Mormon community. For example, the 1969 official statement from the Church Presidency reduced the priesthood ban to "matters . . . [and a mystery] of faith." It urged the faithful to "await" the Lord, as he alone established the restriction and he alone—through "revelation"—could overturn it. Yet echoing the 1844 presidential platform of the first Mormon to run for president, the LDS First Presidency went further than it had in recent decades on the question of civil rights. In the official 1969 statement, the church narrated a past of persecution shared by both blacks and Mormons: "First may we say that we know something of the sufferings of those who are discriminated against in a denial of their civil rights and Constitutional privileges." Asserting that, from Joseph Smith forward, the church had maintained a "deep and historic concern with man's free agency," the First Presidency declared, "We believe the Negro, as well as those of other races, should have full Constitutional privileges as a member of society."[52]

Let me conclude this brief discussion of the civil rights era by pointing to one of the most influential pressure points applied to the perpetuation of the priesthood ban, and one that came from within the Mormon community. In the 1960s and 1970s, historians, mostly Mormons themselves, created a body of scholarship that proved the ban was a historical accretion, based on no specific revelation or sacred scripture. A medical doctor and an amateur historian, Lester E. Bush, conducted an exhaustive ten-year study of church records and found no evidence that Joseph Smith himself started the ban—one of the main historical arguments the church hierarchy had used to justify the restriction. In fact, Bush and, later, Newell Bringhurst and Henry Wolfinger provided conclusive evidence that, in the first decade of the church's history, a handful of black men—most notably Elijah Abel—had been ordained as priesthood holders and recognized by Joseph Smith as such. These historians also showed that Joseph Smith was not antagonistic to the idea of black Mormons. In fact they proved that, in the 1840s, Smith welcomed a few black converts, including Jane Manning James's family, as brethren and sisters in Nauvoo, providing them with housing, protection, and employment.[53] In 1997, Edward Kimball, the son of the late Church President Kimball, wrote a letter to Dr. Bush. In it, Kimball informed Bush that his article, "The Negro Doctrine," first published in *Dialogue: A Journal of Mormon Thought* in 1973, "was a very important event in setting the stage for what happened." What happened, of course, was the 1978 announcement of the revelation lifting the ban on full black membership.[54]

These historians of early Mormonism rediscovered a "black Mormon past," a past that had been lost (or perhaps purposefully forgotten). Yet these efforts weren't simply undertaken out of academic curiosity. Bush, Bringhurst, and other historians of early black Mormonism set out to reconcile the universalism they understood as the core of the Mormon gospel—a universalism that rejected the Puritanical idea that the sons, even the purported sons of Cain and Ham, should be held responsible for the sins of their fathers—with this particularistic, racialized doctrine and policy that limited this gospel to a select set of ancient lineages.[55]

2012: The Mormon *and* Black Moments

Let us return this discussion to the more recent past: the 2012 race for the White House. There is little doubt that Mitt Romney's nomination as the Republican candidate for president brought about unprecedented interest in Mormonism. Much like John F. Kennedy's 1960 campaign forced the American people to consider what it would mean for a nation dominated by Protestantism to have a Catholic in the White House, fifty-two years later, as Americans vetted candidate Mitt Romney, they also investigated his faith. And by the time election day, November 6, 2012, arrived, it was the words, "Willard Mitt Romney," which appeared on presidential ballots around the country. Not "Mormon" Mitt Romney.

Still, it is worth considering that Romney's Mormon faith did have an effect on the campaign of 2012, even beyond the "Mormon Moment." Mormonism's history with race is so complex—at least a "twice-told tale"—that, more than the Catholic Rick Santorum or the Protestant Rick Perry, the Mormon Mitt Romney's selection as the Republican nominee guaranteed that the conversation about race, religion, and politics that America started with the nomination of Barack Obama in 2008 would continue in 2012. In this sense, the "Mormon Moment" also helped extend the "Black Moment" in American presidential history.

NOTES

1. Aaron Blake, "Wealth Replaces Mormonism as Romney's Defining Trait," *The Washington Post*, August 29, 2012.

2. Grant Bennett, "Transcript: Read Grant Bennett's Remarks at the RNC," *Fox News Insider*, August 30, 2012, http://foxnewsinsider.com/2012/08/30/transcript-read-grant-bennetts-remarks-at-the-rnc/.

3. Brigham Young, *Journal of Discourses* 2:184 (February 18, 1855), quoted in Lester E. Bush, "Mormonism's Negro Doctrine: An Historical Overview," *Dialogue: A Journal of Mormon Thought* 8.1 (Spring 1973): 25.

4. Elder Joseph Fielding Smith, *The Way to Perfection* (Salt Lake City: The Genealogical Society of Utah, 1931), 41, 48; quoted in Armand L. Mauss, *All Abraham's Children: Changing Mormon Conceptions of Race and Lineage* (Urbana: University of Illinois Press, 2003), 30.

5. On the history of the Mormon exclusion of people of African descent, see Bush, "Mormonism's Negro Doctrine"; Mauss, *All Abraham's Children*; and Newell G. Bringhurst, *Saints, Slaves, and Blacks: The Changing Place of Black People Within Mormonism* (Westport, CT: Greenwood Press, 1981).

6. "Official Declaration—2," Approved in General Conference, September 30, 1978.

7. Newell G. Bringhurst and Darron T. Smith, *Black and Mormon* (Urbana: University of Illinois Press, 2004), 3.

8. Jason Horowitz, "The Genesis of a Church's Stance on Race," *Washington Post*, February 28, 2012; www.washingtonpost.com/politics/the-genesis-of-a-churchs-stand-on-race/2012/02/22/gIQAQZXyfR_story.html.

9. "Race and the Church: All Are Alike Unto God," Newsroom: The Church of Jesus Christ of Latter-day Saints, mormonnewsroom.org, February 29, 2012.

10. Obery M. Hendricks, "Mitt Romney and the Curse of Blackness," *The Huffington Post*, January 12, 2012.

11. Lee Seigel, "What's Race Got to Do with It?" *New York Times*, January 14, 2012; http://campaignstops.blogs.nytimes.com/2012/01/14/whats-race-got-to-do-with-it/.

12. Stuart Hall, "Race, the Floating Signifier" (Northampton, MA: Media Education Foundation, 1997).

13. Seigel, "What's Race Got to Do with It?" *New York Times*, January 14, 2012.

14. Max Perry Mueller, "Has the Mormon Church Truly Left Its Race Problems Behind?" *The New Republic*, November 15, 2011; www.tnr.com/article/politics/97362/african-american-mormons-lds. In the documentary film *Nobody Knows: The Untold Story of Black Mormons*, an African American Mormon convert, Tamu Smith, recounts how she was called a "nigger" in the Salt Lake City

temple. Margaret Blair Young and Darius Gray, directors, *Nobody Knows: The Untold Story of Black Mormons* (2009), http://blackmormonfilm.com/index.html.

15. In my essay, "History Lessons: Race and the LDS Church," included in the special edition of the *Journal of Mormon History* (Winter 2015), I explore in more detail this new history lesson in the context of the church and its prophets' century-worth of official teachings on race.

16. See LDS Church First Presidency Statement on the Question of Blacks within the Church, August 17, 1949, reprinted in Bringhurst, *Saints, Slaves, and Blacks*, 230–31.

17. "Race and the Priesthood," Gospel Topics, The LDS Church, December 6, 2013, www.lds.org/topics/race-and-the-priesthood?lang=eng.

18. Charles T. Davis and Henry Louis Gates, *The Slave's Narrative* (New York: Oxford University Press, 1991), 70.

19. Note that I use the term "Mormon" here instead of the "LDS Church" to expand the "Mormon" protagonists in this story beyond the "brethren" who make up the hierarchy, while not excluding them from this discussion.

20. I take my cues here from literary theorists, and from literature itself. Mieke Bal, *Narrative Theory: Major Issues in Narrative Theory* (New York: Taylor & Francis, 2004), 108; Joseph R. Urgo and Noel Polk, *Reading Faulkner: Glossary and Commentary. Absalom, Absalom!* (Jackson: University Press of Mississippi, 2010), 73.

21. Due to space restrictions, I am selecting particularly salient examples of the history of Mormonism's relationship with people of African descent as a "twice-told tale." A comprehensive history of both Mormonism's racial exclusion and inclusion of people of African descent has yet to be written.

22. Jared Farmer, *On Zion's Mount: Mormons, Indians, and the American Landscape* (Cambridge: Harvard University Press, 2008), 56; Dan Vogel, *Indian Origins and the Book of Mormon: Religious Solutions from Columbus to Joseph Smith* (Salt Lake City: Signature Books, 1986).

23. Mormon 5:15, Book of Mormon.

24. Richard Delgado and Jean Stefancic, *Critical Race Theory: An Introduction* (New York: NYU Press, 2001), 67–74.

25. Hyrum Smith, "Patriarchal Blessing for Jane James," May 1844 (LDS Church Historical Department, Salt Lake City); cited in Max Perry Mueller, "The Race of the Archive: Writing Race in Early Mormon History" (dissertation in progress, Harvard University).

26. See "From Lamanite to Indian," in Mauss, *All Abraham's Children*, 41–73. Over its 182-year history, in most editions of the Book of Mormon, 2 Nephi 30:6 has read "white and a delightsome people." Yet in both the 1840 and in the most recent 1981 editions of the Book of Mormon, "white" is replaced with "pure." While many small changes to the Book of Mormon's text have occurred over the centuries, this has garnered the most attention, in large measure because it reinforces the semiotic link between Mormon conceptions of purity and whiteness. Though this change does have a historical precedent (the 1840 edition, whose editing Joseph Smith himself oversaw), more than a few scholars have speculated that the change was more about the future: the association between purity and

whiteness would present challenges to missionaries seeking converts in areas populated by people of African descent and other dark-skinned peoples, areas which, up until the 1978 priesthood revelation, were long avoided. D. Michael Quinn, *The Mormon Hierarchy: Extensions of Power* (Salt Lake City: Signature Books, 1997), 876.

27. "Introduction," Book of Mormon.

28. For a biography of Elijah Abel, see Newell G. Bringhurst, "Elijah Abel and the Changing Status of Blacks Within Mormonism," *Dialogue* 12.2 (Summer 1979): 22–36.

29. Louis Agassiz, "The Diversity of Origin of Human Races," *Christian Examiner* 49 (1850): 110–45.

30. Richards, quoted in Lester E. Bush, *Compilation on the Negro in Mormonism*, University of Utah Special Collections.

31. Ibid.

32. Warren Montag, "The Universalization of Whiteness: Racism and Enlightenment," in Mike Hill, ed., *Whiteness: A Critical Reader* (New York: NYU Press, 1997), 281–93.

33. David N. Livingstone, *Adam's Ancestors: Race, Religion, and the Politics of Human Origins* (Baltimore: JHU Press, 2008).

34. Charles F. Irons, *The Origins of Proslavery Christianity: White and Black Evangelicals in Colonial and Antebellum Virginia* (Chapel Hill: University of North Carolina Press, 2008).

35. Joseph Smith, "For The Messenger and Advocate," *Messenger & Advocate* 2 (May 15, 2012): 289–301; Eugene D. Genovese, *Roll, Jordan, Roll: The World the Slaves Made* (New York: Vintage Books, 1976).

36. Smith, Letter to the Editor, *Times & Seasons* 5.10 (May 15, 1844).

37. "An Act in Relation to Service" in Utah Territory, Legislative Assembly, *Acts, Resolutions and Memorials* (Salt Lake City. Published by the Authority of the Legislative Assembly, 1852), 80–81.

38. "The Mormons in the Wilderness," *The North Star*, March 3, 1848; "The Mormons," *The North Star*, March 17, 1848; "The Mormon Temple in Ruins," *The North Star*, November 10, 1848.

39. "Slavery in the Territories," *Frederick Douglass Papers*, October 6, 1854; "Mormon Iniquity," *Frederick Douglass Papers*, January 26, 1855.

40. Sondra Jones, *Trial of Don Pedro Leon Lujan* (Salt Lake: University of Utah Press, 1999).

41. Within a few days of arriving in the Salt Lake Valley, Brigham Young himself taught that along with "strictley" keeping "the law of God" the Saints were called to "form connections with the different tribes of the Indians and by that means they would become a white and delightsum (sic) people." Levi Jackman's Journal, July 28, 1847 (LDS Church History Library and Archives, Salt Lake City).

42. Despite the prohibition on sexual relations with slaves, there is evidence that Mormon slave owners did father children with their slaves, even after relocating to Utah. Max Perry Mueller, "Hemings and Jefferson Together Forever?" *Slate*, March 29, 2012.

43. "An Act in Relation to Service."

44. Faustine C. Jones-Wilson, "Race, Realities, and American Education: Two Sides of the Coin," *The Journal of Negro Education* 59.2 (April 1, 1990): 119.

45. Brigham Young, "Governor's Message to the Legislative Assembly of Utah Territory," January 5, 1852; reprinted in Lester E. Bush, "Compilation on the Negro in Mormonism (1973)."

46. In 1963, the NAACP called off a planned protest of the General Conference only after the First Presidency released a statement clarifying, "Be it known that there is in the church no doctrine, belief, or practice that is intended to deny the enjoyment of full civil rights by any person regardless of race, color, creed." Cited in Bringhurst, *Saints, Slaves and Blacks*, 181.

47. Reprinted in ibid., 231–34.

48. Cited in ibid., 171.

49. This speech has proven so problematic for Brigham Young University and the LDS Church that it is not available on the *BYU Speeches* website, which normally houses such historical pronouncements by leading church officials. Mark E. Petersen, "Race Problems—As They Affect the Church," speech given at Brigham Young University, August 27, 1954. Also see Bringhurst, *Saints, Slaves and Blacks*, 169; and http://en.fairmormon.org/Mormonism_and_racial_issues/Maher_claims_that_blacks_go_to_heaven_as_slaves#endnote_petersen1.

50. F. Ross Peterson, "'Don't Lecture the Brethren'; Stewart L. Udall's Pro-Civil Rights Stance, 1967," *Journal of Mormon History* 25 (Spring 1999): 280.

51. Ibid., 280.

52. "The First Presidency on the Rights of the Negro," December 15, 1969; reprinted in Bringhurst, *Saints, Slaves and Blacks*, 232.

53. Lester E. Bush, *Compilation on the Negro in Mormonism*; Bringhurst, *Saints, Slaves, and Blacks*; Henry Wolfinger, "A Test of Faith: Jane Manning Elizabeth James and the Origins of the Utah Black Community," in Clark Knowlton, ed., *Social Accommodation in Utah* (Salt Lake City: American West Center, University of Utah, 1975), 126–72.

54. Edward L. Kimball to Lester Bush, March 26, 1997, University of Utah Special Collections.

55. Lester Bush, "Writing 'Mormonism's Negro Doctrine' (1973)," *Journal of Mormon History* 25 (1999): 229–71.

11   Mormon Women Talk Politics

Claudia L. Bushman

Women have traditionally been in short supply in politics. Women are seldom the bloc that makes a difference in a political outcome. Women are less often candidates themselves, and so they are not often elected. A few Mormon women have been significantly involved in politics. Ivy Baker Priest was the U.S. treasurer from 1953 to 1961, and her signature appeared on all U.S. currency then issued; Paula Hawkins served in the U.S. Senate from Florida from 1981 to 1987. Esther Eggertsen Peterson was a consumer advocate, both as an activist and as an official, under several U.S. presidents. But in legal realms women have traditionally been considered extensions of their husbands and fathers, rather than individuals in their own right. Although there have been three recent female Secretaries of State in the United States, political women are more often seen as the silent, tight-lipped supporters of their husbands caught in flagrant, usually sexual, misbehavior.

Mormon women, largely thought of as obedient to authority and lacking in ambition to challenge male leadership, would be considered unlikely to have played significant political roles. However, it is a matter of record that Utahn Miss Seraph Young, a niece of Brigham Young, happened to be the first woman to vote with full suffrage in the United States. She was the first woman at the polls who voted in Salt Lake City on February 21,

1870. The Utah women also voted in the general state election in September of 1870. The Territorial Legislature of Wyoming had passed a woman suffrage measure on December 10, 1869, before Utah passed its own law on February 12, 1870, just two months later. But Utah had the first female voters because Wyoming held no election until November of 1870. Utah's women voted from 1870 until 1887 when the right of suffrage, which had been granted by the Territorial governor and legislative assembly, was withdrawn by the national Congress in the Edmunds-Tucker Act as part of the effort to combat Utah's practice of plural marriage. Utah's women voted for seventeen years and then did not vote for nineteen years. When Utah was admitted to the Union as a state in 1896, its constitution carried an equal suffrage clause. Dr. Martha Hughes Cannon was elected a state senator in the first election.[1] We may note that Utah women gained the vote, lost it, and got it back many years before 1920 when women's suffrage became the law of the land.

Mormon women have acted politically on a number of occasions, mostly at the request of the men in their church, sometimes in opposition. They have left lasting records of their activity in print and in memory. This chapter recalls a few of these stirring voices. Their rhetoric is often thrilling and heartfelt as they speak for their own positions against real and assumed opposition. Of the many occasions when Mormon women have had an opportunity to speak out on political matters, I am choosing four: the consideration of the Cullom Bill at the time that suffrage was first established in Utah in 1870; the undated *Utah Woman Suffrage Songbook* of the 1880s or 1890s; a voice from the 1970s during the events related to the Equal Rights Amendment and the meetings of the International Women's Year; and other voices considering California's Proposition 8 in 2008. These few voices are representative of Mormon women's political opinions, the strong public voices and the more nuanced private opinions. We need to find and study more of these private voices to understand the broad range of political feeling.

The Cullom Bill (1870)

In 1870, Shelby Moore Cullom, representative from Illinois, introduced stringent anti-Mormon legislation in the United States Congress. The Cullom Bill prompted the Utah Mormon women, perhaps encouraged by male leaders, to protest its passage. At a mass meeting in the Salt Lake Tabernacle, the articulate and forceful women showed themselves as effective political speakers as well as voters. Their published and widely distributed remarks have been partially credited with the defeat of the bill. Historians have noted that Utah's woman suffrage may well have been instigated to combat Mormonism and especially plural marriage by enlisting women to help do away with their male and church-induced oppression. If so, the mass meetings are evidence of a failed strategy.[2]

The Cullom Bill passed the national House of Representatives, but died in the Senate. Mormon feminists' passionate defense of their way of life resulted in impressive documents that publicized their arguments. Perhaps the most powerful speech, by Mormon High Priestess and Relief Society president Eliza R. Snow, contains many ringing phrases.

Snow contends that women stay in Mormonism by choice. Not only are they not forced to stay, they choose to stay as the best possible living situation.

> Our enemies pretend that in Utah woman is held in a state of vassalage; that she does not act from choice but by coercion; that we would even prefer life elsewhere were it possible for us to make our escape. What nonsense! We all know that if we wished we could leave at any time—either to go singly or we could rise *en masse*, and there is no power here that could or would ever wish to prevent us.

These women consider themselves free, but so devoted to their church that they have willingly done what they could never have been forced to do. Snow proudly notes that Mormon women "have performed and suffered what could never have been borne and accomplished by slaves." They are not only able and independent, they have freely chosen this hard life. But they only do so by choice, by their desire to serve their men and their God. They cannot be forced to take on such duties. So they are not only not enslaved, but they have chosen and prefer to work harder than slaves.

> I will now ask this intelligent assembly of ladies, Do you know of any place on the face of the earth where woman has more liberty and where she enjoys such high and glorious privileges as she does here as a Latter-day Saint? "No!" The very idea of women here in a state of slavery is a burlesque on good common sense. The history of this people, with a very little reflection, would instruct outsiders on this point; it would show at once that the part which woman has acted in it could never have been performed against her will. Amid the

many distressing scenes through which we have passed, the privations and hardships consequent on our expulsion from State to State, and our location in an isolated, barren wilderness, the women in this church have performed and suffered what could never have been borne and accomplished by slaves.

These women identify themselves as refined women, true helpmeets and counselors to their husbands in tones that suggest the Declaration of Independence.

Were we the stupid, degraded, heart-broken beings that we have been represented, silence might become us; but as women of God, women filling high and responsible positions, performing sacred duties, women who stand not as dictators but as counselors to their husbands, and who, in the purest, noblest sense of refined womanhood, being truly their helpmates, we not only speak because we have the right, but justice and humanity demand that we should.[3]

The proceedings of the mass meeting where this and other potent speeches were declaimed were published in 1870 and stand as a strong early feminist credo in the United States, as strong as Elizabeth Cady Stanton's 1848 Declaration of Sentiments. But were these strong independent sentiments orchestrated by the males in their lives? Were they encouraged to take a public stand they might not have chosen on their own? I think the rhetoric can be read both ways.

Mormon women exercised the franchise until 1887 when the federal Edmunds-Tucker Act, a much more stringent antipolygamy bill, snatched back that privilege by preventing all Utah women from voting. Under extensive pressure, the LDS Church discontinued plural marriage in 1890, allowing Utah to join the Union in 1896, with woman suffrage.[4] This next document suggests more independence of composition. Note that it does not speak for the Mormons against the Gentile world as did the first, but from women in opposition to men in general.

The Utah Woman Suffrage Songbook (n.d.)

A more lighthearted contribution from Mormon women was *The Utah Woman Suffrage Songbook*, a publication of words to be sung to familiar tunes at suffrage rallies. This undated songbook, priced at ten cents, would have been published in the years between 1887, when Utah women lost the vote, and when they got it back again in 1896. Many of these lively songs are written by Mormon women and describe the situation in Utah, including this third verse from "Where Is the Suffrage Gone" by M.A.Y. Greenhalgh:

> Be active, dear sisters, and haste the return
> Of the time when your lamps with her brightness shall burn,
> When the polls will be open to you and to all,
> Nor tyranny longer your spirits enthrall.
> With all noble women your forces unite,
> Your watchword be freedom, for right against might.[5]

Another lyric, "The Reason Why," by Augusta Joyce Crocheron, is also a vote for temperance. As she says, in the third of her twelve stanzas,

> The brain that reels with drink and smoke
> Is not so clear as your own wives',
> The step that totters to its place
> Is not the step to lead our lives.
>
> Then true and nobler men, ye need
> A mighty balance in your power,
> A woman's vote goes to the good,
> She is your friend through ev'ry hour.
>
> So, would ye right the many wrongs
> That cloud and pierce our inmost lives,
> Would ye have help through all the world—
> Share votes with mothers, sisters, wives.[6]

Other lyrics are borrowed from suffrage groups in the East and have no LDS references, but some are very specific. In this second verse of the "Song for Equal Rights," Belle D. Edwards emphasizes preparing for the vote with male help:

> We'll learn to wash and bake and brew in the best and quickest way,
> And try to sweep and dust and stew and not consume the day;

But garner time to study, too, and teach our boys the way
To wave the flag of equal rights in Utah.[7]

The best of these songs is called "Woman, Arise." No author is credited, but the words suggest a female voice and are set to an LDS tune, "Hope of Israel" by William Clayson. The words and music work well. The attractive perkiness, rather than the super virtuous tone, makes it a winner. Its short whole goes like this:

Freedom's daughter, rouse from slumber,
See the curtains are withdrawn
Which so long thy mind hath shrouded
Lo! Thy day begins to dawn.

Chorus:

Woman, 'rise, thy penance o'er,
Sit thou in the dust no more;
Seize the scepter, hold the van,
Equal with thy brother, man.

Truth and virtue be thy motto,
Temp'rance, liberty and peace,
Light shall shine and darkness vanish,
Love shall reign, oppression cease.

Chorus: Woman, 'rise, etc.[8]

Now, that's a good song.

So many movements and revolutions ride on the felicitous phrase. And Mormon women have not been lacking in creating those phrases when they have been involved in political matters.

Mormon women were on the politically correct side in seeking the vote in the late nineteenth century. But in the 1970s when the Equal Rights Amendment, which would increase and solidify their rights, was under consideration, they were urged to oppose it. Their political action was orchestrated from on high, and this brief account of the decisions of a Mormon female leader show how far allegiance to that leader could go.

Elaine Cannon (1970s)

I was around in the 1970s for the political activity that accompanied consideration of the Equal Rights Amendment and the meetings of the International Women's Year. Familiar as I was with Utah's sprightly feminist heritage from which I have just quoted, and living far away from Utah in Massachusetts, I expected that the church would embrace the equal rights legislation without question. I did not expect that there would be opposition to the ERA from the Church of Jesus Christ of Latter-day Saints, and there was none until quite late in the game.

Here the most stirring rhetoric came from the Mormon housewife Sonia Johnson. Her phrases were sufficiently memorable and oppositional that she called the wrath of the church down on her head. Rather than supporting the church with her rhetoric as Eliza R. Snow had done, Johnson threatened the organization and its leaders and was duly punished by excommunication. Spunky women were in a new situation where instead of being enlisted as instruments of the church, they opposed it. That story has been often told.

For the 1970s period I will quote the voice of Elaine Cannon in a recently and privately published biography by her daughter Holly C. Metcalf. Cannon, a devoted and dutiful Latter-day Saint, was an immensely successful Utah newspaper writer, leader of LDS organizations, and motivational speaker while also being a working mother, a major family breadwinner, and an independent self-made woman. A voluble journal keeper, she recorded her private feelings while also writing prolifically for the public.

At the Houston meeting of the International Women's Year, where all states met together after their individual meetings, Utah women found themselves true pariahs. Seen as enemies because of their conservative views, their hotel rooms were cancelled, they were refused the key to their caucus room, and no space could be found for their display. Victims of many political dirty tricks, they felt the disapproval of delegates from other states who favored equal rights for women. In searching for space for themselves between the feminists whom they saw denying the importance of motherhood and family and the fear that conservatives were dictating to them, they fastened on the issue of support for minority women. That was the space they needed at the conference.

The Mormon women had originally opposed voting for the minority women's clause because it required heavy cost and additional taxes, but, as underdogs, they were drawn to support it and did. The Utah underdogs felt some unity with the minority women and voted for them. These Utah delegates in the 1970s found themselves at odds with other women and at some odds with church leadership as the women of the 1870s had not. They forged their own compromises. In private they thought for themselves. In public they were more obedient than required.

One of Elaine Cannon's compromises, her effort to show her own freedom by asking no questions and providing more obedience than was asked for, became extremely well known. As a leader of the Young Women of the church, she participated in a broadcast in connection with the church's General Conference in 1978 that brought church women and girls together. In her talk, urging the women to follow the leadership of the then Church-President Spencer W. Kimball, Elaine Cannon spoke these words, here somewhat edited down.

> My firm feeling is that we must pursue a course of a covenant people.... Your priorities ought to be known to you as a daughter of God. Personal opinions may vary. Eternal principles never do. *When the prophet speaks, sisters, the debate is over.* So I urge us all to provide powerful unity as women for those things we can agree upon—family, chastity, accountability to the Lord, responsibility to the community, sharing the gospel ... and sisters, we emphatically and happily declare, "I will be obedient! I will help strengthen others that they may be so too!"[9]

This pronouncement caused quite a stir. President Kimball himself gently asked that she not use the phrase "when the prophet speaks, the debate is over" again. He thought it was too easily misunderstood. He wanted church members to feel free to make decisions about the statements of the prophet for themselves. Later that same year, 1978, one of President Kimball's counselors, President Nathan Eldon Tanner, quoted and then qualified the statement. He said that he continually told people to follow the prophet, that we all needed divine inspiration, but he made the teaching much more dependent on individual agency.[10]

Elaine Cannon had shown her agency by accepting all direction before even being asked. Faced with pledges of such unquestioning obedience, the church asked its members for more individual responsibility. This origin story of a well-known phrase throws the demand for obedience itself into question, although for many this phrase has now come to be required behavior. The official stand, iterated by President Kimball, was to seek divine inspiration for individual direction in following the church prophets.

California's Proposition 8 (2008–2011)

A recent request for political help occurred in California when the LDS Church solicited funds and involvement to build support for Proposition 8, a measure to support traditional marriage between one man and one woman. The women quoted in this essay so far, speaking publicly, have spoken with breathtaking surety and conviction. The women's voices that follow here are silent voices, used anonymously, recorded in quiet rooms for the Claremont Oral History program. These voices are troubled and marked by doubt, shaded by ambiguity and nuance. They are less emphatic than the public speakers.

Few voices wholeheartedly supported the issue of Proposition 8. Some rejected it as a suitable position for the church. Some cited the pain it would cause others. One sister, who observed the situation from another state, said:

> I just felt that the church had no business getting involved in that. They were trying to get people to go out and canvas neighborhoods and vote against it. I wouldn't have gone out there on a bet. I mean I just did not think that the church should have been involved. That just wasn't the church's place. I disagreed with it totally.[11]

Some were more specific as they were more critical and dismissive:

> Mormons were pulled into political activity. Church buildings were used for political purposes. Heavy preaching supported a definition of marriage as between a man and a woman, therefore against any marriage between two people of the same gender. Those unwilling to join the battle were considered to have failed a religious test.[12]

The pain the action brought to others, as well as the ruptures in relationships, were cited by those who opposed the bill—even by some who supported it and worked actively for it, as the woman quoted here.

> I have a really good friend at school [who] is a lesbian. She got married over the summer and found out about my support [of Proposition 8 and] it pretty much destroyed our friendship. We'd been really good friends for about fifteen years. We are collegial now, but we're not friends anymore. That was very painful for both of us. She just can't understand how I could belong to a church that hates her.[13]

Another sister made obedience her major concern. She felt the campaign overreached, but if asked, she would have complied.

> I am so glad I did not live in California and have to go door to door. It appears to me, and I can't even point to anything specific, but it appears to me that the church learned something from what happened in California. I don't think that they will ask other states to fight the battle that way. But I'm obedient. Would I do it? I know I would, but it would be very hard. There's a lot of obedience involved. My husband says that when you raise your hand to the square to sustain somebody in a position, when you sustain them is when you disagree with them. If you agree with everything, it's no big deal. It's when you disagree with maybe how they're doing something. I'm just so glad that I didn't have to do that.[14]

This issue figured in the extended narratives of a number of sisters, taking on a more causal relationship to daily life. Here are some of their stories. The first is from a woman who temporarily left the LDS Church.

> This was an extremely painful moment for me in my history as a Mormon, because I saw . . . good people . . . mobilize to do something that I felt was really at heart unchristian and unkind. People want to marry. How is that a bad thing? We should be affirming this in every way!
>
> At first I went to church every week, valiantly wearing my little rainbow ribbon pinned to my shirt. Eventually, I couldn't continue going to church because it seemed that every Sunday there were talks over the pulpit about it or there would be announcements . . . or comment[s] in Sunday school. Perhaps the breaking point came when a fellow ward member referred to Mormons who didn't support Prop 8 as "tares" that needed to be separated from the wheat. So I was a tare, huh? I couldn't handle it anymore. I retreated and

found my refuge at the [United Church of Christ]. They are an open and affirming congregation. The pastor is gay and has a lifelong partner. He's wonderful. A large segment of the congregation is gay and they are just such good people. I loved their services and their sermons and their music. I felt a real connection with the people there and they were good to me. . . . I had a wonderful experience with the UCC and I'll always be grateful to them for being that refuge when I needed them during the Prop 8 crisis.[15]

Here's another story:

Proposition 8 was bad. Prop 8 was really bad. I left DC in July and they had literally just read the letter over the pulpit in my sacrament meeting there saying, "The elections are coming up in the fall, we do not hand out the ward list, and we do not get involved." This is DC. [That's] what was read in my ward.

Then I show up in [California] and they are reading over the pulpit the letter from the First Presidency saying, "You must get involved in your community to help pass Prop 8." And I'm thinking, wait a minute, these don't match. Here A doesn't match B; in fact they're complete opposites.

We had a woman in the ward who was in charge of sign-ups to do polling in the neighborhood. . . . They were going around asking people how they would vote. Supposedly they weren't trying to influence, but at the same time they would say "Well, here's information on our take on it." I can't even remember if we were "Yes" or "No," this is how much I didn't want to be a part of things.

Every week, the woman in charge would pass a list around and people would sign up to go. I wouldn't do it, in part because I have friends who are gay and I couldn't make it work in my head. Well, one day in Sunday school class this woman bore her testimony and cried for over fifteen minutes, and I am not exaggerating because again I was sitting there thinking, "How much longer do I have to sit here before I can actually get up and leave because I can't breathe." I was basically having an anxiety attack. I had to leave the room, and she kept going. I couldn't deal with it and then they had a fifth Sunday meeting . . .

The one lawyer . . . in the ward explained [all the terrible things that were] going to happen if Prop 8 didn't pass. They handed out copies of the letter from the First Presidency and I was sitting in the back with a couple of radical friends. I finally got the letter and it basically said, "We believe in marriage between a man and a woman. Do what you can." Period. It didn't say go polling. It didn't say stand outside of the polling places and hold signs. It didn't say any of this. It said "Do what your conscience tells you to do." And I thought, "Okay, all of this stuff that the lawyer is telling us may come to pass, and I'm not going to argue with him. But at the same time, none of this is in this letter. None of this." And I did what I could. I voted because that's what was asked of me. And that one was difficult. I think sometimes we tend to take whatever is political and try to fit it into our theology, but that's not what the letter said. [The local people] told us that the stake had to donate money, but that's not what the letter says. The letter says "Do what you can." If the stake interprets it as we need to raise money to support this, well that's fine if that's what they believe, but the letter to me said, "Do what you can." For the woman that was handing out the signup sheets bearing her testimony, that was what she could do. More power to her, but don't do it around me.

I think Prop 8 was really the only time that I have really come down to the point where I had to know exactly what the church said, because the way it was being represented to me was wrong, was incorrect. But people do the best they can with what they have.[16]

Stories of personal involvement in the campaigns against gay marriage now have histories of their own as families face and react to repeated incidents. This story takes a family with a gay son through two ballot initiatives to limit marriage to heterosexual unions.

Difficulties arose as we had to endure California's Propositions 22 & 8 in recent years. As an active LDS family, we found the church's involvement to be difficult and challenging for our family. Prop 22 nearly tore our family apart. I had chosen not to be involved in the campaign at all and I had told my ecclesiastical leaders that I would not participate. My husband was a member of the High Council at the time, and he decided he would not be visibly involved but would allow his offices to be used for phone campaigning. When [our son] later found out about his [dad's passive] involvement, he was extremely hurt. He chose not to discuss his anger with us but mostly kept it to himself for several years. We eventually had to discuss his hurt and apologize and repent for it. I swore I would never let anything be so divisive in our family again.

She then recounted how her family approached the later Proposition 8.

When Prop 8 rolled around, my husband and I both very kindly told our bishop and stake president that we would not be involved on any level. I explained to them some of the problems that our family had had during and after Prop 22, and how we had decided never to let anything like that divide our family again. We gained the full support of our Priesthood leaders in not being involved [in Proposition 8] even though I was the Relief Society president at the time and [my husband] was on the High Council. We felt that [our leaders] had empathy for our situation. However, Proposition 8 left [our son] with definite scars and anger against the LDS Church at a level I don't think he had felt prior to Prop 8. That has been very hard for our family. How could something we love so much, the Gospel, continue to cause deep pain for our son?[17]

This woman's son has recently married his gay partner. Her family members were all involved in the event.

Here's another firsthand account from a woman where the gay issue cut directly into her family. Each family so affected must make serious policy decisions. This woman tells how her family has dealt with the issue. She has decided to speak out about her situation and experience. So far, many are interested in what she has to say, but less interested in joining her to talk about this issue. Here is part of her account.

Our middle child and second son is a homosexual. He came out to us when he was eighteen, after a year at BYU. The fact that he said he was gay was no surprise to me. It was a surprise to his dad, but I had sort of wondered about that possibility, and we had gone about our lives. I didn't wish it on him, but there it is. I think the church has not handled the issue well. I think frankly the church was wrong in California regarding same sex marriage. I do not see that it's causing any damage to traditional couples. It was easy enough for the church to speak against homosexuality and assure members that it was an inclination, a choice, and could be changed. Now the church no longer claims that, but the fact is that homosexuals still do not feel welcome in the Church, unless they stay tightly closeted.

She continues.

> Just recently we had a women's stake-wide reunion of sisters, just a couple of hours on Saturday morning. We had a few groups. One was about women and their hormones and one was about families that face the situation of "same-sex attraction." I don't like that term personally. My husband and I were asked to speak about it. I have made it a point personally to speak openly about it to anyone who is willing to listen. After our son came out, I said it was OK. It took him a while to talk about it to his closest friends in the church whose opinions he valued. It took courage to speak to them so that he wouldn't lose them. Since then I've made it a point that I would speak. But sadly it is still something that's hidden. We know a number of people who are gay or lesbian and a surprising number of families who don't ever, ever mention it. It is an unnamed problem. They may mention a child who may be doing drugs, but never one who is gay. No, I don't think that the church is handling it well.
>
> I understand that it's a difficult situation. It's not only our church, it's other churches as well. But when you say we love them and they are welcome, they are not really welcome. Church members are uncomfortable about asking gay children to stay with them if they come to visit. Should you invite their partners? One leader said that everyone has to make his own decisions, but said that he would consider inviting them for dinner and a visit, but not to stay. My husband was uncomfortable when I brought that subject up, but I think that people have a right to know. Basically I said that we have other children who are not involved in the church. We are in a big city. They may live here with their girlfriends, boyfriends and they may have children. Do we deny them access? Do we deny them our home? I find that so offensive. I said in the meeting that I am just an ordinary woman and my husband and I love our children the best we can. Oftentimes we make mistakes, but it is hard for me to see that our son's mistakes are greater than those of our other children or ours, for that matter. My belief is that God loves them as much as he loves us and more than we can really conceive. For me to make a judg-

ment that our gay children are not good enough to stay in our house is inconceivable.

My husband and I have often wondered if the fact that our son is gay has had an influence on our other children and their inactivity in the church. I would say that it has. The siblings support him. Our oldest son is very passionate. He thinks the treatment of gays is so patently unfair. So, I am afraid that the church has not done well with that issue. But I am learning some things about organizations. They move slowly. And therefore it's very difficult for me to say that the church is always perfect and does everything just right. It doesn't. It's just made up of people. It's made up of very good people who try very hard but they only understand what they understand.[18]

What we see in these potent narratives is a story in which politics and church instructions impinge on family relationships, changing the direction of the story. What we find is much ambiguity, contradiction, and some humor. As another woman concludes,

I often don't know which side [of the gay debate] I am on! . . . Personally, I believe that our son's [same-sex] marriage will be good for him and good for society. His marriage will in no way undermine my marriage . . . or male/female marriage in general. On the other hand, I believe that a prophet stands at the head of our Church who has spoken out against same-sex marriage. It's a good thing I have two hands![19]

These responses to the California marriage debate show some of the variations and differences that we know to exist on many issues. When the church speaks the response is never simple and in one voice. What people say in public, under the pressure of public opinion, is not necessarily what they would say privately. People often speak in an obedient voice when they do not feel that way.

This last issue, reactions to opposition to gay marriage, remains a matter of considerable tension. The issues considered at the beginning of this chapter, suffrage and equal rights, have been resolved or have moved out of contention at the moment. Gay marriage and gay and lesbian rights in general continue to be matters of considerable discussion as voices call both for more open dialogue as well as for an end to debate.

In April of 2012, sociology and psychology professors at BYU organized a panel discussion to cover "everything you wanted to know about being gay at BYU." Bridey Jensen, a 23-year-old lesbian student who was one of the panelists, described her situation. "Both of these things [being a Mormon and a lesbian] are just a fundamental part of me that I never chose," she said. "Just because I accept [that I am gay] doesn't mean I believe in the gospel any less." However, Stephen Graham, president of Standard of Liberty, "an LDS-oriented educational corporation," objected to the event as "ill-conceived," a "soul-destroying situation," because it would threaten traditional values, perhaps depicting homosexuality as healthy and normal. "It will be harmful, harmful to the souls of those giving the talks, harmful to those young minds listening." Bridey Jensen, who led an unofficial student group called "Understanding Same Gender Attraction," didn't take a stand on LDS gay teachings, but did promote compassion. "As Christians," she said, "aren't we missing the mark if we don't embrace these people with compassion and love?"[20]

The unofficial BYU event drew six hundred listeners to hear how the panel members balance the teachings of their church with their own sexual identities. The students said that as they find friends and support that "It gets better." The school has adjusted its Honor Code to allow students to identify as gay without sanctions as long as they remain celibate.[21]

This issue will continue to be discussed openly and quietly for some time as the tensions are considered and resolved. We can expect to hear many more women's voices discussing the problems here, both openly and in private documents.

This chapter provides evidence that there is value in recording strong views, both those spoken publicly and those written silently. If these attitudes are not recorded, they can never be used as historical evidence for attitudes and behavior. Recorded personal views, though they may never be delivered in public speeches or published in the newspaper, may come to light and have a later life. Private attitudes are always more nuanced than a unanimous opinion would seem to be. Let's get those opinions and experiences recorded.

Notes

1. Susa Young Gates and Leah D. Widtsoe, *Women of the "Mormon" Church* (Independence, MO: Press of Zion's Printing and Publishing, 1928), 8–9.

2. Martha Sonntag Bradley (Evans), *Pedestals and Podiums: Utah Women, Religious Authority, and Equal Rights* (Salt Lake City: Signature Books, 2005), 16–17.

3. Eliza R. Snow, *Proceedings in Mass Meeting of the Ladies of Salt Lake City, to Protest Against the Passage of Cullom's Bill, January 14, 1870* (Salt Lake City: n.p., 1870), 4, 5.

4. Claudia L. Bushman, ed., *Mormon Sisters: Women in Early Utah* (Cambridge, MA: Emmeline Press, 1976), 157–75.

5. N.A., *The Utah Woman Suffrage Songbook* (Salt Lake City: Office of the Woman's Exponent, n.d.), 9.

6. Ibid., 11.

7. Ibid., 23.

8. Ibid., 5.

9. Holly C. Metcalf, *Love's Banner: Memories of the Life of Elaine Cannon* (Kenmore, WA: Lamb and Lion, 2011), 204 (emphasis added).

10. Ibid., 204–206.

11. Claremont Oral History Collection, #139, 11 (Special Collections, Claremont Library, Claremont, CA).

12. Ibid., #12, 31.

13. Ibid., #17, 12.

14. Ibid., #141, 10.

15. Ibid., #61, 12–13

16. Ibid., #008, 14–15.

17. Ibid., #071, 17.

18. Ibid., #140, 9–11.

19. Ibid., #071, 24.

20. "Gay and Mormon: BYU Students to Speak on Campus Panel," *Salt Lake Tribune*, March 29, 2012.

21. "Gay BYU Students to Mormon Youths: 'It gets better,'" *Salt Lake Tribune*, April 6, 2012.

12 On the "Underground"

What the Mormon "Yes on 8" Campaign Reveals About the Future of Mormons in American Political Life

Joanna Brooks

In 2008, opponents of same-sex marriage in California sponsored Proposition 8, a ballot initiative that amended the California state constitution to abolish the rights of gay and lesbian couples to civil marriage. Same-sex couples in California had enjoyed the right to marry after the California State Supreme Court issued its *In Re Marriage* ruling on May 15, 2008, nullifying a statutory ban against same-sex marriage established by the Proposition 22 ballot initiative in 2000. After a contentious five-month campaign that cost $83 million—the most expensive social policy initiative in United States history—Proposition 8 passed by a margin of 52.24 percent to 47.76 percent in November 2008.

In the weeks leading up to and following the election, it was disclosed by activists—gay and straight, Mormon and non-Mormon—and reported in the press that the Church of Jesus Christ of Latter-day Saints had played a significant role in funding and staffing the "Yes on 8" campaign. Mormons, who constitute less than 2 percent of California's population, made up a grossly disproportionate share of donors to "Yes on 8": a share estimated at 40 to 70 percent. Acting on instruction from LDS Church leaders, LDS members had also been mobilized as precinct walkers, phone bankers, zip code area supervisors, and child care providers, in voter identification and get-out-the-vote efforts for a far-reaching and professionally orchestrated "grassroots" campaign. Although precise data on the number of hours donated by LDS volunteers as compared to volunteers of other faith backgrounds is not available, those who witnessed the "Yes on 8" campaign in action observe that the volunteer force was overwhelmingly LDS and that no other faith in California approached the level of volunteer mobilization of Mormons.

Even though the LDS Church had previously played outsized roles in campaigns against same-sex marriage in Alaska and Hawaii, the magnitude and intensity of LDS involvement in California's "Yes on 8" campaign exceeded LDS activity in any prior political campaign except the fight against the Equal Rights Amendment. Revelations of the LDS Church's heavy involvement in Proposition 8 stunned many Californians and contributed to a national perception of the church as a leading opponent of LGBT civil equality and as a focus of LGBT activism in postelection 2008 and beyond.

But the way the Mormon "Yes on 8" campaign was understood by non-Mormons does not necessarily match the way the campaign was understood by Mormons themselves, and to understand its intensity and the magnitude of LDS involvement, it is crucial to examine Mormon activism within the framework of LDS history and culture. Political scientist David Campbell has characterized readily mobilizable Mormon populations as "dry kindling" and attributed their quick response to the strongly centralized hierarchical organization of the church and emphasis on obedience to LDS Church leadership.[1]

When and why the "kindling" is lit is another important dimension of the story, for it is not the case that every socially conservative cause elicits such a response from LDS Church members. In fact, Mormons trend in a more moderate direction on issues like abortion and immigration than other conservative Christians. Even on the issue of homosexuality, it would be inaccurate to characterize the quality of LDS discourse about homosexuals as more intense than that of other socially conservative religious denominations, a few egregious and frequently cited statements by specific LDS Church leaders over the last decades notwithstanding. We come closer to understanding how Mormons experienced the "Yes on 8" campaign when we acknowledge theologically distinctive Mormon views of marriage. LDS theology treats marriage as an ordinance necessary to the eternal well-being of the soul. Only through an LDS temple marriage, orthodox theology teaches, can souls enjoy the highest degrees of glory in the eternities.

Although general homophobia contributed to and circulated through the Mormon "Yes on 8" campaign, it is this LDS view of the legalization of same-sex marriage as a threat to LDS theology that served as the prime rationale for Mormon involvement. And, as I will argue, the construction of the campaign in LDS communities as a defense of LDS temple marriage triggered century-old tensions between Mormons and American civil society over questions of family definition, theocracy, and state sovereignty. Under pressure from federal powers, Mormons were forced to go "underground" with the practice of polygamy in the 1880s. After the church's abolition of this-world polygamy in 1890, LDS people withdrew belief in the eternal efficacy of polygamy into the realm of private belief and insider conversation. This private-public split and consequential habits of dualism and guardedness in public speech continue to operate within LDS culture, in a complex of discursive habits I will call "undergrounding": a split between private or insider and public communication that manifests both in practices of social insularity as well as in the careful use of public speech as deflective action rather than communicative reason—the assumed speech norm of modern civic life. This essay will examine how the Proposition 8 campaign reactivated LDS habits of "undergrounding" that continue to shape the Mormon presence in American civic and political life.

The nineteenth-century Mormon "underground" was a system of social networks that harbored LDS men and women evading prosecution or persecution for polygamy or unlawful cohabitation. It developed as a result of open political conflict between Mormons and their host American society over family definition. On one side of this conflict, dominant American society criminalized and instrumentalized polygamy to mark Mormons as aliens and deprive them of the rights of citizens; in defense of polygamy, Mormon communities constructed and maintained themselves as theocracies against United States rule.[2] This nineteenth-century open conflict has exerted profound and lasting consequences on the way Mormons have participated in American public life.

Both the historic practice of polygamy and its continuing theological and residual social power in LDS communities are routinely understated in Mormon studies. At times, apologetic scholars have cited the proportion of Mormons practicing polygamy in the late nineteenth century as 2 to 3 percent; the best scholarship places that number closer to 30 percent.[3] Remarkably few scholars openly acknowledge that polygamy as an eternal principle remains on the books in scripture and in LDS temple sealing practices to this day. And we have yet to see a full and candid assessment of the impact of polygamy on contemporary Mormon society and culture.[4] I believe polygamy is to Mormon experience as slavery is to American experience: defining, materially and ideologically constitutive, contradictory to some of its stated ideals, and lasting in its cultural consequences.

One of the consequences of the polygamy crisis and the practice of undergrounding is a dominant culture image of Mormons as deviant, untrustworthy, and duplicitous, an image that crystallized in popular culture during the Reed Smoot Senate hearings at the dawn of the twentieth century (see chapter 3).[5] While the image itself was sensationalistic and pejorative in its composition and intent, I believe it gestures toward a set of actually existing discursive strategies used by Mormons to maintain their theocratic sovereignty in the face of federal colonization. These strategies have been analyzed and identified by anthropologist Daymon Smith. I summarize five elements of his findings here.

1. *Theological and discursive construction of the temple-sealed family as a unit of LDS theocracy, and LDS temples as its emblem.* The assault on polygamy and LDS theocracy was narrated in LDS culture as an assault on the temple itself.[6] Even after the LDS Church's abolition of this-world polygamy in 1890, the temple-sealed family served as a basic unit of LDS theocracy as well as an incubator of Mormon identity and difference. Defense of temple-sealed families would serve as the rationale for the LDS Church's two major efforts to shape national policy in the late twentieth and twenty-first centuries.

2. *Preference for information through authorized channels and general distrust of noninstitutional sources on Mormonism.* To protect the continuing practice of polygamy and index reliable allies in this project, LDS Church institutional channels of information were to be understood as trustworthy, while all others were suspect and potentially anti-Mormon.[7]

3. *Adoption of a defensive default posture of non-transparency in public relations.* The phrase "Mind your business" circulated in the oral and print cultures of late-nineteenth-century Mormonism as the "Mormon creed." Adherence to this creed through scrupulous non-revelation of one's own private matters and refusal to inquire into the family situation of others indicated reliability and status.[8]

4. *Cultivation of "insider" and "outsider" narratives.* The public abolition of the LDS practice of polygamy in 1890 did not lead to the expulsion

of polygamy from Mormon theology, scripture, or belief. Indeed, belief in polygamy as an eternal principle continued and continues as a mark of orthodoxy and status in LDS societies. This reflects a strong break between "public" and "private" Mormonism, a break initiated when church leaders rejected "upfront, out-in the-open-contest between God and state," opting instead for "a stealthier approach, where public would meet public, politic with politic, and the Church would stay behind the scenes."[9] The maintenance of distinctive LDS beliefs and practices like polygamy depended on the continuation of a robustly insular Mormon society, protected first by geographical isolation and then by elective patterns of social affiliation. This public/private dualism is reinforced by the mind/body dualism that Smith observes as a consequence of the 1890 Manifesto.[10]

5. *Careful public speech* to protect private knowledge. The Underground instituted among LDS people an understanding of public speech as a tool to deflect or redirect public attention and protect private belief and knowledge. This stands in contrast to modern language ideologies that privilege speech as a transparent and efficacious tool of "communicative reason."[11] Tight control of public messaging remained (and still remains) a feature of Mormon discourse and a marker of Mormon status beyond the abolition of polygamy.[12] Secrecy continues to index authority, authenticity, status, and power within LDS culture.

LDS communities developed an ethos privileging opacity, institutional loyalty, hierarchy, and guardedness as they attempted to preserve a residue of theocracy and difference even while being assimilated into broader United States society. The private-public split resulted in a form of self-consciousness described by one Mormon studies scholar as a "divided sense of self" and related habits of double-coding in public speech, especially in situations where LDS people perceive a threat to their way of being.[13]

When same-sex civil marriage became legal in California in June 2008, LDS people were already disposed to view it as a threat to their religious beliefs and practices. This was the result of more than twenty years of efforts by LDS Church leaders—including sizable commitments to the political fight against same-sex marriage that would distinguish the church even among conservative denominations as a singularly committed opponent of marriage equality. Leaked internal documents suggest that LDS Church leaders began to discuss same-sex marriage as a distinct political issue as early as 1984. (The threat of homosexual marriage had been posed during the LDS Church's organized opposition to the Equal Rights Amendment during the 1970s and 1980s but only as an adjunct.) LDS Church leaders first asked members to involve themselves in political activism against same-sex marriage in 1994. LDS Church institutional activism against same-sex marriage began in Hawaii in 1996 as the church and Catholic partners formed the Hawaii's Future Today coalition. HFT filed amicus briefs against the legalization of same-sex marriage by court decision and served as a funding and organizing mechanism to support the passage of constitutional amendments to ban same-sex marriage in the Hawaii legislature.

Significantly, according to leaked documents, LDS Church President Gordon B. Hinckley, a public relations professional, strongly recommended that the LDS Church "not [be] out front" or "singled out" on the issue of same-sex marriage, and that the better-liked Catholics should in fact take the lead in HFT activities.[14] Despite this strategic recommendation, the LDS Church played an outsized role in support of a 1998 Alaskan ballot measure to ban same-sex marriage, making a direct contribution of $500,000 to the Alaska Family Coalition, about 78 percent of the total funding for the campaign in a state where Mormons made up only 3 percent of the population. Hinckley's advice to avoid being "out front" did not hold.

In California, where Mormons make up about 2 percent of the population, LDS Church involvement in same-sex marriage began with Proposition 22, a measure to amend the state constitution, which passed with financial, institutional, and volunteer support from Mormons in 2000. Same-sex marriage opponents brought a second same-sex marriage ban to the initiative process in late 2007, as legal petitions that would eventuate in the legalization of same-sex marriage made their way through the California court system in late 2007 and early 2008. The lead donors in the signature-gathering phase were Catholics. It was not until May 2008 that Mormon participation was formally elicited, by Roman Catholic Archbishop George Niederauer of San Francisco, who had served for eleven years in Salt Lake City. On June 20, 2008, the LDS Church issued a letter to be read over the pulpits in California congregations asking members to "do all they could" in support of Proposition 8. Over the next few months, the church made cash and in-kind contributions to the coalitional sponsor of the initiative, ProtectMarriage.com. But the real financial contributions of the church came through its leveraging of institutional power and member financial records to mobilize congregations, congregational leaders, and regional church officials as bundlers for the "Yes on 8" campaign.

By late August 2008, the church had organized selective solicitation conference calls between potentially large donors and members of the Quorum of the Seventy. Quorum members asked donors to make donations of $25,000 per family, and a surge in five-figure donations began to appear on state donor records in early September. Large- and small-scale giving continued, so that by the end of the campaign, it is estimated that individual Mormons contributed between 50 and 70 percent of the $40 million raised by "Yes on 8." In many areas, Mormons also constituted the majority of the on-the-ground grassroots political operation. Mormons as far away as Massachusetts were solicited for donations, while LDS Church members in Idaho were readied to participate in phone banks. Again, Hinckley's original recommendation that Mormons not be "out front" was disregarded.

Why the intensity? LDS people did not experience their participation in the Proposition 8 campaign as a general coalitional effort in defense of conservative social values. Rather, LDS Church officials and Mormon political operatives successfully particularized the "Yes on 8" campaign so that it was experienced by Mormons as a specifically Mormon effort. This is not to say that the LDS Church's theological outlook on homosexuality and general American social homophobia did not contribute to Mormon "Yes on 8" activism; these were necessary conditions for the "Yes on 8" effort. But these were not the narratives driving the LDS campaign. LDS people were led to experience Proposition 8 as an assault by broader society on what Mormons had for more than a century perceived to be a historically imperiled form: Mormon temple marriage.

There is much that needs to be covered here to fully understand how and why this narrative was so successful. Long overdue in Mormon studies is a critical examination of the roles of temples and temple-building in the Mormon imagination: the politics of temple location, design, and fundraising; the construction of the temple not only as a place of worship but as a status object and a marker of Mormon difference; LDS views on temple marriage as guarantors of status; and how these views differ by social class and global region. But for the purposes of this essay, I am most interested in examining how LDS popular understandings of the "Yes on 8" campaign as a last-ditch defense of LDS temple marriage practices reactivated Mormon discursive tactics of "undergrounding" developed under the pressure of the nineteenth-century battle of polygamy.

I present those tactics here again, with explication of how they were implemented during the 2008 "Yes on 8" campaign.

1. *Preference for information through authorized channels and general distrust of noninstitutional sources on Mormonism.*

First, the LDS "Yes on 8" campaign operationalized Mormon preference for information through authorized LDS channels and distrust of noninstitutional sources—a pattern that dates back to polygamy. Mormons did not receive their information about Proposition 8 primarily through general campaign media. Instead, specifically Mormon campaign content was developed and distributed through familiar institutional channels: letters over the pulpit, instructions from priesthood leaders in congregations, and donation solicitation and video conference training by members of the Quorum of the Seventy. A second set of surrogate institutional channels bearing a trusted conservative LDS brand was also established, particularly through the conservative online LDS *Meridian Magazine*. A third set of trusted insider channels during the campaign was Mormon kinship networks—families, friends, wards—which horizontally distributed discourse and argumentation through face-to-face and online interaction. So effective were these horizontal kinship networks that, during their October 8 teleconference training, LDS Church officials directed members to use horizontal messaging. Institutional, branded surrogate, and kinship networks all served as the primary, trusted source of information for LDS people during the "Yes on 8" campaign. Public sources were disregarded or regarded with distrust.

2. *Adoption of a defensive default posture of non-transparency in public relations.*

The church established through its surrogates a defensive organizational posture of public non-transparency: the operational equivalent of a "mind your own business" creed. Just as authorized campaign communications were fed into Mormon communities through LDS institutional and surrogate channels, surrogate channels of campaign mobilization that piggybacked on LDS Church structures initially gave the church a layer of protection against public scrutiny. Even before the Proposition 8 campaign, observers of the LGBT civil rights movement had tracked close ties between the LDS Church and national anti–marriage equality organizations like the National Organization for Marriage. During the "Yes on 8" campaign, church members were instructed to recognize ProtectMarriage.com as the authorized surrogate LDS campaign agency.

ProtectMarriage.com organized a "grassroots" operational arm that was distinguished (on paper at least) from ecclesiastical structures but which in fact piggybacked onto geographically organized ecclesiastical units—with "regions" mapped onto stakes and "zip code supervisors" assigned by wards. Regional directors and zip code supervisors were authorized to assign campaign responsibilities within their wards and stakes in a practice that mimicked the LDS ecclesiastical practice of assigning members "callings." Financially, the church also deferred to and directed members to support ProtectMarriage.com. The church itself did not make a major direct donation to the campaign, as it had in Alaska; instead, it assisted with fundraising assessments and directed members to donate to ProtectMarriage.com only. Church members were advised to conduct the campaign in ways that might shield the church from scrutiny or deflect attention from its major role. LDS volunteers who did door-to-door voter identification were encouraged not to self-identify as Mormons. Some members regarded these instructions and the use of surrogates that annexed ecclesiastical structures "confusing." Indeed, the main utility of this elaborate surrogate structure was to create a membrane of non-transparency to provide a plausible layer of protection against the church's being identified as a major direct stakeholder in "Yes on 8."

3. *Cultivation of "insider" and "outsider" narratives, including coded language,*

4. *Careful public speech to protect private knowledge, and*

5. *Theological and discursive construction as the temple-sealed family as a unit of LDS theocracy and LDS temples as its emblem.*

Within insider organizational channels, the ways LDS people talked among themselves about the "Yes on 8" campaign differed from the ways they talked about the campaign in public. While it is true that on both channels, the scripted narrative was that a vote for Proposition 8 was a vote to "protect marriage," LDS people narrated the "Yes on 8" campaign as an urgent defense of temple marriage in particular. Insider LDS communications about Proposition 8 depicted marriage equality as an assault on the ability of the LDS Church to continue to perform temple marriages, constructing the "Yes on 8" campaign as defense of the temple and temple-sealed families. In July 2008, *Meridian Magazine* published from Protect Marriage grassroots director Gary Lawrence, who is LDS and whose firm Lawrence Research was contracted by the campaign, an article that framed the Proposition 8 campaign in Mormon theological terms as a sacred war in defense of religious agency—a "defining moment, a tipping point, a critical battle in our existence" (July 7, 2008).[15] On August 9, 2008, *Meridian* published an article by Lawrence's grassroots codirector Glen Greener presenting nine talking points alleging tendentiously that failure to pass Proposition 8 will result in government intrusions on religious and individual liberties, including lawsuits against churches that refused to perform same-sex marriages. Shortly thereafter, a redacted "Six Consequences" document created by Gary Lawrence went viral through Mormon organizational and kinship networks.

What was not said explicitly in "Six Consequences" was elaborated in the oral and unofficial cultures of the Mormon "Yes on 8" campaign. Those who witnessed the campaign firsthand in California report that it was communicated by priesthood leaders in Sunday meetings and widely believed among LDS Church members that the legalization of same-sex marriage would force the LDS Church to marry gay couples, and that the church would be forced to shut down its own temples rather than comply.[16] (Similar narratives were deployed among LDS Church members in Arizona and Massachusetts when those states considered same-sex marriage legalization.) Mormons generally did not incorporate their fear of a threat against temple marriage in their communications with non-Mormon potential voters, because that would have contradicted instructions not to openly identify as LDS during the day-to-day public conduct of the campaign. But day-to-day communications among members consistently telegraphed this threat in language coded to index the Mormon temple. For example, one zip code supervisor described door-to-door voter identification as a "solemn duty." Another described phonebanking as a responsibility with "eternal" consequences.

The idea that the legalization of same-sex marriage would force conservative denominations to offer marriage to same-sex couples or face legal penalties was broadly discredited by legal experts writing in the mainstream media. Mormon supporters of marriage equality also sought to contest this tendentious interpretation, but their efforts were broadly disregarded because they did not reach LDS populations through recognized institutional and authorized surrogate channels. The siege-oriented "undergrounding" mentality insulated LDS populations from robust civil exchange with fellow citizens.

In summer and fall 2008, a small cadre of Mormons worked to document and bring to light the nature and the extent of LDS involvement and funding in the "Yes on 8" campaign. One group of Mormon activists did so by combing through campaign donation records published online by the California Secretary of State and identifying LDS donors, either through personal knowledge, corroboration with accessible congregational directories, or search-engine use. Spreadsheets documenting donor names identified as LDS were published on the internet at Mormonsfor8.com. In using state records and LDS insider knowledge to circumvent Mormon efforts to obscure the extent of LDS influence on the "Yes on 8" campaign, the group sought to hold LDS political participants accountable to the norms of contemporary civic life—including norms of transparency. The activist group itself sought to remain anonymous because its members understood that within Mormon culture such an act would be viewed as a betrayal and potentially could jeopardize their membership within the LDS Church. "What they [church leaders] are doing was just what they did during the Equal Rights Amendment campaign," one Mormonsfor8.com activist who had witnessed the LDS anti-ERA effort told me. "When anyone asks me, 'Why do you want to make the church look bad?,' I say, 'Maybe if you think [LDS involvement in Yes on 8] looks bad, it *is* bad.'" These comments indicate the extent to which consciousness of insider-outsider boundaries and communicative dynamics structure LDS political involvement during high seasons.

They also reveal that tactics of "undergrounding" mobilized during the Proposition 8 campaign were not new. As historian Martha Sonntag Bradley documents in her book *Pedestals and Podiums* (2005), many of these strategies were implemented during the LDS Church's fight against the ratification of the Equal Rights Amendment during the late 1970s and early 1980s. Just as the church had made financial contributions to campaigns against same-sex marriage in states like Hawaii and Alaska that were grossly disproportionate to the percentages of LDS residents, during International Women's Year (IWY) events in 1977, LDS leaders mobilized Mormon women in several states to attend in numbers grossly disproportionate to their percentage of the citizenship and participate in ways designed to overwhelm and disrupt planned proceedings (especially but not exclusively in Utah): in Washington state, where Mormons made up 2 percent of the population, 50 percent of the 4,000 Washington IWY attendees were LDS; in Montana, organizers and LDS priesthood leaders estimated that half of the attendees were LDS. Letters from LDS Church headquarters mobilized and instructed Mormon women attendees in New York state; Mormon women in Hawaii were instructed by local leaders to attend multiday pre-IWY convention trainings and organized into carpools to the convention, where they reportedly outnumbered liberal women by a two-to-one margin. In several states, LDS men with walkie-talkies accompanied the Mormon women's delegations, instructing and guiding their participation.[17]

During the ERA fight itself, Bradley notes, LDS Church leaders particularized the campaign to LDS people by crafting specifically LDS anti-ERA messaging and delivering it through trusted institutional print channels like the *Deseret News* and the *Ensign*. Mormon-specific messaging focused on the need to protect LDS families against worldly regulation of gender, activating deep-rooted historical fears about threats to the Mormon family and deeply held defensive postures. As he would later do during the Hawaii anti–same-sex marriage campaign, then Elder Gordon B. Hinckley encouraged Mormons in the strategic ratification state of Virginia to think of and present themselves as members of a larger trans-faith coalition against the ERA, but the Virginia LDS anti-ERA campaign was implemented by LDS leaders through specifically LDS vehicles. Hinckley recruited and even issued ecclesiastical "callings" to members in strategic ratification states like Virginia to create ostensibly "independent" LDS political organizations such as Virginia's LDS Citizens Coalition. LDS Church members were encouraged to donate to specific church-identified organizational surrogates such as Families Are Concerned Today (FACT), even as the church denied any connection to those surrogates. Virginia's anti-ERA efforts instrumentalized LDS wards, using church meetings and facilities to gather anti-ERA signatures and organizing canvassing efforts. Even when they were not officially appointed by church leaders or "set apart" with an ecclesiastical blessing by the laying on of hands, anti-ERA activists were encouraged by local and general church leaders to understand their campaigning as a religious "calling." Yet even as LDS leaders particularized the campaign to LDS populations in a way that activated specifically LDS fears and sensibilities, they instructed local leaders to foster the sense that LDS Church headquarters was not directing the campaign. This resulted in what Bradley describes as a "tightrope walk" that left priesthood leaders relaying instructions from headquarters like "clandestine operatives." Mormons who organized to distribute literature or canvass door-to-door were instructed not to identify themselves as Mormons.[18] In these tactics, we see precursors of key features of the Proposition 8 campaign, including particularization of the campaign to

LDS motives and sensibilities through authorized channels, public postures of non-transparency that obscure central LDS direction of local efforts, and a focus on the besieged family in internal communications.

There is no question that when these discursive tactics of "undergrounding" were used again during the "Yes on 8" campaign they effectively motivated and mobilized LDS people. But reactivating these old patterns of guardedness, siege mentality, opacity, and insider-outsider boundary maintenance also came at a cost to LDS credibility. As conversations recollected by Mormonsfor8.com activists reveal, LDS people had a sense that if their activities became public they would not be well received by non-Mormons; even so, most Mormons did not interpret this concern as a reason for a moral reevaluation of the campaign and its tactics. More fundamental was the sense that Mormons had been and would continue to be misunderstood or even antagonized by outsiders and that what mattered most was protecting the community, no matter the cost to credibility or relationships with non-LDS people, or to the image of Mormons in political and civic life. Those costs would soon be known.

Thanks in large part to the internet and their own willingness to use insider knowledge in the service of public sphere norms of communication, Mormonsfor8.com activists and others soon documented and made public the extent of church-backed LDS involvement in the campaign, including the fact that between 40 to 70 percent of "Yes on 8" money came from LDS people who constituted less than 2 percent of the California population. Because the church had successfully deflected attention from its own heavy investment in Proposition 8 by mobilizing insulated internal channels of communication, using surrogates to deflect attention from institutional involvement, and fostering private siege narratives to motivate LDS public sphere participation, postelection documentation of Mormon participation took on a sensational air. Even media outlets as carefully toned as the *New York Times* described LDS involvement in the campaign as being "concealed" and then "uncover"-ed. Such coverage fostered a sense of outing a cloaked but pervasive Mormon influence. These revelations hearkened back to and seemed to confirm stereotypes of Mormon deception and untrustworthiness dating back to the late nineteenth century.

Witness, for example, the striking parallels between images that circulated in the early twentieth-century press depicting Mormon theocracy as a secret manipulator of the conduct of LDS Senator Reed Smoot and the official graphic in the award-winning and widely screened documentary *8: The Mormon Proposition* (2010). Notice too how the review quote selected by the producers of *8* position Mormons as a population unwilling to participate in "open dialogue."

As much as I reject negative stereotypes of LDS people, these images point to some painful realities. Most Mormons were only marginally aware of the tactics of insularity, deflection, and careful management implemented by the so-called grassroots "Yes on 8" campaign. "Yes on 8" activities were conducted in plain sight in LDS communities, and LDS people were coached to view themselves as part of a "coalition" to oppose same-sex marriage. Consequently, Mormons were unprepared for the media's ensuing sensationalistic revelations of a Mormon "underground" and bewildered by the postelection LGBT activist response focusing on LDS participation, including demonstrations at LDS temples in California and beyond. These demonstrations recursively confirmed the construction of the LDS temple as an emblem of besieged theocracy and heightened the sense that LDS beliefs and practices were under threat from a hostile secular world. Mormons were also seemingly unprepared for the idea that their disproportionate and carefully managed involvement in the "Yes on 8" campaign would brand the church as a leading opponent of LGBT equality nationwide. All of these consequences highlight the general nonalignment between internal LDS discourse and discursive norms and dominant public sphere discourse and discursive norms. Indeed, LDS and public narratives about same-sex marriage continued to be sharply divided in the years after the campaign. As public opinion transitions steadily toward majority acceptance of same-sex marriage as a civil right, LDS leaders continue to frame the question defensively as a protection of religious freedom. It is worth noting, however, that we have not seen since 2008 a similarly scaled LDS mobilization against same-sex marriage, even as the ballot initiatives in the fall of 2012 reached geographical areas like Maryland (including Washington, D.C., suburbs, where the church had previously activated a strong and cohesive LDS population against the Equal Rights Amendment), and Washington state, where in some counties, LDS people constitute up to 10 percent of the population.

Understanding the insularity, privacy, and residual theocracy of LDS communities is crucial to understanding Mormon participation in American political life. Mormons have not routinely mobilized on socially conservative issues like abortion rights that have motivated other conservative Christian denominations. But if they are directed by LDS Church

FIGURE 12.1 "The Real Objection to Smoot," *Puck Magazine*, April 27, 1904. (J. Ottmann Lithograph Co., New York; copyright 1904 by Keppler & Schwarzmann; at www.loc.gov/pictures/item/2011645528/)

leaders to mobilize on an issue that is perceived to damage LDS interests, they will do so with intensity. The primary site for these high-intensity interventions into American political life have been on issues of gender, especially as they pertain to family definition, inasmuch as the power to create and eternally bind families on a heterosexual-reproductive model is a primary distinguishing feature of LDS theocracy. This pattern held true for more than a century—from the political crisis over polygamy, to the Equal Rights Amendment, to Proposition 8. Even as Mormonism has transitioned from a frontier theocracy toward a minority denomination, Mormons have maintained among ourselves a strong sense of differentiation from, and a residually martial disposition toward, dominant society. A robust sense of our history, vibrant kinship networks, and op-

FIGURE 12.2
Official poster, *8: The Mormon Proposition* (2010). Property of Red Flag Releasing.

positional identity are assets to the Mormon tradition. Old patterns of "undergrounding" are the shadow side of our difference. How Mormon communities continue to manage this shadow side and what it costs us will be key determinants of Mormon participation in American political life in the twenty-first century.

NOTES

1. David E. Campbell and J. Quin Monson, "Dry Kindling: A Political Profile of American Mormons," in J. Matthew Wilson, ed., *From Pews to Polling Places: Faith and Politics in the American Religious Mosaic* (Washington, D.C.: Georgetown University Press, 2007), 105–130. I would add that in addition to this vertical chain of command, strong horizontal kinship networks among Mormons contribute to communication and mobilization as well, as did demographic concentrations of LDS wealth in California, in the case of the "Yes on 8" campaign.

2. Daymon Smith, "The Last Shall Be First and the First Shall Be Last: Discourse and Mormon History" (PhD diss., Philadelphia: University of Pennsylvania, 2007), 30; Edwin Firmage and R. Collin Mangrum, *Zion in the Courts: A Legal History of the Church of Jesus Christ of Latter-day Saints, 1830–1900* (Urbana: University of Illinois Press, 2001), 137.

3. Thomas Alexander, *Utah: The Right Place: The Official Centennial History* (Salt Lake City: Gibbs Smith, 1995), 188–89.

4. Important exceptions here include Richard Lyman Bushman, *Joseph Smith: Rough Stone Rolling* (New York: Vintage, 2007); Todd Compton, *In Sacred Loneliness: The Plural Wives of Joseph Smith* (Salt Lake City: Signature Books, 1997); Kathleen Flake, *The Politics of American Religious Identity: The Seating of Senator Reed Smoot, Mormon Apostle* (Chapel Hill: University of North Carolina Press, 2004); and Richard Van Wagoner, *Mormon Polygamy: A History* (Salt Lake City: Signature Books, 1992). Laurel Thatcher Ulrich is now completing a major study of polygamy.

5. Smith, "The Last Shall Be First . . . ," 315–17.

6. Ibid., 347. Smith quotes a Manti temple worker named Moses Farnsworth writing in 1890, "We must save our temples. . . . There are some things that we are required to keep, i.e., we must not cast our pearls before swine, etc., and it places some in a peculiar position, for they cannot talk neither can they write, and they cannot print, and I want to say to you, when any busybodies come around with their talk and cant, tell them to stand still and see the salvation of God, or else go home and mind their own business" (188).

7. Smith notes in particular the "Religious identity of 'Mormon' indexed reliability with respect to keeping secrets" (ibid., 47).

8. Ibid., 96–97. It also bears mentioning that LDS temple ceremonies enjoining secrecy also contributed to the LDS cultural valuation of non-transparency.

9. Ibid., 165.

10. Ibid., 163–65.

11. Ibid., 321. The concept of communicative reason belongs to Jürgen Habermas, first articulated in his book *The Structural Transformation of the Public Sphere* (1962).

12. Smith, "The Last Shall Be First . . . ," 319, 362. 413.

13. Boyd Petersen, "Hugh Nibley and the 'Inmigration' of Mormon Education," unpublished MS, November 6, 2009. Daymon Smith argues that these practices of undergrounding were forced out with the excommunication of LDS fundamentalists in the 1930s and virtually expunged by the work of the LDS Church Correlation Committee in the middle of the twentieth century (Smith, ibid., 369). I would argue that correlation works in dialectical tension within and against older practices of undergrounding that index Mormon theocracy, difference, and status.

14. Loren Dunn to Russell M. Ballard, Letter, March 4, 1997; accessed online at www.boxturtlebulletin.com/btb/wp-content/uploads/2008/11/mormon20anti-gay20game20plan201997–2008.pdf.

15. Jeremy Hooper, "Lawrence vs. Hexes: The Eye-Opening Spiritual War Behind NOM's New Maryland Poll," *Prop 8 Trial Tracker* (February 17, 2011): www.prop8trialtracker.com/2011/02/17/lawrence-vs-hexes-the-eye-opening-spiritual-war-behind-noms-new-maryland-poll/.

16. Letters from anonymous sources, in possession of the author, January 2012.

17. Martha Sonntag Bradley, *Pedestals and Podiums: Utah Women, Religious Authority, and Equal Rights* (Salt Lake City: Signature Books, 2005), 231–37. On the Mormon anti-ERA campaign, see also Neil J. Young, "'The ERA Is a Moral Issue': The Mormon Church, LDS Women, and the Defeat of the Equal Rights Amendment," *American Quarterly* 59.3 (September 2007): 623–44.

18. Bradley, *Pedestals and Podiums*, 331–68.

13 Mitt, Mormonism, and the Media

An Unfamiliar Faith Takes the Stage in the 2012 U.S. Presidential Election

Peggy Fletcher Stack

A few years before Mitt Romney made his first run at the highest office in the land, a new reporter in the Salt Lake City bureau of the Associated Press was covering his first LDS General Conference, where more than 20,000 people gather in a giant auditorium for two days of announcements, music, and sermons. When the journalist's account of the semiannual church gathering hit the wires, it said that Gordon B. Hinckley, then president of the LDS Church, had been "re-elected unanimously." More seasoned reporters corrected the writer, pointing out that the LDS tradition of sustaining their church leader, considered a "prophet, seer and revelator," was not an election per se, but a symbolic gesture. Hinckley's position was never in question. Still, the AP greenie persisted.

"I heard the man say, 'All in favor, raise your right hand,'" the journalist declared, "and everybody did."

Such confusion was understandable. After all, Mormon founder Joseph Smith borrowed the term "General Conference" from the Methodists, whose representatives still meet every four years to vote for officers and churchwide resolutions, while setting policy for the church.

Therein was the challenge for reporters across the country—indeed, the globe—who were suddenly enlisted to explain the Mormon candidate and his faith to a world that knew almost nothing about the American-born church. For the most part, their experience, knowledge, vocabulary, and perspective came from the Protestant world that long has dominated American religion. This sometimes led journalists to make false assumptions and ask the wrong questions.

Consider a few examples culled from the coverage: Romney was a Mormon "bishop" and "stake president," but that did not make him a "high church official," as some wrote.[1] The fifteen-million member church has thousands of such lay leaders. And, though even the candidate came to use the term "pastor" to describe his role as bishop, the two positions are not equivalent. Romney got no special Mormon perks from paying millions in tithing to his church, as some writers presumed. After losing the presidency, the Republican nominee couldn't then "run for" the LDS Church presidency, as it is not an elected office.[2] The church may be against gambling, but it wasn't going to sanction Romney for proposing a $10,000 bet to Rick Perry.[3] And Mormonism does not forbid military service, as asserted by television host Whoopi Goldberg on *The View*. It is possible that she confused the Utah-based church with Jehovah's Witnesses.[4] Even those who attempted to defend Mormonism from evangelical attacks—including American historian David Reynolds—mischaracterized Romney's faith as "a brand of Protestantism."[5]

The list of errors goes on and on. Here are the top six mistakes reporters made in trying to explain Romney's Mormonism:

1. *Misunderstanding or misusing Mormon vocabulary.* Latter-day Saints have their own lexicon—including such unique terms as sacrament meeting, Primary, Word of Wisdom, ward, stake, general authority, and so forth—which can be daunting to reporters trying to cover the faith. Sermons are "talks," while communion is "the sacrament." An all-too-frequent error was dropping "Jesus Christ" out of the church's formal name, calling it instead the Church of the Latter-day Saints. In addition, a dizzying number of people in a given *ward* or *stake* are called "president." How was a reporter to tell if the opinion of an elders quorum president—a relatively routine congregational position—is as authoritative as that of a stake president, who holds a much more consequential church post?

2. *Misusing common religious vocabulary that means something different to Mormons.* An LDS seminary is not like training for the ministry, but more like a high school catechism class. An "elder" can be a 19-year-old boy, not a lay official in a Presbyterian congregation. A 15-year-old boy can be a priest. LDS missionaries serve for a limited time, not as a permanent calling.

3. *Misunderstanding the relationship between LDS general authorities and leaders at the local level.* The central Mormon hierarchy is as rigidly set as the Vatican, but leadership at the local level rotates frequently. Again, due to the church's unique vocabulary, a "high priest" seems like an important official. Romney is a high priest, having served as a bishop and stake president. But so is everyone who has been in a lay LDS bishopric and most of the faithful men from middle age on up.

4. *Presuming an LDS bishop has the same power and role as other religious leaders.* A Protestant minister, Catholic priest, or megachurch pastor is at the center of a congregation, preaching weekly and representing the views of his or her adherents and the church. In contrast, a Mormon bishop is a volunteer with a separate full-time job who is essentially an administrator and counselor. He doesn't typically give sermons on current events.

5. *Mistaking folk doctrines for core beliefs.* This problem was especially obvious in those writers who used *The Book of Mormon* musical as their source on LDS teachings. The list of beliefs offered up to a newspaper audience often seemed arbitrary and idiosyncratic. It's not surprising that Mormons don't see themselves in these accounts about planets, godhood, and magic underwear. For most members, these are not ideas that are often discussed at their weekly services. The church's health code was also routinely miscast—for example, *New York Times* columnist Maureen Dowd twice mistakenly wrote that Mormons aren't supposed to drink caffeine and, after several LDS complaints, had to write a correction.[6]

6. *Treating all former Mormons as "whistle-blowers" who promise to reveal problems within the faith unknown to outsiders.* This journalistic model may work in certain institutions and for certain ethical or moral lapses such as in cases of abuse, but in this case, journalists' heavy reliance on the testimony of ex-Mormons put forward a skewed view of the LDS Church. Former Mormons often have compelling personal narratives that could and should be included in pieces that balance them with equally compelling stories of satisfaction and conversion. But not many former members are entirely fair-minded observers of the contemporary church.

Between 2007, when Romney began his climb to the presidency, and November 6, 2012, when the first LDS presidential candidate from a major party was defeated, thousands of stories about Mormonism appeared in newspapers, websites, television, and radio. A simple Google search in November 2012 of the words "Mitt Romney Mormon" came up with nearly seventeen million entries. Romney and his faith graced the cover of numerous magazines, including *Time*, *Newsweek*, and the *New Yorker*, the latter with an illustration of the candidate riding a chauffeur-driven white horse.[7] Journalists flocked to LDS Church headquarters in Salt Lake City as well as to Belmont, Massachusetts, where Romney had lived and worshipped for decades, to glean more about the little-known faith as a possible key to the candidate's character. They interviewed church leaders, friends, neighbors, observers, historians or anyone who might add depth and color to Mitt's profile.

Reporters covering the religion beat seemed best able to grasp the details and nuances of Mormonism, writing thoughtful explorations of the faith and how it might influence the candidate.[8] Even some political journalists with no prior knowledge of the LDS Church spent time schooling themselves in its history and beliefs.[9] At the same time, editorial writers, web commenters, and politicos of all stripes weighed in from a position of ignorance and ill will.

Thus began a dance between the mainstream media and the Utah church, which produced some surprising results. Mormons saw themselves reflected in the country's pluralistic mirror, not as outsiders but as part of the crowded field. They faced some of the tougher issues in their history and had a chance to erase false perceptions. Some Mormons discovered more diversity in their own movement than they knew existed. Meanwhile, many other Americans met the real Mormonism for the first time, rather than its tabloid versions.

Yes, there was predictable stereotyping and mockery, including misperceptions and absurdities on editorial pages and websites of even prestigious news organizations. Some accounts exploited easy targets such as the caricature of Mormonism as a cult, its battle with historic Christians, its racist past, and its involvement with polygamy. But there was also remarkable restraint by many in the mainstream media and a conscious decision to avoid certain avenues of discussion that many Mormons had felt certain the media would go. The kind of persecution some prominent Latter-day Saints, including Utah Senator Orrin Hatch, expected failed to materialize.

Cult or Quacks?

When Romney launched his first candidacy for president on February 13, 2007, the stage was set for a major face-off between Mormon and evangelical Christians. Many evangelicals believed that Romney's church did not fit the definition of "Christian" at best and at worst was a dangerous counterfeit faith.

The Reverend Robert Jeffress, a Southern Baptist pastor in Dallas, Texas, called Mormonism a cult in 2007, then again in 2011.[10] Eventually, Jeffress joined the Romney parade, even saying he would vote for the Mormon; however, he never changed his view about Romney's faith. The Reverend Bill Keller said "a vote for Romney is a vote for Satan," and onetime Democratic candidate the Reverend Al Sharpton said, "As for the one Mormon running for office, those who really believe in God will defeat him anyways, so don't worry about that; that's a temporary situation."[11] Finally, when Mike Huckabee—former governor of Arkansas, a Baptist minister, and competing 2008 Republican presidential candidate—was asked if he believed Mormonism was a cult, he claimed he didn't know much about the LDS Church. But he then asked: "Don't Mormons believe that Jesus Christ and the devil are brothers?"[12]

The cult issue was much less in play during Romney's 2012 campaign, with the latter articles much more explanatory than provocative. For example, on the eve of the Florida Republican primary in 2012, religion writer Cathy Lynn Grossman from *USA Today* penned a complicated and comprehensive analysis about why evangelicals were still wary of Mormons. It was well done and fair (with only one error—she said Gordon B. Hinckley rather than Spencer W. Kimball ended the priesthood ban on black men).[13]

Meanwhile, more secular writers scoffed at the notion of a candidate who took seriously Mormon history and beliefs." I wouldn't vote for someone," Jacob Weisberg wrote in the online magazine *Slate*, "who truly believed in the founding whoppers of Mormonism."[14] That was a line of reasoning that several opinion writers followed into the 2012 campaign. The late Christopher Hitchens, a prominent atheist writer, decried what he said was the "weird and sinister belief system of the LDS."[15]

Even literary scholar Harold Bloom, who had written somewhat glowingly about Mormon founder Joseph Smith in his book *The American Religion: The Emergence of the Post-Christian Nation*, seemed to dismiss Romney's Mormonism. "A superb trickster and protean personality, Smith was a religious genius, uniquely able to craft a story capable of turning a self-invented faith into a people now as numerous as the Jews, in America and abroad," Bloom wrote in a *New York Times* guest column. Yet he continued by saying that the "last two decades have witnessed the deliberate dwindling of the Church of Jesus Christ of Latter-day Saints into just one more Protestant sect."[16] Bloom condemned the current LDS Church president, Thomas S. Monson, claiming he was "indistinguishable from the secular plutocratic oligarchs who exercise power in our supposed democracy." He then concluded by attacking both the Mormons and the Southern Baptists, speculating on which would be "more dangerous" in an American president—"a knowledge-hungry religious zealotry or a proudly stupid one? Either way we are condemned to remain a plutocracy and oligarchy. I can be forgiven for dreading a further strengthening of theocracy in that powerful brew."

Biography as Theology

Several writers recognized early that Romney's religious experience—from his two-year LDS mission to France, his time at Brigham Young University, and his stint as lay leader of a Boston-area congregation—might add some contours to the candidate's profile.

In January 2008, the *Salt Lake Tribune* became the first to write about the humanizing effect of Romney's church service in the 1980s and '90s, interviewing many fellow Mormons who had known the candidate in those days.[17] But Romney dropped out of the race a month later, so the topic became moot—until it was resurrected again in 2011 and 2012 by reporters at the *New York Times*, the *Washington Post*, the *Los Angeles Times*, and CNN, to name a few.[18]

"As the presumptive Republican nominee for president, Mr. Romney speaks so sparingly about his faith—he and his aides frequently stipulate that he does not impose his beliefs on others—that its influence on him can be difficult to detect," Jodi Kantor wrote in the *New York Times* on May 19, 2012.[19] "But dozens of the candidate's friends, fellow church members and relatives describe a man whose faith is his design for living. The church is by no means his only influence, and its impact cannot be fully untangled from that of his family, which is also steeped in Mormonism."

Kantor's piece, while generally positive, got a few odd things wrong: she used the word "deseret" as an adjective suggesting "industriousness," when it is a noun in LDS-speak meaning "honeybee." Mormons generally don't "belt out" or even sing the Protestant hymn "What a Friend We Have in Jesus." White temple clothes don't necessarily indicate an "elevated state." And Nephites and Lamanites are Book of Mormon characters only; they are not in the Bible.

Several of the Romney biographical sketches mentioned his relationship with women in his congregations, a sensitive topic for a faith with an all-male priesthood. One episode was repeated again and again in media accounts, including Kantor's: as a young bishop, Romney reportedly pressured a church member against having an abortion, even when the doctors and other Mormon leaders felt it would be the best solution for the married mother with some life-threatening health issues. Feminists pointed to the incident as a clear example of Romney's supposed attacks on women, but it won him bona fides among the antiabortion crowd that had been suspicious of him while he was running for governor of Massachusetts.

In November 2011, Jason Horowitz of the *Washington Post* looked at Romney's evolution in his treatment of Mormon women. Horowitz described episodes where Romney was patronizing, even bullying, toward LDS feminists when he was a stake president in Boston. But the reporter did his homework with more than a few Mormon women, tracing the candidate's evolving attitudes. To be sure, Romney never embraced a feminist point of view, but Horowitz depicted the one-time Mormon leader as a pragmatic problem-solver. The writer seemed to understand some of the dynamics at play between a young bishop and the women in his flock.

Like other reporters, however, Horowitz did not quite capture the dynamic in a Mormon ward, seeing a Protestant congregation as the closest analogue. "As bishop, Romney exercised great power over his congregation. Besides appointing staff members, from the local church librarian to choir master, he interviewed people in the congregation to determine fealty to the church," Horowitz wrote.[20] "He decided who could carry a 'recommend,' a physical card that serves as proof of a person's good doctrinal standing and suitability to enter the sacred temples." Romney may have been a strong Mormon bishop, but this seems to overstate his power and understate the role of a three-member LDS bishopric in the issuing of "temple recommends." Besides, Mormon bishops' roles in determining temple worthiness are clearly spelled out for them in instructional manuals and training by church headquarters. Romney was not freelancing his approach.

Horowitz also repeats a story about a divorced pregnant woman in Romney's congregation. The woman, who no longer considered herself a church member, said Romney had threatened her with excommunication if she didn't give the baby up for adoption. To most Mormon readers, however, that didn't make sense. Romney could have been bullying and exerting pressure, but no one can be excommunicated from the LDS Church for refusing to give up a baby for adoption. It was another one of those cases where a journalist didn't seem to know all the right questions to ask.

Who Are the Experts?

It was not easy for reporters to figure out who were the best guides into the world of Mormonism. Their first call may have been to LDS spokespeople, who could give the official explanations of beliefs and practices. But the church's Public Affairs office kept an arm's length from the campaign, maintaining the church's strict and oft-stated stance of political neutrality. Monson, the church president, gave no interviews during Romney's run, nor did either of his counselors in the governing First Presidency.

Thus, journalists were left to cultivate unofficial choices. Many sought LDS historians, religious studies scholars, writers, and bloggers to explain the candidate and his relation to the faith of his forefathers. Was Romney typical? Were his decisions, policies, and pronouncements born of his religious beliefs?

Among the most articulate of the alternate voices was Joanna Brooks, a professor at San Diego State University, and a passionate Mormon storyteller. Brooks's self-published memoir, *The Book of Mormon Girl*, hit the public in January 2012 (and was later picked up by Simon and Schuster) just as curiosity about Romney's religion was on the rise. She was profiled by Jessica Ravitz of CNN, and later interviewed by Jon Stewart of Comedy Central (*The Daily Show*) fame.[21] In addition to being the go-to source on all things Mormon, Brooks routinely responded to media critiques of Romney and their shared faith in her regular column at *Religion Dispatches*.[22] She waded into complex historical and social issues—women, blacks, gays, tithing, finances, temple rituals—and even explored the whole Mormon "funny underwear" mystique.

Brooks was among a cadre of loyal LDS experts, including historians Richard Lyman Bushman, Matthew Bowman, Kathleen Flake, and Philip Barlow, and writers Jana Riess, McKay Coppins, and Kristine Haglund, who became the most sought-after Mormon observers. Their presence in the church offered journalists a chance to include perspectives generally more multifaceted than official sources, allowing for criticisms and alluding to divisive issues within the faith. This revealed a broader set of beliefs in the Mormon movement than had been known before and helped shape a richer image for outsiders. These experts were, by and large, more liberal and progressive in Mormon matters, but journalists also turned to more conservative but unofficial voices such as members of FAIR (formerly known as the Foundation for Apologetic Information and Research) and so-called Mormon Mommy Bloggers.

Then there were the career critics, typically former Mormons who had written books about their experience or created websites to expose what they felt were the wrongs of the LDS movement. Their purpose was to undermine the credibility of both the LDS Church and Romney. Their views are typically unidimensional, and often hyperbolic.

On several occasions, CNN interviewed Tricia Erickson, the author of *Can Mitt Romney Serve Two Masters? The Mormon Church Versus the Office of the Presidency of the United States of America*. "I cannot explain to you in a few words here just how completely violent, mind controlling and alarming these [temple] ceremonies are," Erickson told CNN. "Just this information on the secret temple ceremonies would send most thinking human beings into 'warning mode' that maybe we all better rethink who our Republican candidate should be. . . . I can't stress enough to you how truly alarming these ceremonies that Mitt and Ann repeatedly went through, and continue to go to and participate in, are."[23] Erickson, a self-styled whistle-blower, said she was waiting for someone else to publicize the evils of Mormonism before jumping in. "It just amazed me," she said in the interview, "knowing what I know, that no one else would expose what has to be brought to light to the American people about this candidate."

Newsweek and *Daily Beast* reporter Jamie Reno published a provocative interview with Sue Emmett, a direct descendent of Brigham Young and a former LDS Church member, who claimed, "Every Mormon grows up with the idea that it's OK to lie if it's for a higher cause."[24]

Another former Mormon, Sally Denton, told the *New York Times* that "male dominance is the essence of the LDS Church." To be sure, the church's patriarchy is a problem for many Mormon women, but Denton made it the faith's central issue. She then cited Sonia Johnson, a Mormon feminist who was excommunicated from the church in 1979. Much has changed in the intervening decades, and it is astonishing that Denton couldn't find more current feminists to showcase. Denton then went on to warn readers that giving Romney the presidency would be tantamount to allowing the LDS Church free rein over the country.[25]

But one name conspicuously absent among the sources was journalist Jon Krakauer, whose bestselling 2003 book *Under the Banner of Heaven:*

A Story of Violent Faith had been read by millions as a primer on Mormonism. Krakauer's thesis was that Mormonism is a destructive, controlling faith that inevitably leads to pain, conflict, and, sometimes, even murder. The book was decried by LDS officials. During the 2008 raid of a Texas polygamist group that is an offshoot of mainstream Mormonism, Krakauer was a regular commenter on CNN. Yet during Romney's 2012 run, few, if any, looked to him as an expert.

Protesting the Faith

Again using a Protestant model, some journalists presumed that if Romney, or any Mormon, was displeased with his church's direction, he should publicly criticize the institution or leave it for another. After all, most mainline Protestants align with congregations that share their political perspective as well as their theological views and, if they are not satisfied, they can seek out another wing of the denomination or switch to another within the umbrella of historic Christianity. But Mormonism is more tribal than that. Even though they might be upset by the church's stances on gays, blacks, or women, most believing Latter-day Saints stay with the faith, trying to change it from within. Thus, Romney responded very typically in a 2007 *Meet the Press* interview when Tim Russert noted that Romney was thirty-one years old in 1978, when the LDS Church lifted its ban against black males holding the priesthood. "Didn't you think, 'What am I doing [as] part of an organization that is viewed by many as a racist organization?'" Russert asked. "I'm very proud of my faith, and it's the faith of my fathers," Romney answered. "And I'm not going to distance myself from my faith in any way."[26]

Journalists did raise the race issue again in the 2012 campaign and, while the candidate didn't give any different answers, seeing its discontinued priesthood ban in the national spotlight had a dramatic impact on the church itself. Indeed, several reporters quickly recognized the historic choice faced by black Mormons—whether to vote their race with President Obama or their faith with Romney.[27] Throughout the campaign, representatives of that tension—including Darius Gray, former president of the Genesis Group, a support organization for black Mormons—could be heard in newspapers and seen on television. This was yet another example of a growing diversity within the faith.[28]

In a February 22, 2012, piece titled "The Genesis of a Church's Stand on Race," the *Washington Post*'s Jason Horowitz explored reasons behind the century-long prohibition on black men being ordained to the Mormon priesthood.[29] The writer interviewed BYU religion professor Randy Bott, who described several theological theories about the ban, including the idea that blacks were somehow "less valiant" in the premortal life or that it was merely about timing. "God has always been discriminatory," Bott told Horowitz, who wrote that Bott compared "blacks with a young child prematurely asking for the keys to her father's car, and explains that similarly until 1978, the Lord determined that blacks were not yet ready for the priesthood."

Bott's comments generated howls of complaints from church members and officials. Within a day, the LDS Church's Newsroom issued a strong statement that the BYU professor's words were his own and that the church condemned "racism, including any and all past racism by individuals both inside and outside the Church."[30]

It was a pivotal moment for Mormonism. Ever since the 1978 removal of the ban, many members had pushed the church to disavow all religious folklore that had arisen to defend the racist policy. With a single article in the midst of a political campaign, LDS officials finally had done just that: "Some have attempted to explain the reason for this restriction but these attempts should be viewed as speculation and opinion, not doctrine." Though some still hankered for an apology, many quietly celebrated the church's strong statement.

The Money Issue

While racism was an issue that most observers admitted was mostly in the Mormon past, the church's wealth was another, much more contemporary, matter. Some 2012 news stories, particularly those dealing with Romney's tithing to the church, subtly suggested ulterior motives surrounding LDS practices.

"Romney Sent Millions to the Mormon Church," an ABC news piece announced in February 2012.[31] The story went on to suggest that Romney, as an LDS lay leader, was helping his church by giving it "millions of dollars worth of stock in some of Bain Capital's most well-known holdings." Though donating stock is a common practice among wealthy and even some middle-class American Mormons, ABC's message was clear:

Romney was doing something nefarious by giving his church "a slice of his . . . lucrative business deals."

Or how about this one, from the *Christian Science Monitor?* "The strength of Romney's religious conviction now has a dollar sign attached to it. Will his tithing invigorate the unease that many Americans feel toward the Mormon church?"[32]

For Mormons, tithing is a religious practice that is about their relationship to God and their commitment to building his church, not about hiding assets or winning plaudits by being a big donor. Toward the end of the campaign, the issue of Romney's methods of church donations did raise some legitimate concerns about his use of the church to get out of paying some taxes; however, it was not a well-understood critique for most Americans, even Mormons.[33]

Mostly, questions about Mormon finances continued to intrigue and vex writers, who often got the details right while missing the larger picture. In an October 2011 cover story for *Harper's*, "Pennies from Heaven: How Mormon Economics Shape the G.O.P.," writer Chris Lehmann put together a harangue about Romney's supposed view of economics.[34] He quoted Mark Skousen—a professor of economics who is the nephew of author Cleon Skousen—referring to Mormon teachings on success as "the Protestant ethic on steroids." In the article, Lehmann asserted that "today's Mormons are model free-market apostles" who "have very little ambivalence about the acquisition of wealth," paying no attention to the faith's long-standing communitarian strain of thinking.

Lehmann assembled quotes from various leaders, conservative members, and scripture to argue that Mormons believe more than any other Christians in the "prosperity gospel"—a term that has been applied to some Protestants' theology but that Latter-day Saints do not use—suggesting that the accumulation of wealth is a major goal for Mormons and symbolic of God's favor. Mormons like Romney may be wealthy and some may credit their success in life to their righteousness, but those are not official LDS teachings. In fact, the church's signature scripture, the Book of Mormon, constantly condemns economic inequality and neglect of the poor. Along those lines, several other media outlets, including NBC's magazine program *Rock Center*, went to great lengths to showcase the LDS Church's extensive welfare system and humanitarian efforts.[35]

At the same time, both *Businessweek* and Reuters attempted to uncover the sources and patterns of LDS corporate finances.[36] Although the church is run by volunteers at the local level, it pays a vast bureaucracy in Utah to manage what some say is a billion-dollar budget. The two articles described the church's recent development of a downtown Salt Lake City shopping mall, City Creek Center, its real estate holdings, and its pay scale for some of its top managers—all for-profit ventures that reportedly did not use current tithing dollars. The *Businessweek* cover was especially offensive to the LDS faithful. It carried an illustration of John the Baptist giving the priesthood to Joseph Smith and Oliver Cowdery, with the thought bubbles over their heads reading, "And thou shalt build a shopping mall, own stock in Burger King and open a Polynesian theme park in Hawaii that shall be largely exempt from the frustrations of tax . . ."

Both articles were extensively researched and seemed to get the data right, yet the overall perception did not match with how most Mormons view church finances. The church's Public Affairs office took issue with the findings and posted a rebuttal called "The Church and Its Financial Independence" on its Newsroom website.[37]

Unexpected Attacks, Restraints, and Conclusions

In March 2012, John Sweeney, a freelancer with the BBC, did a classic video exposé on Mormonism, complete with what is known as "ambush journalism."[38] He managed to film during services inside the LDS chapel in Belmont, Massachusetts, where Romney worshipped, and to get an interview with Mormon apostle Jeffrey R. Holland, promising a broad look at the faith. Instead, Sweeney hit the apostle with probing questions about the LDS temple ceremony, which Mormons do not discuss outside of that sacred sphere. His piece was all told from the perspective of former members out to "expose" what they view as a secretive, deluded, dangerous sect, which is often cruel to those who leave.

In the last weeks of the 2012 campaign, another former Mormon began to pitch an undercover video taken inside an LDS temple ceremony, saying he had footage of the candidate himself dressed in holy clothing and swearing total allegiance to the faith. The man, who identified himself only as "Newnamenoah," put the footage on YouTube. Within days it had attracted more than a million page views, though no one in the clip could be identified as Romney. Astonishingly, the only semi-mainstream reporter to use the clip was Andrew Sullivan at the *Atlantic*. Every other media outlet the former Mormon approached declined to touch it.

In the end, Mormonism was not Romney's undoing. There was handwringing among evangelicals who worried aloud about voting for a Mormon, but they still stood behind their Republican candidate. Romney virtually swept the Bible Belt, with nearly the same percentage of evangelicals voting for the Mormon candidate as had voted for George W. Bush.[39] The Mormonism-is-a-cult claim didn't stick with the larger population. Mormon underwear jokes came and went during Romney's candidacy, but ultimately became just another "so what?" to most Americans. Mormons developed thicker skins about their unusual beliefs and practices, while their friends of other faiths discovered that Latter-day Saints may have some quirky beliefs (what religion doesn't?), but they also have a strong work ethic and do lots of good—and they're not Protestants.

Romney's first campaign revealed that "latent misunderstanding" about Mormonism existed in America, LDS spokesman Michael Otterson told the *Washington Post* on Election Day 2012. The second campaign talked about how LDS beliefs differ from other faiths, then moved into a broader discussion of what Mormons do.[40] "The media started to ask more questions about what do Mormons actually do, how do they live their lives, what is different about the community?" Otterson said. "And that was a conversation that made a lot more sense to us."

Some longtime observers believed that Romney's run was a net gain for his church, while his defeat actually helped it sidestep a potential avalanche of negative publicity. Romney's loss "may be a blessing for Mormons concerned about further public scrutiny of their faith," Utah Valley University administrator Brian Birch told the *Salt Lake Tribune* on Election Night. "A Romney presidency would almost certainly have kept Mormonism under the microscope for many years to come."[41]

The day after Romney's defeat, the phone stopped its incessant ringing in the church's Public Affairs office at its Salt Lake City headquarters. No calls from French reporters wanting to know about polygamy. No texts from video producers in India or China or Brazil asking about missionaries. The so-called "Mormon Moment" surrounding Romney's two failed bids to be the first Mormon to lead the free world was over.

In December 2012, the Pew Forum on Religion and Public Life found that Romney's run for the White House had not educated Americans about his faith. Eight in ten (82 percent) told pollsters they "learned little or nothing about the Mormon religion during the presidential campaign."[42] Most were still unable to correctly answer basic questions about LDS

224   INTO THE TWENTY-FIRST CENTURY

history and sacred texts. And three in ten continued "to consider the Mormon religion a non-Christian faith."

Nearly two years later, the LDS Church was once again working to offer the general public a glimpse into its faith and people. This time it was a documentary film, *Meet the Mormons*, which profiled six everyday members of the Utah-based faith—a Nepalese humanitarian; a head football coach of the U.S. Naval Academy in Annapolis, Maryland; an amateur kickboxing champ in Costa Rica; an African American Mormon bishop in Atlanta; a Utah mom of a biracial LDS missionary; and a retired U.S. airman, who dropped candy tied to parachutes to children during the 1940s Berlin Airlift.

On hand for the October 7, 2014, premiere at a Salt Lake City cinema were many of Mormonism's glitterati. According to a Utah news report, "famous athletes, big-name entertainers, international rock stars, Mormon cultural icons" were all on hand, as well as "lots of others who wouldn't necessarily need to introduce themselves."[43]

Romney, who had spent considerable time since his 2012 defeat supporting Republican candidates and assuming the role of senior statesman to party hopefuls (stoking speculation of a potential 2016 return), moved easily among others in his faith that night. The former standard-bearer and still-revered politico, who sometimes seemed ill at ease on the stump, was most at home among his Mormon people.

NOTES

1. Howard Fineman, "Mitt Romney, Former Mormon Bishop, Unveils New Emphasis on His Faith," *Huffington Post*, August 30, 2012.

2. Albert R. Hunt, *Bloomberg News*, November 2011.

3. Elizabeth Tenety, "Did Mitt Romney's $10,000 Bet Violate Mormon Church Teaching?" *Washington Post*, December 11, 2011.

4. Kevin Cirilli, "Ann Romney Corrects Whoopi Goldberg on LDS," *Politico*, October 18, 2012.

5. David S. Reynolds, "Why Evangelicals Don't Like Mormons," *New York Times*, January 25, 2012.

6. Truth be told, many Mormons get the caffeine question wrong, too, showing the sway that folk beliefs sometimes hold over actual dogma.

7. *The New Yorker*, October 1, 2012.

8. Examples include Laurie Goodstein of the *New York Times*, Rachel Zoll of the Associated Press, and Ann Rogers of the *Pittsburgh Post Gazette*.

9. Examples include Jason Horowitz of the *Washington Post*, Leon Wieseltier of the *New Republic*, and Hendrik Hertzberg of the *New Yorker*.

10. Richard A. Oppel and Erik Eckholm, "Prominent Pastor Calls Romney's Church a Cult," *New York Times*, October 7, 2011.

11. "Christian Leader Follows Up Attack by Sharpton," *World News Daily*, May 10, 2007.

12. Zev Chavets, "The Huckabee Factor," *New York Times Magazine*, December 12, 2007.

13. Cathy Lynn Grossman, "Few Informed, Many Wary of Mormon Beliefs," *USA Today*, January 25, 2012.

14. Jacob Weisberg, "A Mormon President? No Way," *Slate*, December 20, 2006.

15. Christopher Hitchens, "Romney's Mormon Problem," *Slate*, October 17, 2011.

16. Harold Bloom, "Will This Election Be the Mormon Breakthrough?" *New York Times*, November 12, 2011.

17. Peggy Fletcher Stack, "Mitt and his Faith: Remembering When Candidate Romney Was Bishop Romney," *Salt Lake Tribune*, January 11, 2008.

18. Jessica Ravitz, "The Shaping of a Candidate: A Look at Mitt Romney's Faith Journey," CNN, October 29, 2011; Alana Semuels, "Romney: An Active Man of Faith," *Los Angeles Times*, November 8, 2011.

19. Jodi Kantor, "Romney's Faith, Silent but Deep," *New York Times*, May 19, 2012.

20. Jason Horowitz, "In Boston, Mitt Romney 'Evolved' in Mormon Leadership, Some Churchwomen Say," *Washington Post*, November 21, 2011.

21. Jessica Ravitz, "Crossing the Plains and Kicking Up Dirt," CNN, February 5, 2012.

22. See www.religiondispatches.org.

23. CNN, July 7, 2011.

24. Emmett, quoted in Jamie Reno, "Brigham Young's Great-Great-Granddaughter on Mormonism and Mitt Romney," *The Daily Beast*, August 7, 2012.

25. Sally Denton, "A Male-Dominated Church," *New York Times—Room for Debate*, January 30, 2012.

26. *Meet the Press*, December 17, 2007.

27. Religion News Service and Peggy Fletcher Stack, "Black Mormons Face Historic Presidential Choice," *Salt Lake Tribune*, June 11, 2012.

28. Jessica Williams, "The Black Mormon Vote," *The Daily Show with Jon Stewart*, October 9, 2012.

29. Jason Horowitz, "The Genesis of a Church's Stand on Race," *Washington Post*, February 22, 2012.

30. "Church Statement Regarding *Washington Post* Article on Race and the Church," Newsroom: The Church of Jesus Christ of Latter-day Saints, mormonnewsroom.org, February 29, 2012.

31. *ABC News*, January 18, 2012.

32. Gloria Goodale, "Mitt Romney's Tithing: Do Voters See It As Very Generous or Very Mormon?" *Christian Science Monitor*, January 25, 2012.

33. Joanna Brooks, "Romney's Tax Secret Revealed—And It's About Religion," *Religion Dispatches*, October 30, 2012.

34. Chris Lehmann, "Pennies from Heaven: How Mormon Economics Shape the G.O.P.," *Harper's*, October 2011.

35. NBC's *Rock Center*, August 22, 2012.

36. Caroline Winter, "How Mormons Make Money," *Businessweek*, July 18, 2012; Paul Henderson, "Insight: Mormon Church Made Wealthy by Donations," Reuters, August 12, 2012.

37. "The Church and Its Financial Independence," Newsroom: The Church of Jesus Christ of Latter-day Saints, www.mormonnewsroom.org/article/church-financial-independence, July 12, 2012.

38. John Sweeney, "The Mormon Candidate," BBC TWO, *This World*, March 27, 2012.

39. Thomas Burr, "No Mormon Spike for Romney on Election Day," *Salt Lake Tribune*, November 9, 2012.

40. Jason Horowitz, "Mormon Press Office: Church's Image Survived the Campaign," *Washington Post*, November 6, 2012.

41. Peggy Fletcher Stack, "Mormon Moment Ends with a Loss—But His Religion Still Won," *Salt Lake Tribune*, November 7, 2012.

42. "Americans Learned Little About the Mormon Faith, But Some Attitudes Have Softened," Pew Research Center, Religion and Public Life Project, December 14, 2012.

43. Aaron Shill, "Big Names Attend Screening of *Meet the Mormons*," *Deseret News*, October 9, 2014.

Contributors

Randall Balmer is Dartmouth Professor in the Arts and Sciences, chair of the Religion Department, and director of the Society of Fellows at Dartmouth College. He gave the Tanner Lecture for the Mormon History Association in 2003, and he is the author of more than a dozen books, including *Mine Eyes Have Seen the Glory: A Journey into the Evangelical Subculture in America* (Oxford, 1989), now in its fifth edition, and *Redeemer: The Life of Jimmy Carter* (Basic Books, 2014).

Philip L. Barlow is the author of the updated edition of *Mormons and the Bible* (Oxford, 2014), and the coeditor, with Terryl Givens, of the forthcoming *Oxford Handbook to Mormonism* (Oxford, 2015). He is the Leonard J. Arrington Professor of Mormon History and Culture at Utah State University.

Matthew Bowman is the author of *The Mormon People: The Making of an American Faith* (Random House, 2012) and *The Urban Pulpit: New York City and the Fate of Liberal Evangelicalism* (Oxford, 2014). He teaches history at Bowling Green State University.

Joanna Brooks is Associate Dean of Graduate and Research Affairs at San Diego State University. She is the author or editor of six scholarly and popular books on religion, gender, colonialism, and American culture, including *The Book of Mormon Girl* (Simon and Schuster, 2012) and *Mormon Feminist Thought: Essential Writings from Forty Years of the Movement* (Oxford, 2015).

Claudia L. Bushman has taught at Columbia University, Claremont Graduate University, and the Joseph Fielding Smith Institute for Church History. She is the author or editor of many books, including *Contemporary Mormonism: Latter-Day Saints in Modern America* (Praeger, 2006), *Mormon Sisters: Women in Early Utah* (Utah State, 1997), and *Mormon Women Have Their Say: Essays from the Claremont Oral History Collection* (Greg Kofford Books, 2013).

Richard Lyman Bushman is Gouverneur Morris Professor of History, Emeritus, at Columbia University and author of *Joseph Smith: Rough Stone Rolling* (Knopf, 2005). His books on American culture include *The Refinement of America: Persons, Houses, Cities* (Vintage Books, 1992). From 2008 to 2011 he was Howard W. Hunter Visiting Professor of Mormon Studies at Claremont Graduate University. He lives with his wife Claudia Bushman in New York City.

David E. Campbell is professor of political science at the University of Notre Dame, and director of the Rooney Center for the Study of American Democracy. He has published in a variety of publications for both scholarly and general audiences. He is the author of *Why We Vote: How Schools and Communities Shape our Civic Life* (Princeton, 2010), and coauthor of *American Grace: How Religion Divides and Unites Us* (Simon and Schuster, 2012) and *Seeking the Promised Land: Mormons and American Politics* (Cambridge, 2014).

Russell Arben Fox is Professor of Political Science at Friends University in Wichita, Kansas. His teaching and research interests include communitarianism, urban sustainability, American political thought, German romantic philosophy, Confucian political theory, radical democracy, and Mormonism. His writings have appeared in *American Behavioral Scientist*, *Philosophy East & West*, *Polity*, and *The Review of Politics*; he is the coeditor with Jon Carlson of *The State of Nature in Comparative Political Thought: Western and Non-Western Perspectives* (Lexington Books, 2014).

Christopher F. Karpowitz is the Associate Director of the Center for the Study of Elections and Democracy and an Associate Professor of Political Science at Brigham Young University. Much of his research examines participation in democratic institutions and processes, with special attention to democratic and deliberative theory. He is a coauthor of *The Silent Sex: Gender, Deliberation, and Institutions* (Princeton, 2014) and *Deliberation, Democracy, and Civic Forums: Improving Equality and Publicity* (Cambridge, 2014).

J. Quin Monson is Associate Professor of Political Science and Director of the Center for the Study of Elections and Democracy at Brigham Young University. His research has appeared in journals such as *Public Opinion Quarterly, Political Research Quarterly, Political Analysis, Political Behavior*, and the *Journal for the Scientific Study of Religion*. He is a coauthor of *Seeking the Promised Land: Mormons and American Politics* (Cambridge, 2014).

Max Perry Mueller holds a PhD in American religious history from Harvard University. His dissertation, "Black, White, and Red: Race and the Making of the Mormon People, 1830–1880," examines the importance of literacy and religious literature in the creation and contestation of racial categories in the nineteenth-century American Republic. He is also cofounder and contributing editor of *Religion & Politics*, the online journal of news and analysis of the John C. Danforth Center on Religion & Politics at Washington University in St. Louis. He currently teaches in the religion department of Mount Holyoke College.

Jana Riess has a PhD in American religious history from Columbia University and has worked for fifteen years as an editor in the publishing industry. She is the author or coauthor of numerous books, including *Flunking Sainthood* (Paraclete, 2011) and *Mormonism for Dummies* (Wiley, 2005). She blogs about Mormonism for Religion News Service and has taught at Barnard College and Miami University of Ohio.

Jan Shipps is professor emerita of history and religious studies at Indiana University–Purdue University Indianapolis. She is widely recognized as a media expert on Mormonism and is the author of *Mormonism: The Story of a New Religious Tradition* (University of Illinois Press, 1987) and *Sojourner in the Promised Land: Forty Years Among the Mormons* (University of Illinois Press, 2000), as well as other works.

Peggy Fletcher Stack is a senior religion writer at the *Salt Lake Tribune*, where she has covered Mormonism and other faiths for more than two decades. She reported on issues of religion during both Romney campaigns. She was a member of the Religion Newswriters Association executive committee for three years, and was named George Cornell Religion Writer of the Year in 2012.

John G. Turner teaches religious studies at George Mason University and is the author of *Brigham Young: Pioneer Prophet* (Harvard, 2012).

Index

ABC news (American Broadcasting Company), 220–21
Abel, Elijah, 163, 168, 169–70
abolition, 161, 164
abortion, 140, 143–45, 146, 148, 193, 216
Addams, Jane, 55–56, 63
African Americans, 156–71; Abel, Elijah, 163, 168, 169–70; "black problem," 156, 157–60; the Book of Mormon and, 158, 160, 161–64, 172n26; church membership and, 157, 158, 159, 170; Clinton, William J. "Bill" and, 126; Douglass, Frederick, 166; equality and, 127–28; evangelical Christians and, 159; Faith Matters survey and, 142, 153n26; Genesis Group (black Mormon organization), 219; Hendricks, Obery M., 158, 161; James, Jane Manning, 162, 163, 168, 170; Mormon kinship and, 160, 165, 166, 169; Mormon missions and, 157, 160; National Association for the Advancement of Colored People (NAACP), 167, 174n46; "Negro Doctrine, The" (Bush) (article), 170; "Negro question," the, 121, 123; *Nobody Knows: The Untold Story of Black Mormons* (documentary), 171n14; "On [the] Position of Blacks with The Church and Civil Rights" (statement), 167; priesthood ban and, 129n10, 157–60, 167–70, 214, 219, 220; Quorum of the Twelve Apostles and, 157; "Race and the Priesthood" (essay) and, 159–60; Romney, George Wilcken and, 119, 121, 123, 125; Romney, Mitt and, 157, 158, 159, 219; Smith, Joseph and, 170; Smith, Joseph Fielding (son of Hyrum Smith) and, 156–57; spiritual inferiority belief and, 156–57, 161, 163, 164; Utah and, 165–67; Wright, Jeremiah, 126; Young, Brigham and, 156, 167. *See also* civil rights; Obama, Barack; race; slavery
Agassiz, Louis, 163

INDEX

Alaska, 193, 197, 200, 202
Alaska Family Coalition, 197
Allen, Corinne Marie, 45, 48n6
Alma (prophet), 104
Alsop, Stewart, 121
American exceptionalism, xii, 102–103, 106–112, 113n7. *See also* religious exceptionalism
American Freedom and Catholic Power (Blanshard), 116, 124
American progressivism, 53–67; Addams, Jane and, 55–56; evolution and, 59–60; Mormon theology and, 53, 57–63; Mormon women and, 63–65; optimism and, 54–55, 58, 61; Patten, Simon and, 54, 56; Protestantism and, 58–59; social sciences and, 55–56, 59, 67n4; twenty-first century and, 54; Ward, Lester Frank and, 56
American Religion: The Emergence of the Post-Christian Nation, The (Bloom), 214
American republicanism, 16–17
antipolygamy. *See* polygamy
Arizona, 19–20, 201
Arrington, Leonard, 82
Associated Press, 210
Atlantic (magazine), 222
auxiliaries, 62, 78–79, 157. *See also* individual auxiliaries

Babbitt, Almon W., 22
Bakhtin, Mikhail, 91–92
Baptists, 32, 38, 39, 40–41, 117, 125, 214, 215. *See also* Protestantism
Barlow, Philip, 95, 98, 217
BBC (British Broadcasting Corporation), 222
Beacon Press, 116
Bederman, Gail, 47
Beehive House mansion, 16–17
Bellah, Robert, 87
Bennett, Grant, 156
Benson, Ezra Taft, 73–83; as Agriculture Secretary, x, 74, 79–80, 81, 108; American exceptionalism and, 108, 110; communism and, 80, 81–82, 108; conservatism and, 80–83; politics and, x, xii; as president of the Church of Jesus Christ of Latter-day Saints, x; Quorum of the Twelve Apostles and, 80, 81; youth of, 80–81
Benson, Reed, 80, 81
Bernhisel, John, 20–21, 25–26
Biden, Joe, 86
Birch, Brian, 223
"black problem," 156, 157–60. *See also* African Americans
Blanshard, Paul, 116
Bloom, Harold, 214–15
Blumell, Bruce D., 77
Boggs, Lilburn, ix, 4, 19
Book of Abraham, 113n4
Book of Mormon, the: African Americans and, 158, 160, 161–64, 172n26; American exceptionalism and, 102, 107–108, 109; Benson, Ezra Taft and, 82–83; Brigham Young University (BYU) and, 110; Deseret and, 19; finances and, 221; *General Smith's Views of the Powers and Policy of the Government of the United States (Views)* (Phelps) and, 7–12; government by judges and, 8–9; history of, 5–7; Jews and, 109; media errors and, 212, 215, 221; multi-language versions of, 34; Native Americans and, 110, 162–63; political leadership and, 5–7; politics of harmony and, 10; religious exceptionalism and, 104; revelation and, 91–93; Roberts, Brigham H. and, 38; Smith, Joseph and, 5, 7–8, 11, 108, 163; testimony and, 94
Book of Mormon, The (musical), xi, 212
Book of Mormon Girl, The (Brooks), 217
Bott, Randy, 158, 220
Bowman, Matthew, 217
Boy Scouts of America, 62, 70n35, 81
Bradley, Martha Sonntag, 202, 203

INDEX   233

Brandebury, Lemuel, 22
Brigham Young University (BYU): the Book of Mormon, and, 110; Bott, Randy and, 158, 220; Cheney, Dick protest and, 149–50; civil rights and, 167, 168; homosexuality and, 187, 190; Peterson, Mark E. and, 168, 174n49; Romney, George Wilcken and, 121; Romney, Mitt and, 215; Skousen, W. Cleon and, 80; Utah Colleges Exit Poll (UCEP) and, 140; Wilkinson, Ernest and, 80
Bringhurst, Newell G., 122, 169–70
Brocchus, Perry E., 22
Brooks, Joanna, 217
Brown, Hugh B., 82
Bryan, William Jennings, 135, 136–37
Buchanan, James, 25, 26
Building the City of God: Community and Cooperation Among the Mormons (Arrington, Fox, May), 82
Bullock, Thomas, 22
Buren, Martin Van, 4–5
Burr, David, 26
Burrows, Julius, 46
Bush, George H. W., 54, 115, 117, 118, 126
Bush, George W., 126, 139–40, 223
Bush, Lester E., 169–70
Bushman, Richard Lyman, 217
Businessweek (magazine), 221
BYU (Brigham Young University). *See* Brigham Young University (BYU)
BYU Studies (journal), 122

Calhoun, John C., 3–4, 20
California, 19–20, 192. *See also* Proposition 8 (California); "Yes on 8" campaign, the
California State Supreme Court, 192
Campbell, David E., 90, 93–94, 99n12, 193
Campbell, William, 43
Canada, 10–11
Can Mitt Romney Serve Two Masters? The Mormon Church Versus the Office of the Presidency of the United States of America (Erickson), 218
Cannon, Elaine, 181–83
Cannon, Martha Hughes, 176
Carter, Jimmy, 125–26, 127, 139
Cass, Lewis, 20
Catholicism: *American Freedom and Catholic Power* (Blanshard), 116, 124; America's political apostasy and, 15; civil religion and, 85–86, 88, 96; conservatism and, 140; Faith Matters survey and, 142–48, 153n26; Mormonism comparison and, 212; presidency and, 115–16, 117, 124; same-sex marriage and, 197; two-parties and, 150. *See also* Kennedy, John F.
Center for the Study of Elections and Democracy, 140
Cheney, Dick, 149–50
Chicago Daily News (newspaper), 122
Christian Endeavor (magazine), 39
Christianity, 90–91, 92, 96. *See also* Baptists; Catholicism; evangelical Christians; Judeo-Christian; Presbyterians; Protestantism
Christian Science Monitor (news organization), 221
"Church and Its Financial Independence, The" (Public Affairs Office), 222
"Church and the Public Square(s), The" essay, 101n52
Church Welfare Program, 66–67, 78, 79, 143
civil liberties vs. security, 146
civil religion: America's, xii, 85–88, 96–98; revelation and, 88–93; testimony and, 93–96
civil rights, 119, 120, 121, 123, 125, 161, 167–70, 174n46
Civil War, U.S., 27, 28
Claremont Oral History program, 183
Clark, J. Reuben, 108
Clay, Henry, 3

Clayson, William, 180
Clinton, William J. "Bill," 126, 139
CNN (Cable News Network), 215, 217, 218, 219
Colorado, 19–20
Columbian Exposition, 35
communism, 79, 80, 81–82, 108, 138
Compromise of 1850, the, 21
Concordia Lutheran College, 123
Congress: antipolygamy legislation and, 24–25, 26, 27; Democratic, Republican parties and, 74; Deseret and, 19–21; *General Smith's Views of the Powers and Policy of the Government of the United States* (*Views*) (Phelps) and, 7; Mormon representation and, x, 83n3; Morrill, Justin and, 24; Roberts, Brigham H. and, x, 32–33, 40, 41, 43. *See also* Mormonism, U.S. Government and; Smoot, Reed; Utah, U.S. Government and
Connor, Patrick E., 27
conservatism, 73–83; abortion and, 144, 146, 205; Benson, Ezra Taft and, 80–83; Mormons and, xii–xiii, 134, 138–39, 148, 193; Republican Party and, 73–74, 76, 133, 140; same-sex marriage and, 146, 196, 198
conservative Christians. *See* evangelical Christians
Coppins, McKay, 217
Coronet (magazine), 79
Correlation, 66, 95–96, 208n13
Council of Fifty, 19–20
Cowdery, Oliver, 222
Cox, Archibald, 117
Crocheron, Augusta Joyce, 179
Cullom, Shelby Moore, 176–77
Cullom Bill, the (1870), 176–78
cult, Mormonism as, 159, 213–15
Cumming, Alfred, 26
Cushing, Caleb, 23

Daily Beast (website), 218
Daily Show, The (television), 217

Darwin, Charles, 60
Davies, Douglas, 62
Declaration of Independence, 8, 106, 165
Declaration of Sentiments (1848), 178
Democratic Party: Benson, Ezra Taft and the, 83; Mauss, Armand data and the, 138; Mormons and the, 150, 152n16; presidential elections and the, 3, 75*fig.*, 77, 80, 135–40; progressivism and the, 54; Smith, Joseph and the, 74; Utah and the, 73–74
Denton, Sally, 218
Depression, the, 65, 66–67, 77–78, 79, 81, 82, 119
Deseret, ix–x, 19–21
Deseret Books (publisher), 82
Deseret News (newspaper), 24–25, 77, 122, 203
Deseret Sunday School Union, 62
Detroit Free Press (newspaper), 120–21
Detroit News (newspaper), 122
Dialogue: A Journal of Mormon Thought, 170
Diefenderfer, Frances J., 47–48
Doctrine and Covenants, the (D&C), 100n21, 103
Douglas, Stephen, 20, 21, 25, 26
Douglass, Frederick, 166
Dowd, Maureen, 212
Drummond, W. W., 25–26
dualism, Mormon, 194–96, 200, 202, 204–205
Dukakis, Michael S., 54, 126
Dulles, Avery, 91

Edmunds Act of 1882, 118–19
Edmunds-Tucker Act of 1887, 118–19, 176, 178
Edwards, Belle D., 179–80
Edwards, John C., 19
Edwards, Jonathan, 106
8: The Mormon Proposition (2010) (documentary), 204–205, 207*fig.*

INDEX   235

Eisenach, Eldon, 88
Eisenhower, Dwight D., x, 74, 79, 80, 81, 108, 119
Embry, Jessie, 49n19
Emmett, Sue, 218
Ensign (magazine), 203
Equal Rights Amendment (ERA), 140, 153n28, 176, 180–83, 197, 202–203
Erickson, Tricia, 218
"eternal progression," 53, 60
evangelical Christians: African Americans and, 159; Bush, George W. and, 126; Carter, Jimmy and, 126; civil liberties and, 146; Mormons and, 90, 133–34, 141–48; Nixon, Richard and, 130n24; presidential elections and, 117, 126; Republican Party and, 116, 126, 133, 134, 140, 142; Romney, Mitt and, 86, 126, 156, 213–14, 223
evolution, 59–60, 61, 69n23
exceptionalism, American, xii, 102–103, 106–112, 113n7
exceptionalism, religious, xii, 102–106
experts, on Mormonism, 217–20
expulsions, 16, 18, 166. *See also* persecutions; protection of Mormons
"Extermination Order" of 1838, ix, 4

FAIR (Foundation for Apologetic Information and Research), 218
"Faith in America" (Romney) (speech), 86, 94–95
Faith Matters survey, 142–48, 153n26
Families Are Concerned Today (FACT), 203
Farmer, Jared, 161
"Father and the Son: A Doctrinal Exposition, The" (proclamation), 60–61
fellowship, 93–94
feminism, x, 44, 140, 177, 178, 181, 216, 218. *See also* Equal Rights Amendment (ERA); women's suffrage

Fillmore, Millard, 21
First Presidency: Benson, Ezra Taft and the, x; church membership and the, 154n32; Church Welfare Program and the, 78; civil rights and the, 167, 168, 169, 174n46; Clark, J. Reuben and the, 108; "Father and the Son: A Doctrinal Exposition, The" (exposition) and the, 60–61; political activity and the, 65; priesthood ban and the, 157, 168; Proposition 8 (California) and the, 185–86; Richards, Willard and the, 163; Romney, Mitt and the, 217; Young, Brigham and the, 17
Flake, Kathleen, 46, 217
Fluhman, Spencer, 35
food storage policy, 79
Ford, Gerald, 139
Foster, Craig L., 122
Fox, Feramorz, 82
Frederick Douglass Papers, The, 166
Freehling, William, 27

Galbraith, John Kenneth, 117
Gates, Susa Young (daughter of Brigham Young), 64–65
Gedicks, Frederick Mark, 89, 94–95, 96–97
gender, 40–44, 47, 142–43, 203, 206. *See also* men; women
Genealogical Society of Utah, 36
genealogy, 36, 78, 79
General Assembly of the Presbyterian Church (1906), 46
General Motors (GM), 128n7
General Smith's Views of the Powers and Policy of the Government of the United States (*Views*) (Phelps), 7–12, 165
Genesis Group (black Mormon organization), 219
"Genesis of a Church's Stand on Race, The" (Horowitz) (article), 220
"Gentile" Bureau of Information, 35
Givens, Terryl, 90–93

Goldberg, Whoopi, 211
Goldwater, Barry, 84n22, 120, 122–23, 137
Gordon, Lou, 121
Gospel Topics website, 159–60
Gould, Helen, 38
government of God, 8, 15, 18
Graham, Billy, 116, 128n2, 130n24
Graham, Stephen, 190
Grant, Heber J., 63, 65, 77
Gray, Darius, 219
Great Basin, 19
Greater Houston Ministerial Association, 118, 124, 125
Greener, Glen, 201
Greenhalgh, M.A.Y., 179
Grossman, Cathy Lynn, 214
group-think, 96

Haglund, Kristine, 217
Haldeman, H. R. (Bob), 130n24
Hamilton, Andrew, 79
Harper's (magazine), 221
Harris, Broughton, 22
Harris, T. George, 122
Hatch, Orrin, x, 112, 213
Hawaii, 193, 197, 202–203
Hawaii's Future Today coalition (HFT), 197
Hawkins, Paula, 175
health code. *See* Word of Wisdom (Mormon dietary code)
Hebrew Bible, 7, 8, 61, 107
Hendricks, Obery M., 158, 161
Hinckley, Gordon B., 197, 203, 210, 214
Historical Department, Church LDS, 82
Hitchens, Christopher, 214
Holland, Jeffrey R., 222
Home Mission Monthly (periodical), 38–39
homogeneity, 90, 94, 95, 96, 134, 149
homosexuality, xiii, 140, 146, 187–90, 193–94. *See also* Proposition 8 (California); same-sex marriage; "Yes on 8" campaign, the
Hoover, Herbert, 115
"Hope of Israel" (Clayson) (song), 180

Horowitz, Jason, 216–17, 220
House Un-American Activities Committee (HUAC), 138
Huckabee, Mike, 117, 214
Huffington Post (online news), 158
Hull House, 55
Humphrey, Hubert, 116, 151n10
Huntsman, Jon, x, xi, 112

"I Am a Child of God" (hymn), 53
Illinois, 15, 16, 27, 166, 176. *See also* Nauvoo (Illinois)
immigration, 146–47, 193
Independence, Missouri, 12n2
Indians. *See* Native Americans
In Re Marriage ruling, 192
Interdenominational Council of Women for Christian and Patriotic Service (ICWPS), The, 44–45, 52n60
International Women's Year, 176, 181, 202
Iversen, Joan Smyth, 41–42

Jackson, Andrew, 4, 15
Jacobs, Norton, 18
James, Jane Manning, 162, 163, 168, 170
Jeffress, Robert, 214
Jensen, Bridey, 190
Jensen, Marlin, 147, 150
Jesus the Christ (Talmage), 59, 61
Jews, xiii, 94, 104, 105, 107, 109, 128, 142–48, 153n26, 214. *See also* Judaism; Judeo-Christian
"JFK speech," 115, 117–18, 123, 124
John Birch Society, 81–82
Johns, Andrew L., 122
Johnson, Lyndon, 74, 80, 84n22, 120, 124–25, 137
Johnson, Sonia, x, 181, 218
Jory, Victor, 79
Joseph Smith As Scientist (Widtsoe), 59
journalism. *See* media
Judaism, 89, 91. *See also* Jews
Judeo-Christian, 87, 88, 92, 95, 96. *See also* Christianity; Jews
judgeships, 8–9. *See also* priesthood rule

Kansas-Nebraska Act, 23, 24
Kantor, Jodi, 215, 216
Kathleen Flake, 28
Keller, Bill, 214
Kennedy, John F.: civil religion and, 87; faith, presidential candidacy and, xiii, 83n4, 116, 124; Graham, Billy and, 116, 128n2; "JFK speech," 115, 117–18, 123, 124; Romney, George Wilcken and, 120, 125, 126; Romney, Mitt and, 115, 117–18, 127; Utah and, 137
Kimball, Edward, 170
Kimball, Spencer W., 53, 157, 158, 182–83, 214
King Follet Discourse (Smith), 61
Kinney, John F., 23, 26
kinship, 57, 62, 63, 64
Kinsman, The (anti-Mormon newspaper), 32, 48n1
Krakauer, Jon, 218–19
Ku Klux Klan, 115

Laman, 5–6
Lamanites, 6, 10, 161–62, 163, 215
Landon, Alf, 77
Laurie, Annie, 50n24
Lawrence, Gary, 200, 201
Lawrence Research firm, 200
LDS Citizens Coalition (Virginia), 203
lds.org (LDS Church official website), 144, 154n32
League of Nations, 66
Lehi, 107
Lehmann, Chris, 221
Lemuel, 5–6
libertarianism, 146
Lilla, Mark, 91
Lincoln, Abraham, 26, 27, 87, 106
Linker, Damon, 88, 90, 96
Lion House mansion, 16–17
Logan (Utah), 76
Los Angeles Times (newspaper), 123, 215
Lyman, Amasa, 22

Lyman, Amy Brown, 63–65
Lyman, Richard R., 63
Lythgoe, Dennis L., 122, 129n14

Madison, James, 11
Mangum, Garth L., 77
Manifesto of 1890 (Woodruff), x, xii, 32–33, 36–37, 58, 82, 196
Manti (Utah), 76
Marriott, J. Willard, 120
Marty, Martin, 88
Maryland, 205
Mason, C. E., 52n60
Massachusetts, 155, 201, 213, 215
Matheson, Scott, 137
Mauss, Armand, 95, 138–39, 152n13
May, Dean, 82
McCain, John, 140
McCarthy, Eugene, 121
McGovern, George S., 125, 130n24
McKay, David O., 74, 81–82, 123, 169
McKinley, William, 41, 135–37
McMurrin, Sterling, 79
McNiece, Robert, 33
media, 210–24; attacks and the, 222; experts and the, 217–19; Mormon finances and the, 220–22; Mormonism as cult and the, 213–15; Mormonism misunderstanding and the, 211–13, 221, 223–24; Protestantism and the, 210–11, 212, 214–15, 219, 221; Romney, Mitt and the, 210–24. *See also individuals*; *individual news sources*
Meet the Mormons (documentary), 224
Meet the Press (television), 157, 219
men, 42–43, 47, 62, 203, 218. *See also* gender
Meridian Magazine (online magazine), 199, 200–201
Messenger & Advocate, The (newspaper), 164
Metcalf, Holly C., 181
Mexico, 10–11, 18–19, 20, 118–19
Michigan Historical Review (journal), 122

Mickelson, Jan, 117
Miller, Johnny, 79
mission field, 76
missions. *See* Mormon missions; Protestant missions
Missouri, 12n2, 15, 16, 19, 26, 27
Missouri Compromise, 21, 23
Monson, Thomas S., 215, 217
Morford, Mina, 33–34
Mormon Battalion, 19
"Mormon creed" (Mind your business), 195, 199
Mormonism: American exceptionalism and, 102–103, 106–112, 113n7; bureaucratic organization and, 62; Congress and, x, 83n3; conservatism and, xii–xiii, 134, 138–39, 148, 193; correlation and, 66, 95–96, 208n13; as cult, 159, 213–15; Democratic Party and, 150, 152n16; differentiation and, 206–207; dualism of, 194–96, 200, 202, 204–205; evangelical Christians and, 90, 133–34, 141–48; evolution and, 59–60, 61, 69n23; Faith Matters survey and, 142–48, 153n26; fear of, 33–35, 36, 41, 43, 48n6, 85, 86, 98n7, 213–15; fellowship and, 93–94; finances and, 220–22; geographic disbursement of, 36, 67, 76, 78; government protection and, 3–5, 12; homogeneity of, 90, 94, 95, 96, 134, 149; as an institution, 66, 195, 196, 199; international growth and, 109–110; 1950s decade and, 78–79; partisanship of, 134–39; "People's Party" (Mormon) and, 73–76, 135; Protestantism and, 94, 212, 214–15, 219, 221; religious exceptionalism and, 102–106; Republican Party and, x, 133, 134, 136–41, 142, 147–50, 152n16, 170–71; revelations and, 37, 88–93, 95–96, 100n21; twentieth century ethos and, 53; two-party system and, 43, 51n47, 149–50; U.S. Government and, 17–18, 22–23, 25; vocabulary of, 211–12; voting instruction and, 43, 75 fig., 83n11. *See also* African Americans; American progressivism; civil religion; *individuals*; media; peculiarity; polygamy; presidential elections; Proposition 8 (California); theology; "Yes on 8" campaign, the
Mormonism and Politics conference, xi
Mormon missions, 34, 40–41, 78, 146–47, 157, 160, 172n26, 211
"Mormon Moment," the (2012 election), xiii, 86, 98, 156, 161, 170–71, 223
Mormon Octopus, the, 35 fig.
Mormon presidency. *See* First Presidency
Mormon protection, 3–5, 12. *See also* expulsions; persecutions
Mormon question, the, xiii
Mormonsfor8.com, 202, 204
Mormons' War on Poverty, The (Mangum, Blumell), 77
Mormon Tabernacle Choir, 79
Mormon temple marriage, 193, 194, 195, 198, 200–201, 208n6
Morrill, Justin, 24
Morrill Anti-Bigamy Act, 27
Morrison, Toni, 126
Mountain Meadows Massacre (1857), 28

National Association for the Advancement of Colored People (NAACP), 167, 174n46
National Era (newspaper), 26
National League of Women's Organizations, 45
National Order of Antipolygamy Crusaders, 47–48
National Organization for Marriage, 199
National Press Club, 120
Native Americans, 110, 162–63, 166, 173n41
Nauvoo (Illinois), ix, 3, 4, 18, 28, 118, 134

Nauvoo Legion, 26
Nauvoo Neighbor (newspaper), 163
Nauvoo Press, The (publisher), 7
NBC (National Broadcasting Company), 221
"Negro Doctrine, The" (Bush) (article), 170
"Negro question," the, 121, 123. *See also* African Americans; civil rights; race
Nephi (prophet), 5–6, 102, 104, 107, 108, 109, 161, 172n26
Nephites, 6, 8, 9, 10, 104, 161–62, 215
Nevada, 19–20
New Deal, xii, 76, 77, 81, 82
New Jerusalem, 12n2. *See also* Zion
New Mexico, 19–20
Newnamenoah, 222
New Republic (magazine), 159
"News Analysis" (Wicker), 123–24
Newsweek (magazine), 128n7, 212–13, 218
New West Education Commission, 37
New Yorker (magazine), 212–13
New York Herald (newspaper), 25–26
New York state, 202–203
New York Times (newspaper), 123, 159, 168, 204, 212, 214, 215, 218
New York Times Magazine, 121
Niederauer, George Hugh, 197
Nixon, Richard, 74, 83n4, 121, 122, 125, 130n24, 137, 139, 151n10
Nobel Peace Prize, 55
Nobody Knows: The Untold Story of Black Mormons (documentary), 171n14
North Star (newspaper), 166

Obama, Barack, xiii, 54, 110–11, 112, 126–27, 140, 161, 219
Ogden (Utah), 76
Oman, Nathan, 85–86
"On [the] Position of Blacks with The Church and Civil Rights" (statement), 167
Oregon, 19–20
Otterson, Michael, 223

Parsons, Emma, 44
Pascoe, Peggy, 36
"patriarchal blessing," 162
Patten, Simon, 54, 56
peculiarity, 134–50; as Bible term, 151n2; Mormon history and, 134–39; Mormon politics (1972–2010) and, 139–41; Mormon politics (current) and, 141–48; partisan homogeneity and, 134, 148–51
Pedestals and Podiums (Bradley), 202
"Pennies from Heaven: How Mormon Economics Shape the G.O.P." (Lehmann), 221
"People's Party" (Mormon), 73–76, 135
Perry, Rick, 211
persecutions, ix, 18, 19, 22, 24, 26–27, 165, 169, 213. *See also* expulsions; Nauvoo (Illinois); protection of Mormons
Peterson, Esther Eggertsen, 175
Peterson, Mark E., 168, 174n49
Pew Forum on Religion and Public Life, 223
Phelps, W. W., 7, 11, 16
Pierce, Franklin, 23, 24
plural marriage. *See* polygamy
"Political Aspects of Mormonism, The" (Williams) (tract), 43
political autonomy (self-government), 16, 17–18, 19, 23
political parties. *See* Democratic Party; "People's Party" (Mormon); Republican Party
politics of harmony, 10, 11, 12
Polk, James, 3, 19
polygamy: antipolygamy legislation, 24–25, 26, 27, 118–19, 176, 178; antipolygamy movement, 36–45, 47–48; discontinuation of, 36–37, 53–54, 57, 196; Edmunds Act of 1882 and, 118–19; Edmunds-Tucker Act of 1887 and, 118–19, 176, 178; federal government and, x, 21, 194, 195; Manifesto of 1890 (Woodruff) and,

polygamy (continued)
  x, xii, 32–33, 36–37, 58, 82, 196;
  men, women and, 42–43; Mormon
  theology and, 195–96; Morrill
  Anti-Bigamy Act and, 27; popular
  sovereignty doctrine and, 18, 21, 24,
  27; Protestantism and, 32–33, 36–38,
  42–48; Protestant missions and,
  33–34, 36–40, 41, 44–45; Republican
  Party and, 24, 25, 135; Roberts,
  Brigham H. and, xi, 32–33, 37–44,
  48, 48n6; Romney forebears and,
  118–19; slavery and, 24–25, 135,
  165–66, 195; Smith, Joseph Fielding
  (son of Hyrum Smith) and, 27, 28;
  southern Democrats post–Civil War
  and, 28; undergrounding and,
  194–95, 196, 198; Utah and, 18,
  27–28, 134–35. See also Smoot, Reed
popular sovereignty doctrine, the, 18,
  20–29
Pratt, Parley and Orson, 57, 163
Presbyterians, 33, 34, 37, 39, 43, 46.
  See also Protestantism
Presbyterian Woman's Board of Home
  Missions, 37
presidential elections, xiii, 74–76, 80,
  83n11, 84n22, 117, 125, 126, 135–40.
  See also Faith Matters survey;
  individuals
Priest, Ivy Baker, 175
priesthood ban, 129n10, 157–60, 167–70,
  214, 219, 220
priesthood rule, 15, 16–18, 22, 23, 41,
  42–43, 46, 94. See also judgeships
Primary organization (children's
  auxiliary), 62, 78–79
prisoners, 11, 12
Prohibition, 65. See also temperance
Prophet (newspaper), 163
Proposition 8 (California), 183–90,
  192–207; Catholicism and, 197;
  "Church and the Public Square(s),
  The" essay and, 101n52; 8: The Mormon
  Proposition (2010) (documentary),
  204–205, 207 fig.; finances and,
  197–98, 200; Mormon theology and,
  193–94, 200–201; Proposition 22 and,
  192, 197; temple marriage and, 193,
  194, 195, 198, 200–201, 208n6;
  undergrounding and, xii, 194, 198,
  201, 202–204, 205; women's voices
  on, 176, 183–90. See also same-sex
  marriage; "Yes on 8" campaign, the
Proposition 22, 192, 197
protection of Mormons, 3–4, 12. See also
  expulsions; persecutions
ProtectMarriage.com, 197, 199–200
Protestantism, 32–48; American
  exceptionalism and, 106; American
  progressivism and, 58–59; Faith
  Matters survey and, 142–48, 153n26;
  fear of Mormonism and, 33–35, 36,
  41, 48n6, 85, 86, 213–15; Kennedy,
  John F. and, 115, 116, 124; media
  and, 210–11, 212, 214–15, 219, 221;
  Mormonism comparisons and,
  94, 212, 214–15, 219, 221; polygamy
  and, 32–33, 36–48; Republican Party
  and, 142; Roberts, Brigham H. and,
  32–33, 35, 37–44, 48, 48n6; Romney,
  Mitt and, 86, 211; Utah statehood
  and, 33–34. See also Christianity;
  evangelical Christians
Protestant missions, 33–34, 36–37,
  38–39, 41, 44–45
Public Affairs Department, 79, 222, 223
Puck Magazine, 206 fig.
Putnam, Robert, 90, 93–94, 99n12

Quorum of the Seventy, 37, 58, 198
Quorum of the Twelve Apostles, 3, 18,
  25, 28, 58, 66, 80, 81, 82, 157

race, xii, 119, 157–61, 163, 164, 167–71,
  174n46, 181–82, 219–20. See also
  African Americans; civil rights;
  Native Americans
"Race and the Priesthood" (essay), 159–60
Rampton, Calvin, 137

INDEX   241

Ravitz, Jessica, 217
Rawls, John, 96–97
Reader's Digest (magazine), 79
Reagan, Ronald, 106, 139, 140
Reed, Rose Marie, 79
Reid, Harry, 112, 150
Relief Society, the, 62, 63–65, 78–79, 157, 177, 187
Religion Dispatches (column), 217
religious belief and practice survey (Putnam and Campbell), 90, 93–94, 99n12
religious exceptionalism, xii, 102–106
Religious Right, 116, 118, 126. *See also* evangelical Christians
Reno, Jamie, 218
Reorganized Church of Jesus Christ of Latter Day Saints, 119
Republican Party, 73–83; abortion and the, 144; conservatism and the, 73–74, 76, 133, 140; early history of, 24, 28–29; evangelical Christians and the, 116, 126, 133, 134, 142; Mormons and the, x, 133, 134, 136–41, 142, 147–50, 152n16, 170–71; 1964 National Convention and, 120; "Pennies from Heaven: How Mormon Economics Shape the G.O.P." (Lehmann), 221; polygamy and the, 24, 25, 135; as progressive, 74; Protestantism and, 142; Romney, George Wilcken and, 119; Utah elections and, 74–76, 80. *See also* Romney, George Wilcken; Romney, Mitt
Reuters (news agency), 221
revelations, 37, 88–93, 95–96, 100n21
Reynolds, David, 211
Reynolds, M. C., 32
Richards, Willard, 163
Riess, Jana, xi, 217
Roberts, Brigham H.: antipolygamy and, xi, 32–33, 37–44, 48; the Book of Mormon and, 38; Congress and, x, 32–33, 40, 41, 43; Manifesto of 1890 (Woodruff) and, 32–33; politics and, 65–66; theology of, 50n24, 58, 59, 61, 62; wives of, 49n19; World Parliament of Religions (1893) and, 35
Rock Center (television), 221
Rockefeller, Nelson A., 122
Romney, George Wilcken, 118–27; African Americans and, 119, 121, 123, 125; as businessman, 119, 128n7; civil rights and, 119, 120, 121, 123, 125, 168; forebears of, 118–19; Goldwater, Barry and, 120, 122–23; as governor, 119, 120, 128n7; Kennedy, John F. and, 120, 125, 126; as liberal, xiii; Mormon faith and, 120–21, 123, 126; "Mormon question" and, xii; politics entry and, 119; as presidential candidate, x–xi, 118, 120–27, 128n7, 129n14, 129n16; Republican Party and, 119, 120
Romney, Mitt, 115–28, 210–24; African Americans and, 157, 158, 159, 219; American exceptionalism and, 110–12; biography and, 215–17; as bishop, 216; Book of Mormon and, 163; as businessman, 155–56; *Can Mitt Romney Serve Two Masters? The Mormon Church Versus the Office of the Presidency of the United States of America* (Erickson), 218; civil religion and, 96; evangelical Christians and, 86, 126, 156, 213–14, 223; "Faith in America" (Romney) (speech) and, 86, 94–95; "JFK speech" and, 115, 117–18; as liberal, xiii; media and, 210–24; Mormonism as cult and, 213–15; "Mormon Moment," the (2012 election) and, 98, 156, 170–71; "Mormon question" and, xii; as presidential candidate, x–xi, xiii, 85, 110–12, 116–17, 124, 126–28, 128n7, 155–56, 159; Protestantism and, 86, 211; women and, 216–17
Romney, Vernon, 120
Roosevelt, Franklin D., xii, 75*fig.*, 77, 81
Roosevelt, Theodore, 47, 54

"runaway judges," 21–22
Russert, Tim, 219

Salt Lake City (Utah), 34–35, 76, 109, 119, 222
Salt Lake City Ministerial Association, 123
Salt Lake City Winter Olympics (2002), 155
Salt Lake Herald (newspaper), 37
Salt Lake Ministerial Association, 35, 123
Salt Lake Tabernacle, 14
Salt Lake Tribune (newspaper), 150, 215, 223
same-sex marriage, 140, 145–46, 153n29, 156, 196–97. *See also* homosexuality; Proposition 8 (California); "Yes on 8" campaign, the
San Francisco Examiner (newspaper), 40
Saturday Evening Post (magazine), 121
Scott, Anne Firor, 44
security vs. civil liberties, 146
Seigel, Lee, 159
Sermon in the Grove (Smith), 61
Sharpton, Al, 214
Shaw, Albert, 55
Shipp, Margaret Curtis, 37, 49n19
Shipps, Jan, 36
"Six Consequences" document (Lawrence), 201
Skousen, Mark, 221
Skousen, W. Cleon, 80, 221
Slate (online magazine), 214
slavery: Congress and, 20–21, 23, 24; Kansas-Nebraska Act and, 23, 24; Native Americans and, 166; polygamy and, 24–25, 135, 165–66, 195; popular sovereignty doctrine and, 20–21, 23; Republican Party 1856 platform and, 24; Smith, Joseph and, 7, 10, 12, 164–65; Utah and, 21, 156, 161, 165–67, 173n42; Wilmot Proviso and, 20; Young, Brigham and, 165, 166, 167
Smith, Alfred E., 115
Smith, Daymon, 195–96, 207n1, 208n13
Smith, George A., 17
Smith, Hyrum, 18, 19, 28, 162, 163

Smith, Joseph: abolition and, 161, 164; African Americans and, 168, 169, 170; American exceptionalism and, 108; the Book of Abraham and, 113n4; the Book of Mormon and, 5, 7–8, 11, 108, 163; contemporary political positions and, 7–8; as Democrat, 74; foreign relations and, 11; *General Smith's Views of the Powers and Policy of the Government of the United States* (*Views*) (Phelps) and, 7–12, 165; *Joseph Smith As Scientist* (Widtsoe), 59; murder of, ix, 12, 14–15, 16, 18, 19, 28, 163; politics of harmony and, 10, 11, 12; presidency and, xi, xiii, 3–12, 164–65; priesthood ban and, 168, 169; as prophet, 14, 88, 91–92, 103; protection of Mormons and, 3–4, 12; Quorum of the Twelve Apostles and, 3, 28; religious exceptionalism and, 103, 104, 105; slavery and, 7, 10, 12, 164–65; theology of, 57, 59, 60, 61; youth of, ix
Smith, Joseph Fielding (son of Hyrum Smith), 27, 28, 62, 156–57, 167–68
Smoot, Reed, x, 17, 45–47, 48, 58, 77, 83n3, 195, 204–205, 206 *fig.*
Snow, Eliza R., 177–78
social sciences, 54–56, 59, 63–65, 67n4
Sorenson, Ted, 124
Spanish-American War (1898), 41, 136
Spencer, Herbert, 59–60, 61, 69n23
Stafford, Robert T., 121–22
Stanton, Elizabeth Cady, 178
Steptoe, Edward, 23, 24
Steptoe Expedition, 23–24
Stewart, Jon, 217
St. George (Utah), 76
Sullivan, Andrew, 222
Sunday School, the, 78–79
Swainson, John B., 119
Sweeny, John, 222

Talmage, James, 58, 59, 60, 61–62
Tanner, Nathan Eldon, 182
Taylor, John, 14, 27–28, 163

Taylor, Zachary, 22
temperance, 45, 179, 180
temple marriage, 193, 194, 195, 198, 200–201, 208n6
"Ten Reasons Why Christians Can Not Fellowship the Mormon Church" (resolution), 39
testimony, 93–96
Texas, 10–11
theocracy, 18, 22, 28, 46, 89, 96, 194, 206, 208n13
theodemocracy, 16, 17, 18, 22, 74, 79, 89
theology, 53, 57–63, 85–86, 87–88, 93–96. *See also* revelations; Roberts, Brigham H.; Smith, Joseph
Thirteenth Article of Faith, 104
Thompson, Jacob, 25–26
Thomson, Charles, 113n7
"Those Amazing Mormons" (Hamilton) (article), 79, 82
Tidings (magazine), 39
Time magazine, 119
Times and Seasons (newspaper), 4, 212–13
tithes, 36, 211, 220–21, 222
Tocqueville, Alexis de, 87
Twelve Apostles, The. *See* Quorum of the Twelve Apostles
Tyler, John, 7

Udall, Morris, x
Udall, Stewart, 168–69
undergrounding, xii, 194–95, 198, 201, 202–204, 205, 207, 208n13
Under the Banner of Heaven: A Story of Violent Faith (Krakauer), 218–19
USA Today (newspaper), 214
U.S. Constitution, 5, 8, 19, 41, 102, 106, 108–109, 121
U.S. Government, 15–29; Mormonism and the, 17–18, 22–23, 25; popular sovereignty doctrine and the, 20–29; Utah and the, 17–29; Young, Brigham and the, 15–29. *See also* Congress
Utah, 16–29, 134–41; African Americans and, 165–67; agriculture and, 76–77; civil rights and, 167; Columbian Exposition and, 35; the Depression and, 77–78, 82; as industrialized state, 76–77; Manifesto of 1890 (Woodruff) and, x, xii; political parties and, 73–77; polygamy and, 18, 27–28, 134–35; popular sovereignty doctrine and, 20–29; presidential elections and, 134–41, 151n10; "runaway judges" and, 21–22; slavery and, 21, 156, 161, 165–67, 173n42; statehood and, x, xii, 27–28, 33–34, 40, 83n3, 134–35, 149, 176, 178; as territory, 16, 21, 74; U.S. Government and, 17–29; Washington vs., 21–29; women's suffrage and, 38, 44, 175–80; Young, Brigham and, 16–17, 21, 23. *See also* Roberts, Brigham H.; Smoot, Reed; *individual cities*
Utah Colleges Exit Poll (UCEP), 140
Utah Methodist Episcopal Conference, 34
Utah War, the, 27
Utah Woman Suffrage Songbook, The, 176, 178–80

Vietnam, 121, 123
View, The (television), 211
Views (General Smith's Views of the Powers and Policy of the Government of the United States) (Phelps), 7–12, 165
Virginia, 203
voting instruction, 43, 75 *fig.*, 83n11

Walker, Graham, 88
Wallace, George, 137, 151n10
Ward, Lester Frank, 56
Washington Post (newspaper), 155–56, 158, 215, 216, 220, 223
Washington Star (newspaper), 26
Washington state, 202, 205
Webb, Ann Eliza, 47
Webster, Rose, 38
Weisberg, Jacob, 214
welfare, 77, 143, 221. *See also* Church Welfare Program

Wells, Emmeline, 51n53
Wharton School of Business, 54
white American culture, 159
Wicker, Tom, 123–24, 129n16
Widtsoe, John, 58, 59–60
Wilkinson, Ernest, 80
Wilmot Proviso, 20
Wilson, Woodrow, 66
Winthrop, John, 106
Wolfinger, Henry, 169–70
"Woman, Arise" (song), 180
Woman's American Baptist Home Mission Society, 32
Woman's Christian Temperance Union (WCTU), 45
women, 175–90; African American, 157; antipolygamy movement and, 36–45, 47–48; Brocchus, Perry E. and, 22; Cullom Bill, the (1870) and, 176–78; Faith Matters survey and, 142–43; Interdenominational Council of Women for Christian and Patriotic Service (ICWPS), The, 52n60; minority, 181–82; National League of Women's Organizations, 45; oppression of Mormon, 36; politics and, 175; Proposition 8 (California) and, 176, 183–90; rationalized progressive Mormonism and, 63; Romney, Mitt and, 216–17; Steptoe Expedition and, 24; "Woman, Arise" (song), 180; Woman's American Baptist Home Mission Society, 32; Woman's Christian Temperance Union (WCTU), 45; Young Women's Mutual Improvement Association, 64, 78–79, 182. *See also* Equal Rights Amendment (ERA); gender; *individuals*
women's suffrage, 38, 44, 175–80
Woodruff, Wilford, x, 18, 27–28, 33, 36, 82. *See also* Manifesto of 1890 (Woodruff)
Woods, Robert A., 56
Word of Wisdom (Mormon dietary code), 36, 65, 212

World Parliament of Religions (1893), 35
World War II, 78, 81, 115
Wright, Jeremiah, 126
Wyoming, 19–20, 176

"Yes on 8" campaign, the, 192–94, 197–207; dualism and, 194–96, 200, 202, 204–205; Equal Rights Amendment (ERA) and, 202–203; finances and, 192, 197–98, 200, 201–202, 204; institutional channels and, 199; kinship networks and, 199, 207n1; Mormonsfor8.com and, 202, 204; "Six Consequences" document (Lawrence) and, 201; surrogate organizations and, 199–200, 204. *See also* Proposition 8 (California)
Young, Brigham: African Americans and, 156, 167; assassination fear and, 26, 28; ca. 1850, 16 *fig.*; Native Americans and, 173n41; politics and, ix–x, 16, 17, 18, 19; polygamy and, 26, 27–28; presidency and, ix, 17; religious exceptionalism and, 105; revelation and, 89; Romney forebears and, 118; slavery and, 165, 166, 167; Smith, Joseph and, 14, 18, 28; Taylor, John and, 14; theology of, 61; U.S. Government and, 15–29; as Utah Territory governor, 16–17, 21, 23; Utah war and, 27; Webb, Ann Eliza and, 47. *See also* popular sovereignty doctrine, the
Young, Seraph, 175–76
Young Men's Mutual Improvement Association, 78–79
Young Women's Journal, 64
Young Women's Mutual Improvement Association, 64, 78–79, 182
youth organizations, 62
YouTube, 222

Zion, 12n2, 36, 76, 109, 165–66. *See also* New Jerusalem
Zoramites, 104

GPSR Authorized Representative: Easy Access System Europe, Mustamäe tee 50, 10621 Tallinn, Estonia, gpsr.requests@easproject.com

www.ingramcontent.com/pod-product-compliance
Lightning Source LLC
Chambersburg PA
CBHW021359290426
44108CB00010B/305